Twenty-first Century Schools
Knowledge, Networks and New Economies

Gerard Macdonald
and
David Hursh

SENSE PUBLISHERS
ROTTERDAM / TAIPEI

A C.I.P. record for this book is available from the Library of Congress.

ISBN 90-77874-16-X

Published by: Sense Publishers,
P.O. Box 21858, 3001 AW
Rotterdam, The Netherlands
http://www.sensepublishers.com

Gerard Macdonald is Visiting Fellow at the Centre for Research in Innovation Management, University of Brighton, UK.

David Hursh is at the Warner Graduate School of Education and Human Development, University of Rochester, USA.

Cover photo: Ornan Rotem

Printed on acid-free paper

Twenty-first Century Schools

U
S.

EDUCATIONAL FUTURES
RETHINKING THEORY AND PRACTICE
Volume 1

Scope
This series maps the emergent field of educational futures. It will commission books on the futures of education in relation to the question of globalisation and knowledge economy. It seeks authors who can demonstrate their understanding of discourses of the knowledge and learning economies. It aspires to build a consistent approach to educational futures in terms of traditional methods, including scenario planning and foresight, as well as imaginative narratives, and it will examine examples of futures research in education, pedagogical experiments, new utopian thinking, and educational policy futures with a strong accent on actual policies and examples.

Many people have influenced my thinking about schools, networks and new economies. Among them are Richard Aldrich, Sandy Campbell-Smith, Vincent Carpentier, Anne Casey, Ivor Goodson, Celia Hoyles, David Hursh, Raphie Kaplinsky, Diana Laurillard, Richard Noss, Seymour Papert, John Parry, Mitch Resnick, Marlene Scardamalia, John Schostak, Roger Wassell-Smith, Chris Watkins, Peter Weiss, Michael White and Michael Young. Errors and omissions are of course my own. GM

Over the last several decades many people have pushed me in my political thinking and academic research. Some of the many people who deserve thanks include: Pauline Lipman, Michael Peters, Angela Valenzuela, Michael Apple, Susan Robertson, Roger Dale, Linda McNeil, E. Wayne Ross, Gloria Ladson-Billings, and Dave Hill. In Rochester, public school administrators William Cala and Dan Drmacich have been both inspirational in their reform efforts and helpful in providing memos, articles and other artifacts regarding local and state education policies. I also thank the students in my courses who have read more versions of my different papers than either I or they care to remember. Lastly, I cannot thank enough my wife, Camille Martina, who supports my work in more ways than I can say. DH

CONTENTS

In the old story Rip van Winkle wakes and stumbles, bleary, to the street. He tries to cross.
A nice young woman called Clara yanks him back to the kerb.
'My god,' she says, 'that car could've killed you.'
Catching his breath, clutching Clara's hand, van Winkle asks, 'What is a car, exactly?'
So Clara – once she's established that the man has been asleep for three hundred years
– educates van Winkle by showing him around the city.
It's a tiring business. Everything is new: cars, trains, planes, radios, phones, mobiles, television, factories, computers. It's all too much. The old man stares, uncomprehending.
He can't understand how so much could have changed
while he slept. He can't understand what he is seeing.
By the end of the day, both exhausted, they're passing an institutional building.
Van Winkle peers in a window to see a teacher, shouting at her class.
For the first time he relaxes, and smiles.
Clara registers the change of expression.
'Why are you smiling?' she asks. 'Do you know what that is?'
'Sure,' says van Winkle. 'I went to one of those. It's a school.'

I INTRODUCTORY

Training is a preparation for a future we know.
Education prepares for a future we don't know.

CHAPTER 1

WHAT THIS BOOK IS ABOUT

'Yet for all our reverence for education, we have paid little enough attention to its content: a vague reference to 'the three R's' has often seemed sufficient.'
Jerome Bruner

'You teach a child to read and he or her will be able to pass a literacy test.'
George W Bush, Tennessee, February 21, 2001

This book is about school systems – mainly British and American – in the first years of this century, and about what happens to people who come, as most of us do, through such systems. It takes schooling to be primarily a political and economic project, not an educational enterprise. (If the main aim of state schooling were education we should have a very different system.)

The book's American section deals with state and charter schools; the British chapters deal mainly with state schools. But not all state schools. We are not particularly concerned with outstanding schools (and there are many of them) which give a good education to a minority: those schools from which young people leave with a curious and critical cast of mind. Rather, we are interested in the mass of schools which fail to educate the majority. No one knows precisely the proportions of each group, but our guess is that it is somewhere around the 80:20 mark. British governments have always cosseted a minority of pupils – through fee-charging ('public') schools, grammar schools, city technology colleges, academies, and so on – rather than aiming for a universally high standard of schooling. Providing good schools for a minority of pupils is easier, perhaps more congenial to politicians, and might have made economic sense in the nineteenth and twentieth centuries. But for the new economies of the twenty-first, that may no longer be the case. Poor schooling is of course bad for those compelled to undergo it. It may also be bad for the country.

Our second assumption is that state school systems are controlled by politicians; and that (whatever they may say in public) politicians' first interest is not education. They are, understandably, primarily interested in schools as a means of support for the national economy. In this view, schools' first function is to train a productive workforce, and to look after children while their parents labour in that workforce.

There is a problem though. In the nature of things, schools deal with the future; school pupils will be joining some future workforce, in which they may spend the next half century. But politicians are commonly unclear about what that workforce will be like. It follows that they will be unclear as to how schools should train or educate young people for this dimly foreseen future. But lack of clarity has rarely been a political impediment. We note that politicians now set rules for the future of schooling with the unshakeable confidence they have shown over the past century – which may explain, among other things, why schools are still preparing pupils for a vanishing industrial economy.

This book's third assumption is that schools will continue in some physical form not too different from what we know now. This is not because schools do what they do particularly well. It is because contemporary economies cannot function without the work of both men and women.[1] Of course parents will not go out to work unless they know their children are kept safe and – in the best of all worlds – are being educated. So schools need to contain pupils and, to some extent, separate them from the surrounding community, even though this seclusion may hinder their education.

Our fourth assumption is that we shall, in a future economy, need to distinguish more clearly between education and training; and to limit the role of training in schools. What we now call 'education' is, very often, training (for example, learning to decipher print, learning to write, or learning the basic functions of a computer).

We also assume that the state will continue to be the main financier of school systems, since both liberals and conservatives commonly agree (for different reasons) that schooling young people is worth doing, and that most families cannot – or will not – pay for it. The state will, therefore, continue to finance most schooling and will retain a large degree of control over schools.

A further assumption is that globalisation and economic change will alter education in different ways in different countries; but it will significantly shift patterns of schooling in all of them. It is just possible that this shift will result in school systems that are more equitable, and more friendly to learning.

Twenty-first Century Schools looks critically at educational myth-making. One constituent of our current educational myth is that schools can be 'improved' so that real learning will happen in classrooms with one teacher and thirty or so pupils. A second myth (perpetuated by many politicians) is that good education occurs only in selective schools. A third constituent of the scholastic belief system is that schools are shaped by educators; a fourth is that systemic change stems from teachers' initiatives – that the system evolves when teachers decide to do things differently.

This book questions those beliefs. A change in teaching patterns is certainly part of any systemic change. Inspiring, innovative instances of teaching are not uncommon but, individually or collectively, they do not transform school systems. Educational innovations rapidly reach limits. There are geographical boundaries (they are confined to a school, or a group of schools) or there are political limits: innovations clash with government policies. In 2006, for example, a teacher in England may well have better ways of encouraging children to read than by implementing the government's 'literacy hour'. But this innovative teacher's methods cannot be generalised, because the state has decreed that its literacy hour embodies the best possible method of teaching reading. Teachers are, therefore, obliged to use it. And when the current literacy hour goes out of fashion (as indeed it did, at the time of writing[2]) there will undoubtedly be some other centrally imposed solution – at least so long as the state believes that its methods of centralised control produce the kind of school system we need and deserve. Innovations which encourage collaborative learning, originality, knowledge building, and creativity (all among the preconditions of a knowledge-based economy) have become marginal in British schools. But that is unsurprising: our present regime is not built on research, creativity, or even on deep knowledge of how people learn. Rather, it is founded on the fact that, these days, 'everyman has become his own education expert (particularly every politician or businessman) and the practice of education has become increasingly open to critique, reform and experiment from all sides.'[3] At the other extreme are certain unquestioned facts which seem not to be open to reform or experiment. Among these is the fact that education is best carried on in a classroom with one teacher transmitting information to many pupils. While this may be true of teaching, it is not true of learning.

A pervasive theme of the book is the interaction of school systems with national economies and national politics. Perennially optimistic, educators continue to believe (in the absence of evidence) that governments pay for mass schooling in order to advance education; and that, presented with better ways of educating, politicians will rapidly adopt them. Neither of these propositions is true. But it does not follow that education can ignore politics. Politics will certainly not ignore education. Though teachers commonly believe that schooling should be (and is) outside politics, school systems are, in practice, one of the most politicised areas of contemporary society. An obvious, often overlooked, truth about school systems is that while they are principally financed by politicians, not by educators, those who pay the piper will call the tune.

Of course this does not mean that school systems are shaped solely by political imperatives or economic needs. Many other factors produce particular school formations at particular moments in history. But it is still true that politicians dispense public funds; and politicians are not primarily interested in education; at least not in the context of mass schooling. They have other interests, which are not always made clear.

Government ministers do talk constantly about education and, at times, about education for our future. Campaigning for election in 1997, Mr Blair asserted that 'in today's world there is no more valuable asset than knowledge. The more you learn, the more you earn. It's as simple as that.' Neither knowledge nor learning has turned out, for Mr Blair, to be as simple as that; or, indeed, to be simple at all.

One of the difficulties for the post-1997 Labour government, as for others, is that Ministers use the word 'education' in a different sense from those who are interested in learning. Mr Blair added to the statement quoted above that 'education is an economic imperative'. Ministers are interested in education as an economic adjunct.[4] They are interested in productivity: in better ways of training a future workforce. ('A nation's standard of living is determined by the productivity of its economy, which is measured by the value of goods and services produced per unit of the nation's human, capital and natural resources' but 'the levels of productivity and prosperity in the UK still lag behind many other advanced economies. With labour force utilisation already at a high level, only further catch-up in labour productivity will be able to reduce the gap'.[5]) Yet even when Ministers are dealing with questions of educational productivity, rather than with education *per se*, they do, as we shall see, often get things wrong. They are right, though, in thinking that our school system could make a more significant contribution to the nation's productivity if it focused on the present and future, rather than the past. School systems are inescapably a part of our political and economic process; but, since they are products of an industrial age, they are now a dysfunctional part.

It is worth noting that other Whitehall ministries than Education mistake the outcomes of schooling. The most powerful department in British government, the Treasury, 'has for a long time nurtured a close interest... in the field of education' particularly 'in its potential linkages with questions of employment' but, understandably in this context, 'the Treasury has had a detachment from education as a process of teaching and learning'.[6] That detachment (reflected also in research on 'the economics of education'[7]) may be one reason why the UK Treasury is so often disappointed in school systems' performance, and in its absence of a desired economic effect.

These politico-economic concerns are not of much interest to most people working in schools. Teachers and educators shy away from such issues. Reasonably enough, they concentrate on the domestic affairs of their school, and on the everyday business of classroom discipline, satisfying parents, fighting for better salaries, minimising bureaucracy, reducing contact time, having roofs that don't leak, and lightening workloads.

Battling with such problems, who has time to worry about the economics and politics of schooling? Yet, in the last analysis, these decide the shape of school systems, and shape their daily business. School systems do what governments think they should do. That is part of the political process. And behind the politics are economic constraints. Our political system is increasingly ruled by international economics, as Britain, kicking and screaming, becomes an integral part of the European Union, and recognises that, individually, it has become a middleweight player in a globalising economy, soon to be overtaken in economic leagues by China.

EDUCATION FOR INDUSTRIAL DECLINE

A Nobel laureate recently noted that economics is now a more powerful agent of change than politics.[8] More accurately perhaps, societal and educational changes occur when economic shifts are articulated – often tangentially – through politics, and thus they change other social sectors, school systems among them. As we shall see, these politico-economic changes may be slow, and consequent social changes even tardier; but they cannot be indefinitely postponed.

The orientation of Anglo-American school systems toward a vanishing industrial economy reflects this lethargic pace of change. Both the UK and US have had long experience in training for industry. Britain did, after all, have the world's first industrial economy. Training for industry started there in the late eighteenth century, was refined in the nineteenth, and elaborated in the twentieth. But in the twenty-first century we have difficulties. Britain's industrial economy is declining. It is estimated that Britain lost 12% of its manufacturing jobs in the five years between 1998 and 2003; and in the slightly longer period 1995–2002 thirty-one million manufacturing jobs (out of about 164 million) were lost in the twenty largest manufacturing nations.[9] Traditional industry now accounts for a quite small fraction of UK gross domestic product. Even in good times, thousands of jobs still vanish every month. We are training young people for types of work which are disappearing now, and will have pretty much gone in the span of their working lives. This is a waste of time, an expense of spirit, and a misuse of money. So a central question – which this book tries to answer – is, why do we still train and educate for a past age? Why do school systems change so little? And how might we do things differently?

A moment's pause here. Surely there is frequent change in schools? In England, at least, there seems to be a new schooling initiative every week. There are Green Papers and White Papers (twelve under the post-1997 Labour government) and programmes with catchy titles which, these days, often incorporate the word 'learning', and sometimes even 'e-learning'. But those have little to do with learning; and nothing to do with significant change. Over the past half-century, the only real shift in British school systems has been a measure of financial and management devolution (from central government to school administrations, often with the aim of bypassing local government) and an increase in central control of school knowledge and teaching method. If we take change to include negative movement, we should also include those governmental initiatives which – intentionally or not – have increased the inequality of schools, and hence inequality of opportunity for pupils. In short, adaptation to a new economy, and to twenty-first century society, is something politicians may talk about but undertake in only token ways. To cite a single example, this twenty-first century quotation from a British government paper says many of the right things:

> People who generate bright ideas and have the practical abilities to turn them into successful products and services are vital not just to the creative industries but to every sector of business. Our whole approach to what and how we learn, from the earliest stages of learning, needs to adapt and change in response to this need. Academic achievement remains essential, but it must increasingly be delivered through a rounded education which fosters creativity, enterprise and innovation [which] depends on the very highest standards of teaching and learning and on the ability of teachers and lecturers to enhance the way young people learn so as to develop those capabilities ... We will foster creativity and enterprise through radical new approaches to teaching and learning.[10]

Unfortunately – though this is a paper produced by two influential Whitehall departments – none of these admirable sentiments has been translated into government policy for schools. There are no 'radical new approaches to teaching and learning'. The test of policy commitment is action. In Britain, there has been very little.

As for real education, there is a venerable British tradition that those who need it – the people who will run businesses, go into the professions, become scientists, or run the country – will be educated either outside the state school system, or after they leave it. Their education will start when they go somewhere more promising than school. This book's later chapters argue that Britain's time-honoured separation of sheep from goats will not sustain an economy which depends on new knowledge. Our expensively educated elite has many sterling qualities, but innovation and inventiveness are not the first which come to mind.

The British tradition of schooling was functional, if not particularly equitable, when the kingdom had an industrial economy and an empire; when its ruling classes were running benighted parts of the world, and most homeland workers were employed in factories, or in associated enterprises. As Burton-Jones says, our current publicly funded infrastructure of schools 'was built to satisfy a model of educational needs derived from an industrial era, in which an educated and wealthy elite employed the less-educated masses.'[11] Basic training was of course all that those less-educated masses needed in order to join the workforce.

But that is no longer the case as we move to some sort of 'new' or 'post-industrial' economy. There is of course energetic debate about what this post-industrial economy is, and what it will become. The current consensus is that we are in the early stages of a globalised knowledge-driven economy; that 'globalisation is a force reorganising the world's economy, and the main resources for that economy are knowledge and information'.[12]

We look more closely at this issue later in the book (see chapters 12 and 14). Amid the arguments over the shape of a new economy, one thing is clear. Schools cannot prepare learners properly for life and work in a new economy while they are educating for an old one. At some stage schools will have to change what they do, and what they are. When they come, these changes will be radical; but they do not imply a new national plan for education. Rather, the reverse: government departments will need to moderate their addiction to centralised planning; they will need to stop imposing twentieth-century regimes on a twenty-first century school system.

Such changes will not happen just to make labour more productive and workers more innovative, though that may be the proximate cause. There is a wider planetary imperative. Growing populations, the pressures of global capitalism, raised expectations, increased demand for diminishing reserves of fossil fuels, wars over water, and increasing pollution will combine to make the world humanly intolerable if our present industrial-economic patterns continue. Planetary malaise will not always exempt the rich. Altering those global trends – as we shall have to – demands a variety of technological, social, economic and political innovations. Our societies will either become more innovative or they will regress to a

Hobbesian state of nature.[13] Schooling will be part of the process of change; but clearly it will not be schooling as we know it now.

If our school system is not working well for most pupils, or adequately preparing them for the economy and society in which they will live and labour, how does the system now survive without significant change? A large part of the answer has to do with the way schools are evaluated. Evaluation is done almost entirely by those who have a vested interest in avoiding systemic change. Curricula are designed by bureaucrats; exams and tests are set by those within the system; school inspections are organised by educational quangos. Pupils can fail; from time to time schools are classed as 'failing'; the system itself – being its own judge and jury – cannot fail. But if its main function is to support the contemporary economy it will, at some point, be seen to be failing. Then we are likely to witness radical and systemic changes to schooling.

The following chapters, then, are not simply an analysis of how schools came to be as they are, and the impossibility of their being otherwise. Rather, they suggest that school systems have been shaped by the politics and economics of their time; and that, as the economy changes, they will be otherwise. That must mean a new focus on learning and knowledge; and very different uses of digital technologies.

The book's later chapters suggest that new economies, since they are based around new knowledge, may well increase school systems' attention to education and 'learning to learn'. We are beginning to see degrees of political and economic change which, when they coalesce, may offer us school systems which more actively encourage learning.

For all of us, this is difficult terrain. We find it hard to foresee a different future for schooling. We take it for granted that school, certainly in the secondary years, is mainly a training ground for an industrial workforce. But, in the early years of this century, there are other futures for schooling. Our conclusion is that knowledge-based economies may bring us school systems which not only serve those economies, but might also serve those who must spend time at school.

---

[1] This may (with the emphasis on may) change if the long-heralded replacement of people by machines (at least for some types of work) becomes a significant reality (see chapter 14)

[2] From 2006, reading teachers in England were instructed to abandon formerly mandated methods in favour of synthetic phonics, an instructional method widely used in the nineteen-fifties. The methodological change was made on the basis of a report from Ofsted, one of the British government's educational proxies (see chapter 7)

[3] Hoskin, KW in Messer-Davidow et al 1993

[4] Ministers are aware that, though British productivity is increasing, others are increasing faster. 'What was a modest productivity gap, vis-à-vis the US in the 1980s, has since 'widened into a yawning chasm. American productivity has shot ahead while the eurozone's has stagnated.' (McRae 2004) The 'Europe of innovation and knowledge', confidently predicted in the EC Lisbon summit of 2000, has not yet arrived

[5] Porter and Ketel 2003

[6] Deakin and Parry 2000

[7] See Chapter 12

---

[8] Stiglitz 2003
[9] Rifkin 2004
[10] DTI and DfEE 2001
[11] Burton-Jones 1999
[12] Carnoy 2000
[13] For a particularly depressing view of an oil-starved future see Kunstler 2005

CHAPTER 2

PARAMETERS

'The shift to a knowledge-based economy demands that traditional relationships between education, learning and work are fundamentally reappraised. The long-running debate over whether and to what extent education should be a preparation for work as well as life, is being overtaken by events, with work and learning becoming increasingly interrelated and interdependent.'
  Alan Burton-Jones

'Today, in industrial countries, most people are doing jobs that did not exist when they were born. The most important skill determining a person's life pattern has already become the ability to learn new skills, to take in new concepts, to assess new situations, to deal with the unexpected. This will be increasingly true in the future. The competitive ability is the ability to learn.'
  Seymour Papert

These pages briefly enlarge on some of the assumptions which were noted earlier, and which are thematic in following chapters. If we seek systemic change in schooling, these are the issues we need to address.

MONEY AND CONTROL

In Britain politicians annually spend over thirty billion pounds of our money on state schools. As elsewhere, who pays the piper calls the tune. Our school system is controlled by politicians. A deep knowledge of education is not a prerequisite. At times, indeed, it seems that 'everyone has views on education because it is one of the few fields in which everyone can claim to have had some direct experience. Those with the strongest views tend to be those on whom the experience has had the least lasting effect'.[1] Most politicians, we shall argue, do not see education as the primary purpose of schooling. Rather, the evidence suggests, they see the main use of schools as a means of preparing a future workforce. This may be synonymous with education, but usually is not.

Nor are politicians always well advised even in the business of training a workforce. We contend that there is now a significant disjunction between such training and the needs of the economies in which school-leavers will, in future, work. If we are moving toward a rapidly changing knowledge-based economy, then school-leavers' most valuable attribute will be the ability to learn, and to continue learning throughout life. For most young people, this is not a quality which schools are well equipped to develop. Nor, apparently, do our politicians have a clear idea of how to achieve it.

11

Political control of school systems goes some way to explaining why the efforts of teachers and educators to improve schools are likely to be short-term, localised, or finally fruitless. Schools will not become better places for learning until educators understand that systemic change is essentially a political process; and politicians, in turn, understand that a fundamental reshaping of our school system may serve education, as well as serving a new economy.

CONTROL AND CREATIVITY

In the mid-twentieth century the management writer Peter Drucker argued that organisations should have a clear direction, but that control should be decentralised, and those in control should refrain from micro-management. Otherwise, Drucker wrote, those who work in the organisation are reduced to cogs in a machine, and this manifest lack of trust in workpeople will mean that creativity is devalued or eliminated.[2]

Some years later the UK government, in managing England's state school system, turned these ideas on their head. For decades the system has had no clear educational direction; control is increasingly centralised; teachers are distrusted to the extent that their performance is constantly monitored by agents of central government and their pupils are repeatedly performance-tested. Unsurprisingly, creativity is stifled.

The British government persuades us, in a phrase made famous by Mrs Thatcher, that there is no alternative to its draconian policies. This ignores – to take one example – the practice of the Finnish school system which has, for many years, led the OECD's rankings of school-system performance in the industrialised world. There, 'no selection [of pupils] is involved at any stage ... all students are taught in the same class, and there is no streaming whatsoever. Moreover, the private sector is extremely small, which means that almost everyone attends a state school.'[3] There is, in the Finnish system, an absence of external testing. There are no school league tables, and there is a high degree of trust in teachers. While the Finnish board of education lays down a national core curriculum 'schools and teachers are able to timetable and teach it in whatever way they think best. Creativity in pedagogy is encouraged rather than suppressed.'[4]

In the early years of the twenty-first century the UK government, perhaps belatedly, concluded that, in Mr Drucker's words, we are moving from 'an economy of goods' to 'an economy of knowledge'[5] and, in such economies, 'politicians had to realise that knowledge, and hence education, was the single most important resource for any advanced society'.[6] But not just any education: creativity was central (see chapter 14). Therefore, Downing Street has concluded, schooling should foster this now valuable attribute.

Following that logic, the British Prime Minister has promised that, from 2006 (if he can get the necessary legislation through Parliament), previous policies will be reversed. Rather than government's centralising control and suppressing creativity in schools, they will in future 'be accountable not to government at the centre or locally but to parents, with the creativity and enterprise of the teachers and school leaders set free'.[7]

We must hope that this Pauline conversion is all that it seems and, drawing another biblical parallel, that creativity in schools can, like Lazarus, be swiftly resurrected.

SCHOOLING AS INDOCTRINATION

Schools have always been seen as an opportunity to indoctrinate. In Britain, churches began a tradition of using schools literally to indoctrinate: to immerse children in the doctrine of whatever church controlled the school. As we see in chapter 3, churches' influence over the UK school system slowly declined in the twentieth century; and in the US there has always been a constitutional separation between church and state – and hence between church and state schooling.

In the twenty-first century, Britain's Labour government – without making clear its reasons – has reversed the secular trend by inviting traditional churches (and others, both Muslim and Christian, with an interest in indoctrination) to run state schools.

Indoctrination may of course be exactly what young people need. But, if we see education as the cultivation of curious and critical minds, indoctrination should not be confused with education.

EDUCATION AND TRAINING

These are terms that have something in common (both involve learning) and are commonly confused. But they denote different things. Education is concerned 'with the acquisition of knowledge, skills and values which are generally considered to be worthwhile'. It is a process that is always incomplete: it makes sense to say 'she is now trained in that specific thing' but it makes no sense to say 'she is now educated; she should stop learning'.

Training is preparation for what is known; education prepares us for what we don't yet know.

Education implies participation by all involved. Despite current talk of 'defining educational outcomes', education does not have precisely defined outcomes. A process of learning with precisely defined outcomes ('at the end of this session she will be competent in the use of a chainsaw') implies a training activity.

Central to training is 'the transmission of knowledge, skills and values from one person to another' without implying that transmission is intrinsically valuable, or that it needs the active participation of the trainee.

Training does have (or should have) precisely delineated outcomes. For that reason, private companies often run training programmes very well, while they perform poorly with the slow, ill defined and complex process of education. On the principle that if all you have is a hammer everything looks like a nail, private firms (and some politicians) commonly try to reduce the multifaceted educational process to series of simpler training exercises.

13

This helps to explain why much of what now called education – for instance, the basic teaching of reading – is misnamed, and is, in practice, a training activity. Often that suits those who control schools. Though training is not easily done, it is simpler to train than to educate; and it is certainly simpler to assess a training activity than to assess the quality of education. It is easier to show that standards are rising (if that is what you wish to show) when you assess training, rather than evaluating education.

In the process of education, learning is often misconceived. Teachers and politicians commonly believe that learning is a necessary consequence of good teaching. That may not be so. Clearly teaching and learning are closely connected. But even good teaching does not mean that students will learn in more than the most superficial and transient way. Real learning implies students' active participation. Whether accidental or deliberate, the confusion has serious consequences. It means that those who control schools focus on teaching, rather than on learning. That elision of teaching and learning is unfortunate both for learners and for the society of which they are a part.

EIGHTY: TWENTY

For centuries Britain has offered a good education to a minority of young people. Well educated students are curious and critical; they go out into the world having learned how to learn. That process may start within state-supported schools, in fee-charging schools, or outside schools altogether. Often worthwhile education begins when schooling stops.

No one knows quite how many young people are well educated, and how many are not, but an educated guess suggests a ratio of around eighty to twenty. In terms of power and economics (though clearly not of equity) the 80:20 ratio has, so far, worked well enough for both the US – still the world's richest country – and for the UK. Britain ran the world's largest empire with a profoundly unequal education system. It turned the industrial revolution into what was for a while the world's leading industrial economy, with a small managerial class controlling a much larger working class. Today the UK, still with a highly elitist education system, remains one of the world's five leading economies – though maybe not for long.

For this book, though, there is a question: will the 80:20 ratio work well in a future, knowledge-based and globalised economy, with a changing north-south, and east-west, global balance? For several reasons we shall argue that the answer is, probably not.

A CLOSED SYSTEM

State school systems, in the UK and elsewhere, are closed. In order 'to keep young people safe' schools are commonly enclosed, and separated from the community around them. This clearly implies something very different from pre-school and non-school ways of learning, where young people learn from direct experience of the world around them. Cut off from the outside world, schools have constructed a special category of 'legitimate school knowledge' which means that, even where pupils are learning something with the same name as something in the world outside ('mathematics', for instance, or 'biology') the two activities are likely to be quite different.

Most discussion and writing about schools has a hermetic quality. Openly or otherwise it reflects the system's assumptions, and is commonly couched in a sub-language of semi-scholastic discourse. This explains the astonishing dullness and claustrophobic quality of most educational debates. Since they are inward-looking, and since they are not carried on in the English most of us speak, it is difficult for outsiders to assess the issues.

Evaluation of schools, teachers and pupils also reflects the closure of the system. Evaluative instruments are designed by educators or put in hand by the political administrators of education. As with any hermetic system, there are no reality checks: we know only what the school system wants us to know about pupils, about teachers, about schools, or about the system itself.

With non-monopolistic businesses, customers can go elsewhere. With democratic governments, we can, if we wish, vote for change on polling day. Some of us can leave our country – or try to leave it – if we dislike what is happening and (as with East Germany under Ulbricht and Honecker) this may be a reality check for the ruling class.

In normal times, school systems have no such reality checks. With schools, those outside the education system (or learners within it) have no recognised means of implementing significant change. Parents can move their children to a new school; schools may be classed as 'failing'; but the system continues, largely unaltered. (This issue is considered more fully in chapter 7.)

Closure also affects research and development in school systems. Collectively, educators resemble other closed and introverted congeries – trainspotters, twitchers, bellringers and the like – in having a language which is comprehensible within the group, but only partially understood by those in the real world. For similar reasons, most research, established within system assumptions, is flawed: vitiated by failure to recognise that schooling is primarily a politico-economic project, not an educational one. Conversely, work on the economics of school systems – which does set them in political and economic context – treats schooling itself as a black box.[8] The research measures the relationships and effects of various inputs and outputs but, since there is no serious examination of what actually happens within schools, we have no sense of how different types of schooling might affect ambient economies, or how those economies might affect the business of schooling.

THE PRACTICE OF SCHOOLING DOES NOT ACCUMULATE WISDOM

Everyone has been to school. Everyone knows about schools. We habitually deny that there is anything to be known about schools that is not common knowledge, or common sense. Schools do not build up a store of wisdom that would improve their practice, and the practice of schools in the future. 'Curiously enough, teachers at the elementary and secondary level ... do not fit the template of the modern knowledge-based communities, even though they make intensive use of knowledge. There may be a massive amount of innovation going on as individual instructors strive to find solutions to their teaching problems, but, perhaps because those problems involve working with "unstandardised materials", i.e. their students, relatively few of those pedagogical innovations are passed on to, and shared by the rest of the community.'[9]

SCHOOLS AS THINGS

There is a centuries-old dissenting tradition of education outside the classroom. Last century, deschoolers brought new energy to the argument and, more recently, networked technologies have made it possible (at least in theory) to bring education to learners, rather than bringing pupils together in a place called school.[10]

In this view schools as physical things are unnecessary for the process of education. Most politicians, who pay for state schools, do not agree, for they do not see schools as primarily educational. In the accepted political vision, schools' primary function is to keep children safe, enabling both parents (whether or not they are together) to be part of the national workforce. At the time of writing, there are plans to lengthen school days in Britain, to make it possible for parents to work longer hours, unimpeded by children.

Clearly, if child-minding is a central function of schooling, we need schools as physical places – as buildings more or less insulated from the community around them. Doubtless some schools will be built in new configurations: at the time of writing British architects are putting forward novel and interesting designs. But these are still schools as built environments. Even if (as is likely) increasing numbers of young people are educated outside the scholastic system, schools will continue, for the foreseeable future, to be physical things.

A NETWORKED WORLD

A vignette. Not long ago, an English school, in a traditional Victorian building, became the proud possessor of six new desktop computers. But the teacher in charge of the equipment had a problem: the school still had only one phone, which was in the headmaster's office. The problem was solved when the teacher found that she could call her computer helpline and, when asked the content of current error message, could run upstairs, read the message, and run down again to the phone. It made her evening step class unnecessary.

New economies will be networked economies. Twenty-first century societies, in most of the world, will be networked societies. Schools cannot prepare students for a networked world by 'teaching computing', or by adding static computers to a print-based, industrially-oriented organisation. School systems will prepare for a networked world when they are, themselves, a functioning and integrated part of that world.

EDUCATION AND ECONOMIC CHANGE

If politicians finance school systems mainly to support the national economy, there will come a point, in the process of economic change, when schools – for various reasons – are manifestly not offering that support. When this lack of support for new economies becomes clear to politicians, there will be pressure (as there has been at times in the past) for significant change across the school system. Since politicians have the power to make such changes, they will probably happen, as they have in the past.

Which leads to other questions: *are* economies changing? Will they change significantly? For Britain and the US, the answer is clearly yes. There will be internally and technologically driven changes; but there will also be shifts brought about by external factors. There is widespread consensus that the former are leading economically developed nations (and some which are now less developed) toward economies in which the principal dynamic of growth is knowledge, rather than land, labour or capital (see chapter 14). Of external factors, the most publicised are global competition, climate change and oil depletion. Those three issues, together with economic shifts, mean that, in the working lifetime of those now at school, the world will be a very different place; and of course schools too will need commensurate alteration.

---

[1] Reich 1992
[2] Drucker 1996
[3] *The Guardian* 16.9.2003
[4] Ibid
[5] Quoted in *The Economist* 19.11.2005
[6] Ibid
[7] Mr Blair, speech in Downing Street, 24.10.2005
[8] See, for instance, the interesting collection of essays edited by Machin and Vignoles 2004
[9] David and Foray 2003
[10] See for example Bentley 1998

II THE POLITICAL ECONOMY OF SCHOOLING

CHAPTER 3

FROM CHURCH TO FACTORY

*'That which our school-courses leave almost entirely out, we thus find
to be that which most nearly concerns the business of life. Our industries would
cease were it not for the information which men begin to acquire, as best
they may, after their education is said to be finished.'*
    Herbert Spencer

The history of schooling in Britain is, for over a thousand years, a history of
religious education or, more accurately, religious indoctrination. The nineteenth
century saw a slow move – more for the poor than for the rich – toward industrial
education, or training. In the twenty-first century that shift remains incomplete.

Schools were first recorded in Britain in the sixth century AD. We know little
about them, but we can be fairly sure of one thing: their way of working would
have been didactic. That guess stems from the nature of schooling. Traditionally,
school classes have had one teacher whose task was to transfer information to a
group of students. The teacher talked; learners listened or, at times, wrote. Though
this may not be ideal as a way of learning, it was dictated by the one-to-many,
teacher-led logic of the situation. With minor changes, and a number of different
names, didactic teaching has survived to the present day. What has (quite slowly)
altered is the content taught in schools, and the way they are controlled.

The dominant church of the time organised not only schools, but also the
knowledge they dealt in: all knowledge-transmitting institutions were, for a while,
in the shadow of the church. Debora Spar notes that, in the pre-industrial era,
'information was a highly guarded, tightly controlled commodity. The Catholic
Church (which essentially performed a quasi-governmental function at that time)
sat at the centre of all information flows. Only priests and a handful of scholars
could read; only monks were permitted to write and copy the manuscripts that
formed the backbone of knowledge in the Middle Ages. All information then was
written (aside of course from knowledge passed through the oral tradition) and the
Church controlled the writing process. Indeed, one of the major tasks of the
Catholic Church during this period was to act as a kind of labour-intensive,
multinational publishing operation.'[1]

By the seventeenth century 'Anglican control of [England's] principal
educational institutions … remained strong. It was not until 1860 that endowed
grammar schools were formally opened to the children of Dissenters…'[2] Some of
these church-controlled schools were, in a sense, vocational, as well as academic;
but the vocation was both specialised and limited. 'Mediaeval schools, whether
monastic, cathedral or collegiate church in origin were training grounds for clerics
in such professional skills as song, Latin grammar, theology and canon law.'[3]

This training in 'professional skills' was offered to a small number of older children. For the young, schooling was a moral and religious experience, or at least it was so intended. What we would now call primary schooling began in Britain with the Society for Promoting Christian Knowledge in 1698. Its method was, as ever, didactic. Education consisted of learning the catechism by heart. In subsequent decades 'Sunday schools' continued this tradition. Young people, who had often spent the week in underpaid employment, were lectured on Sundays by men of the church, or they worked from carefully chosen texts. This mode of part-time instruction was extended in 1802, when the British Parliament passed a 'Health and Morals of Apprentices Act'. The Act obliged all apprentices to attend religious education classes each Sunday, as well as having some instruction in reading, writing and arithmetic. It is not clear where health came in.

If some church schools were, in a limited sense, vocational, most were characterised by academic – which is to say bookish and backward-looking – curricula. Traces of this tradition continued long after school systems became predominantly secular and, ostensibly, servants of industry. 'One way of viewing ... characteristics of the academic curriculum is to see them as the historical outcome of how mass education was established on a model of bookish learning for priests which was extended first to lawyers and doctors but which increasingly has come to dominate the curricula of all older age groups in industrial societies.'[4]

In the early eighteenth century there was, across Britain, a scattering of religious schools which took in poor children. Beyond that there was no formal schooling for those who could not pay (a nostalgic state for some deschoolers). The family home was likely to be both adult workplace and, at times, school for the children of the family. But adults' going out to work – as that became more common in the eighteenth century and later – was matched by an increase in children's 'going out to school'; and in schools for them to go to. For the poor, these were likely to be church schools, charity, or 'ragged' schools. In ethos, such schools reflected their ecclesiastical or monastic origins. Centuries later, some still do.

Charity schools were funded by the rich for the deserving poor; church schools were financed by one or other religious institution. In the early nineteenth century Sunday schools and ragged schools had spread more widely across the land. What these schools did was called education, but education was seldom a main concern. As in earlier centuries, schools' mission was, usually, indoctrination.

Church-controlled schooling for the poor initiated traditions which continue, less explicitly, to the present day. The first is a belief in schools as a force for gentling young people, in particular young people of the lower orders: a domestic *mission civilisatrice*. Religious studies in schools were not mainly intended to deepen understanding of God and His works. Religion was seen, often explicitly, as a way of subduing poor children. 'In the hymns they sang, the prayers they recited, and the sermons they had to listen to, charity children were constantly reminded of their low estate and the duty and respect they owed to their betters.'[5] Still further down the social scale – at the bottom, in fact – workhouse schools also invoked God, in the hope that 'children of the poor, instead of being bred up in ignorance and vice to an idle, beggarly and vagabond life, will have the fear of God before their eyes, get habits of virtue, be inured to labour, and thus become useful to their country'.[6]

The belief that religion would lead children of the poor into good behaviour and industrious habit extended well beyond the industrial revolution which had its origins in the second half of the eighteenth century. In 1840 the British Parliament's Committee of Council on Education instructed school inspectors that 'no plan of education ought to be encouraged in which intellectual instruction is not subordinate to the regulation of the thoughts and habits of the children by the doctrines and precepts of revealed religion.'[7] In 1864, the Annual Report of the British and Foreign School Society asked, rhetorically, 'To what but the spread of a sound and scriptural education can we attribute the improved tastes, the orderly demeanour, the patient endurance, the kindly sympathy, now so prevalent among the poorer portion of our fellow countrymen and countrywomen?' As late as the 1940s, the Norwood Report – which helped to shape Britain's postwar schools – argued that schooling should be based, not on natural science but on 'a religious interpretation of life, which for us must mean the Christian interpretation of life'.[8]

But Britain's industrial revolution did of course bring about extensive social and educational change. Its cluster of inventions 'gave birth to a new mode of production – the factory system'. In turn, factory production transformed British society and, more slowly, the schools within it. Social change, then as now, 'placed vast intervals between the classes'[9]: between school as well as social classes. Britain's population grew fast and became younger. Employment patterns shifted. In 1840, agriculture, horticulture and forestry, combined, still provided the largest source of employment in England and Wales. By the end of the century more men were employed in metal manufacture than in agriculture.[10]

Workers displaced from the land moved into the expanding, industrialising towns. Child crime spread. Urban 'street children' were a new (or at least more visible) phenomenon. They disturbed the rising middle class who were, by mid-century, 'engaged in a sharp struggle on two main fronts – against the landed aristocracy on the on the one hand, and against the emerging proletariat on the other'.[11] To those who financed education, schools were increasingly seen as places for reconciling the poor to their straitened condition. More than ever, state-supported schools had a duty to keep the young in order, as well as preparing them for factory work.

We can only guess at the percentage of working-class children who went to some sort of school: it could have been somewhere between a third and a half. But most of those who did go to school would have gone on Sundays, when they were not employed. As in earlier times, Victorian pupils were exhorted – often in the context of religious training – to be socially submissive, and to recognise the instantiated evil of their nature. The 'primary object of early education' was 'to awaken in the tender mind a sense of its evil dispositions and habitual failings, before it is become callous by daily intercourse with vice'.[12] Young people came to school, not only to prepare themselves for work, but also to learn to order themselves lowly and reverently before their betters – of whom they were likely to have many. But, though some aspects were unchanged, schools' central business was (very slowly) moving toward preparation for industry. Schools – at least schools for the poor – were becoming places for the basic training of an expanding industrial workforce.

The skills of reading-writing-arithmetic may not have been generally useful before the nineteenth century. Thereafter they were necessary for young people who hoped for anything more than the most demeaning work in the new manufactories. Factory managers and owners preferred workers who had the elements of reading and figuring.[13] Elementary schools in the nineteenth century, and secondary schools in the twentieth, were seen as supplying 'basic survival and employment skills', as well as serving, for a time, 'to keep young people out of the labour market'. And of course school systems themselves also provide a means of employment for 'a considerable number of educated people'.[14]

Beside their ostensible uses, reading-writing-arithmetic recommended themselves in other ways to teachers and employers. Print and numbers reduce life's chaos to an orderly arrangement of twenty-six letters, ten digits. Imposing alphanumeric codes on the lower classes was part of a slow technical and social systematisation which saw human-scale measurements (hands, feet, fingers) and oral traditions displaced by more precise written documents and numeric measures. Over two centuries, memorised stories were replaced by books; sundials and one-handed clocks by accurate measurement of minutes and seconds.

There is no intrinsic virtue in orderliness of mind. But those who employ people in factories quite reasonably prefer order to disorder. The industrial order prefers tidiness to creativity. The bell-punctuated routine of school days, and the disciplines of figuring, copybook and text – all of these commended themselves to the new industrial class. Schools for the poor ceased to be an expensive beneficence. They became a functional and accepted part of the late Georgian and Victorian social and industrial regime.

Schools, supplying 'basic skills', entered what was to be a long, still continuing, partnership with industry. The interpenetration went deep: schools' organisation and administration came, in many ways, to match that of the new manufactories – notably through the monitorial system, that 'steam engine of the moral world'. Andrew Bell (one of the system's self-proclaimed originators) noted that his method of group instruction was 'like spinning machinery: it diminishes labour and multiplies work'. And it seems that the idea of school inspectors was taken from an early tradition of factory inspection. Once introduced into school systems, of course, the business of inspection flourished wonderfully. It continues in rude health to the present day; its stated aim, now as then, to raise educational standards. Whether or not it does depends on who is counting, as Stalin once said of elections.

Another import from industry was division of labour. In factories, this meant splitting manufacture into a succession of simple stages. Schools' labour was similarly divided into what might now be called bite-sized chunks – not for ease of learning, but for ease of teaching, and ease of control. The monitorial system, mentioned above, was division of labour's finest scholastic hour: a piece of social machinery which was 'both simple and economical', though not in any sense educational. As with the new industrial order, the small increments of the system could be executed by the cheap and semi-skilled (or unskilled) labour of 'monitors'. These were the school's older pupils. Some were unpaid. Others were paid up to two pence a week. They were drilled by a master, and went on in turn to drill younger children. Monitors were often less than twelve years of age: they were, in fact, not much older than their unfortunate pupils.

The industrial model of schooling was further refined under the Revised Code, introduced in 1862. Its mechanism was succinctly described by its architect as one which 'if it is not cheap, shall be efficient' or 'if it is not efficient, it shall be cheap'.[15] That centralised system of control escalated the level of testing and inspection in state-supported schools. In a foretaste of what was to come at the end of the twentieth century, the Revised Code introduced payment by results. Teachers could claim annually a few shillings for each pupil who attended more than a given number of 'morning and afternoon meetings' at school. However, part of the payment was 'subject to examination' of pupils. Teachers' forfeit amounted to 2s 8d if a child failed to satisfy school inspectors in reading; similar sums were subtracted for pupils' 'failure in writing' or 'failure in arithmetic'. A child who failed in all three would cost his or her teacher the entire 8s grant. This was a scholastic production line. Schools had, in a sense, become factories. It was a model for what we might call 'industrial schooling' or, more critically, deskilling. Traces of both persist to the present day.

School training regimes thus took on, and retain, an industrial aspect. 'Children were divided into year groups; knowledge was subdivided into subjects; teachers became specialists, were credentialed (certificated, like tradespersons) and ordered into hierarchies; students were controlled in class groups or batches, moving in linear progression through graded curricula, from easy to more complex, from lower grades to higher grades, 'promoted' (as are workers in factories) up the steps until they graduate.'[16]

The Revised Code was not the first or last scholastic system calculated to set pupils against teachers, but it certainly achieved that end. It was, as Matthew Arnold remarked at the time, designed to be hostile to real learning. Its emphasis on repeated testing and obligatory teaching to achieve centrally imposed and educationally debased targets may be seen, with hindsight, as a rather desperate attempt to come to terms with rapid social and economic change. In this it brings to mind (as we shall see later) Thomas Kuhn's description of the ways in which 'normal science' tries, and eventually fails, to explain phenomena which do not easily fit within whatever may be the current scientific paradigm. The Revised Code also resembles in many ways the targeting-and-testing regimes of the late twentieth and early twenty-first centuries: another dispensation that reflects intellectual and educational bankruptcy in the face of rapid social, economic and technological change (see chapter 7).

There is another interesting parallel between the funding arrangements of the Revised Code, and those instituted by Conservative and Labour administrations a century and a half later. Funding in the mid-nineteenth century was designed to give richer districts more, and poorer less. As in the twenty-first century, Victorian school funding arrangements were, effectively, 'a penalty on poverty'.

By the mid-nineteenth century, schools prepared the poor for industrial work through a settled system of teaching. In this, there were three main, and still familiar, elements. Much of the time, the teacher talked at pupils. Pupils were gathered in a single classroom but – whether sitting at desks or benches – were physically separated from each other. At times pupils read from a textbook (if one was available), or wrote in a copybook. Their writing was related to something in their text, or to something the teacher had said. These elements of teaching continue to the present day, and are still taken for granted as 'the way schools are'. In American terms, this is 'real school'. The fact that it is hard to imagine classrooms otherwise is one reason for their success in resisting significant change.

Clearly the mix of lecturing-reading-and-writing is designed for teaching, not for learning. We all know that being talked at is not an ideal way to learn. Reading is another odd choice. Reading had advantages over the teacher's lecture (with which it has always co-existed) but reading is not most people's first choice as a way of learning. We all have preferred ways of getting and conveying information. For most of us conversation, watching and practising are easiest, and most effective. Reading, writing and figuring are harder, less natural. (Manufacturers of machines know that reading the instruction book is always a last, desperate resort.) Print reduces the rich variety of life to the orderly alphanumeric codes you have in front of you – a cramped set of signs unrelated to what they signify. To make sense of written words involves a significant decoding task, and one which comes easily only to a small part of any population. Yet schools for the poor – as they spread in eighteenth and nineteenth century England – chose to make reading and writing central, though it was not originally valuable to most of their pupils. Nor was it meant to be. 'The realistic purpose of mass instruction under the protestant ethos was to develop the mastery of reading a limited number of religious works'.[17] We might say that the teaching of reading was originally a justification for schools' existence, rather than schools' purpose being, as advertised, to make the unlettered literate.

The enforced primacy of reading was another foretaste of schools to come. Two centuries later, schools' preferred communication modes still make learning difficult for most of their students. The first publicly-supported classrooms foreshadowed what would be continuing intellectual discrimination against the children of the poor. Their preferred ways of learning did not, and do not, usually include what schools choose to offer.

In Britain, the early twentieth century saw the belated birth of what we would now call a national school system, and the start of compulsory mass schooling. The years of compulsory school attendance were steadily extended throughout the twentieth century. The penalties for non-attendance have now been increased, to the point where, in Britain, parents can be jailed for not sending their children to school. (Of course, as Freud remarked of the Austria of his youth, the draconian character of laws may be mitigated by the arbitrary inefficiency of their application.)

If school systems were primarily educational, making attendance compulsory would be a curious decision. In the nature of things, schooling will not, and does not, suit everyone. In practice, it may suit few people. Making most young people go through a fairly standardised system is not, therefore, likely to encourage learning. Nor does obligatory attendance encourage most people's desire to learn. Compulsion is explicable only if education is not the primary purpose of school systems. Yet if schools are now primarily designed for industrial training, and if they are now also useful for child minding while parents work in paid employment, then compulsory school attendance does make sense.

Extended compulsory schooling is a logical outcome of a move from religious to industrial education. But, as we shall see, that shift has been erratic, uneven, incomplete and, in many ways, misguided. Compared to her competitors Britain was late in establishing a national system of schooling and slow to provide effective training for manufacturing industry. And we have hardly begun to design education for life and work in the twenty-first century.

[1] Spar 2001
[2] Aldrich 1995
[3] Ibid
[4] Young 1998
[5] An account of several workhouses ... as also of several charity schools for promoting work and labour London 1732
[6] Ibid
[7] Quoted in Maclure 1986
[8] Committee on Curriculum and Examinations 1941-44, ED 136/681
[9] Minutes of the Committee of Council on Education 1840-41 (London 1841)
[10] Aldrich 1982
[11] Simon 1974
[12] Minutes of the Committee of Council on Education 1840-41 (London 1841)
[13] Exceptionally, some schools were themselves genuine mini-manufactories, such as the 'day school of industry' founded at St Marylebone, London, in 1791. A few eighteenth-century schools professed to train pupils 'for apprenticeship' – which is itself, of course, a form of training – often a more successful one than that which schools offered.
[14] Aldrich 1982
[15] Quoted in Maclure 1986, p79
[16] Beare 2001
[17] Aldrich 1982

CHAPTER 4

WHAT DO POLITICIANS PAY FOR?

'Western technological creativity [has] rested on two foundations: a materialistic pragmatism based on the belief that the manipulation of nature in the service of economic welfare was acceptable, indeed commendable behaviour, and the continuous competition between political units for political and economic hegemony.'
    Joel Mokyr

'Initial education alone can no longer satisfy the rising and changing demand for skills ... However, the intensity of participation in non-formal job-related education and training is comparatively low in the United Kingdom and, like in most other countries, job-related education and training continues to be least common among those who need it most.'
    'Education at a Glance' OECD 2005

What do politicians pay for? More precisely, when it comes to schools, what do politicians think they are paying for? To answer that question we need to know what politicians have paid for and (as far as we can tell) why.

Until the late eighteenth century politicians had little to do with the upkeep of schools. Schooling in Britain was 'local rather than national, diverse rather than uniform' and, in rural areas – that is, in most of the country – such schooling as there was 'took firm account of season, harvest, distance, weather, and economic necessity'.[1] 'Economic necessity' here means that many parents needed their children as workers and were too poor to pay for their schooling.

By the last decades of the century, though, 'a growing population, agricultural change, the growth of towns and dissemination of new ideas, had given rise to deeper uncertainties and a sense of precariousness in the social structure'.[2] Many were driven off the land. They then had to buy food, and were hit by taxation which (in order not to discommode the rich) was largely indirect. There was little alternative employment for rural workers since, as yet, there were few industries which employed large numbers of people. It was, in short, an unusually bad time to be poor. As more labourers were forced off the land, it got worse.

During this 'classic period of the first industrial revolution', 1790-1820, investment in machinery and plant took precedence over expenditure on education. The need for more formal scientific and technological education was not acknowledged.[3] But in the turbulent years of the early nineteenth century, mass education – mass schooling – did become, for the first time, an issue of wide public concern. Social unrest brought forth a small group of radical educators, Tom Paine among them. Paine was that unusual quantity, an Englishman who had radical plans for schooling the poor. Not surprisingly, given his inclination to dissidence, Paine found himself unwelcome in several English towns. Benjamin Franklin suggested emigration to America. That restless colony seemed likely to welcome a radical thinker and, in the event, did. Paine settled in Pennsylvania and influenced the colonial revolutionaries. After American independence he again found himself out of place, and returned to England. This was unwise. Having recently published *The Rights of Man*, Paine was charged with seditious libel. He moved to France before he could be imprisoned. Not fated to a peaceful life, Paine was imprisoned in France, and sentenced to death for opposing the execution of the king.

Before these troubling events, Paine had turned his attention to schools. He argued that a remission of taxes on the poor (and, presumably, increased taxes on the rich) would allow the government of the day to grant families ten shillings a year, enabling parents to send children to school 'to learn reading, writing and common arithmetic'. This 'education grant' would cost the state approximately two and a half million pounds. It would relieve parents' poverty because (then as now) 'it is from the expense of bringing up children that their poverty arises'. The grant would also, not incidentally, abolish ignorance. Paine believed that the school system should provide for children in inaccessible areas, where their education allowance of ten shillings a year would mean that they could be taught by local people: distressed clergymen's widows, for instance. Since Paine's plan was to pay the scholar, not the school, it has been hailed, usually by rightwing thinkers, as the first educational voucher scheme. Paine also believed, it now seems optimistically, that his decentralised scheme would avoid governments' 'despotism over the minds of the people' and would frustrate their practice of retaining power by depending on ignorance. Clearly he failed to foresee governments' control of school knowledge.

Paine held that schooling should be widely extended among the children of the poor. A more general opinion among the affluent was that mass education would be a dangerous innovation which should be limited to the gentry and, perhaps, to the children of the emerging middle classes. The lower classes were, after all, known for 'their irresponsibility, their openness to deception and their inevitable ignorance',[4] all of which made them a threat to the social order. To school the poor was to take a risk: it might well give boys, and men, ideas above their station. Would a ploughman who could read 'be content to whistle up one furrow and down another from dawn in the morning to the setting of the sun?' Probably not. Worse, education would turn the young man into a disaffected person 'not satisfied with the station in which God has placed him': a man who 'forgetting the humility that belonged to his condition, was contriving to raise himself out of his proper place'.[5] (Those potentially disaffected were male. Not even the radical followers of Rousseau imagined that girls would be offered sufficient education to make them restless.)

When mass schooling reached Europe, it came first not to Britain but to Prussia. Its spread there, from 1810 onward, had more to do with nationalism – with reaction to Prussia's recent defeat by Napoleonic France – than with any desire to elevate the Prussian poor. Britain, undefeated by France, had no such motivation, and no such school system. Until the nineteenth century Britain's scattering of schools was financed sometimes by the philanthropy of rich families or, more commonly, by one or other church. Denominational competition for souls had much to do with the spread of British schooling. Sunday schools multiplied, and paved the way for a growing number of weekday schools, still commonly church-financed: notably by the Lancasterian Society and the National Society for Promoting the Education of the Poor in the Principles of the Established Church. The second was, as the name suggests, an evangelical arm of the Church of England.

Politicians came late into the schooling business. Parliament's first attempt at organising some payment to schools came with a Bill, in 1820, intended 'for better promoting the means of education for His Majesty's subjects in England and Wales'. This measure proposed that schools should be aided from local taxes ('rates') and that teachers should be members of the Established Church. Understandably that notion was opposed by churches which were not established – all churches except the Church of England. The Bill failed.

In 1833, the first successful bid to institute a parliamentary grant for education avoided such destructive rivalry by having funds (an annual grant of £20,000) distributed through both established and unestablished church societies. (It has been noted that for some time after this Parliament would continue to spend more on the Queen's stables than on educating the nation's children.) The state funds which were spent on schooling went to churches, in the first place, because Britain lacked effective local government capable of instituting and managing a national school system. (Prussia and France, which then had such systems, were briskly rejected as exemplars.)

In the absence of local government, 'practical administrative considerations, as well as national prejudice, impelled Britain to embark from the very start on a "permissive" course of offering financial support to existing bodies that already gave elementary schooling, instead of embarking on direct provision of schools by the state. The existing bodies in the 1830s being the churches, and especially the Church of England, it was to them that the government began allotting subsidies, so that they could open more schools. From this fatal, if politically inevitable, first step there grew an ever more powerful, vested interest which was to complicate and obstruct educational reform right the way down to the Butler Education Act of 1944.'[6]

Far from being grateful for state assistance, the churches were deeply dissatisfied both with its amount and distribution. In the decades after the 1830s, the Church of England took most of any parliamentary grant for schooling, while complaining that it was insufficient. Church dignitaries believed they should have the whole amount. Dissenting churches, understandably, dissented.

Unsatisfactory as church control may have been, the 1833 Act was a turning point in the financing of education. Since that time (from the mid-nineteenth century to the present) government funding has fluctuated, but has – with few interruptions – increased in real terms decade on decade.[7]

In the years after 1833, Parliament made other education-related grants. £30,000 was allotted, in 1846, for salaries of teachers in workhouse schools. That action was prompted by a finding that over half of workhouse teachers were themselves illiterate, as well as being otherwise incompetent. Since this predated the educational research industry, outcomes of the additional funding were not recorded. Teacher training (as it was called) expanded thereafter, but was still largely financed and controlled by the established church, rather than the state. (The Church of England ran thirty-four out the forty training colleges existing in the mid-nineteenth century.) In status, however, teachers, whether trained or untrained, remained near the bottom of any social or professional hierarchy.

At mid-century, various church societies continued to believe that education of the lower orders would widen the influence of religion. (Religion, in this context, meant of course their own brand of Christianity.) But the state was beginning to rival the church as a financial contributor to the cost of schooling. Annual Parliamentary expenditure under this heading rose from £125,000 in 1848 to over £800,000 in 1861.[8] Legislators invested of necessity in religious schooling, but were inclined to see it more as a defence against child crime (converting 'incipient criminals to Christianity') than as a purely evangelical venture. Since established churches supported an established order, their schools were seen as an insurance against that radicalism which grew from then rapidly increasing social and economic inequality throughout Britain. Members of Parliament feared particularly and equally the 'seductions of socialism' and the 'armed political monster' of Chartism.

Religious and other opponents of Parliamentary influence managed for decades to limit any significant extension of state funding – and hence control – of schooling. This changed with the 1870 Elementary Education Act. The Act funded School Boards and 'board schools' for (mainly working class) children 'for whose elementary education efficient and suitable provision is not otherwise made'. Surprisingly, the Treasury – presumably with an eye to the training of future workers – put a case for universal and free schooling, something which would not be achieved for another half century. Speaking of the masses, W E Forster, author of the 1870 Act, argued that 'now we have given them power, we must not wait any longer to give them education'. For some, this implied free schooling, paid for by the state. That, Forster went on to say, would be 'not only unnecessary, but mischievous'. On this issue, as on others, Forster won the day.

Despite the limitations on free education, and despite extensive concessions to religious educators, the 1870 Act was a major extension of state influence on elementary schooling. It marked a partial – a very partial – shift from primarily bible-based teaching to preparation of a future workforce. Some thirty years later, the National Union of Teachers could describe the 'six million children', in the public elementary schools of England and Wales, as 'the children of the workers, to be themselves England's workers a few years hence'.[9]

The reluctant extension of state funding for schools in the late nineteenth century was prompted, in part, by increasing international industrial competition. Prussia's technically oriented schooling had now become a pan-German system. It was educating a workforce increasingly competitive with that of United Kingdom.. Belatedly, Britain's decision-makers saw a need to train their own – or, more probably, other people's – children: those who would soon be assigned to England's industrial labour force. In this ambition they were commonly opposed by those who believed that 'liberal education' could not coexist with technical; and by the vast vested interests of the churches. Despite this formidable opposition, an Education Act in 1899 established a Board of Education, 'a department of state consolidating central direction over the educational system'[10]; and, in 1902, a further Education Act set out to rationalise Britain's still haphazard school system. Two and a half thousand elected school boards were amalgamated into local education authorities, which were given powers to fund, 'not elementary', but secondary and technical education. (Neither of these existed in any way we would now recognise.)

The 1902 Act achieved the considerable feat of infuriating equally all the churches, established and unestablished. All foresaw the ending of their educational influence. In this they were wrong or, at the very least, premature. The churches – notably, but not only, the Church of England – maintained their grip on British schooling for many decades to come. Despite this, in the years before World War One it did seem that schooling for the poor might be extended, and made more accessible.

The war put such changes on hold. In the depressed postwar years, state-supported schooling regressed. State-supported and fee-charging secondary schools 'aped public schools' but lacked their prestige, while also failing to offer their pupils an education which might have been of use in their life and work. Though it was clear that Britain was declining as an industrial power, it was rare that any connection was made in public discourse between education and economic success or failure. By the late 1920s leading politicians of the three main parties, ably supported by the Federation of British Industries, aimed not to educate skilled workers, but to save money by undoing certain 'intolerably expensive' provisions of the 1902 Education Act. In this campaign they were assisted by Lord Percy, conservative President of the Board of Education from 1924 to 1929. The London *Daily Mail*, as ever combining misinformation with vituperation, accused Lord Percy of communist sympathies. He belonged, the paper believed, 'to the Socialist or "pink" wing of the Cabinet. And he is always thinking of "pink" measures in the hope of pleasing the "Reds".'[11]

Much of the argument at this time revolved around the issue of schooling for pupils after the age of eleven or twelve. To some it seemed obvious that, if compulsory schooling were extended, there should be free secondary schools – either on the model of existing grammar schools, or in some yet-to-be-settled form of technical school. Both options were resisted by secular opponents and, more particularly, by churchmen. Ecclesiastics 'both Roman Catholic and Church of England' insisted that, unless all their demands were met, 'they would arrest all advance ... by any means to hand'.[12] In this negative aim they were successful. A national system of free secondary schools had to wait for the 1944 Education Act.

Even then the churches, unlike the Axis powers, were not about to admit defeat. In preparing this historic Act, the wartime Education Minister, R A Butler, found that his main task was not to plan a school system for the second half of the twentieth century, but to deal with endless delegations of church notables. The churchmen were concerned, first, with making sure that religious indoctrination would continue to be mandatory in schools (in which they were successful) and, second, with seizing a large part of the proposed education budget – in which they did better than they, or the school system, probably deserved. Butler, driven to distraction, suggested abolishing Oxford University, the alma mater of many troublesome priests.

First among Butler's own priorities was 'the need for industrial and technical training and the linking up of schools closely with employment'. But the churches, as a pressure group, forced him instead to concentrate on a lower priority – 'a settlement with the Churches about Church schools, and religious instruction in schools'. This was so time-consuming that the Minister's third issue – 'the question of the public schools' – was left unresolved, to the manifest relief of that elite, but then indigent, sector.

The potential cost of the 1944 Education Act provoked Treasury unease, assuaged only partly by Butler's and Churchill's opposition to paying women teachers a salary equal to that of their male colleagues. (The Government, narrowly defeated on this issue, forced a vote of confidence which re-established unequal pay.) Despite Treasury's misgivings, education budgets increased steadily, in real terms, through the second half of the twentieth century and into the twenty-first. By 2004 Parliament's annual funding for state schooling had risen to around £35 billion. But why? Why, over almost two centuries, do governments hand out these ever-increasing sums? What do politicians believe we, or they, get in return?

This is not an easy question, for politicians are not in the habit of telling the rest of us what they believe. Politicians tell us what they think will be welcome news, which may not be a close fit with what is happening, or what is being planned. To take just one example, Stanley Baldwin, when Prime Minister, announced in 1929 that, while hitherto 'a youth's school badge has been his social label' the interests of social unity 'demand the removal of this source of class prejudice, and that the national structure of education should be drastically remodelled to form one coherent whole' – a 'great new fabric' which was already taking shape. Brian Simon, who quotes this remarkable flight of fancy, comments that 'it is difficult to conceive of any contemporary statement further removed from the truth'.[13] In more recent times we have been repeatedly told by Conservative and Labour Ministers that Britain's school system is now designed to offer all pupils a good education, with equal opportunity for all. Again this is, intentionally or otherwise, some distance from the truth.

In the past, before spin doctors were conceived, politicians and their civil servants were more open in their assessments of the reasons for supporting schools. In 1816, Parliamentary Committees reported on 'the Education of the Lower Orders in the Metropolis [London] and Beyond'.[14] Giving evidence, the Treasurer of the British and Foreign Bible Society estimated that 'if the sum of £400,000 could be devoted [to schooling] every child requiring this sort of education could be provided with it throughout England and Wales, so as to leave not an uneducated person in the country; and, in my opinion, a much smaller sum would suffice'. But, the Committee heard, there were difficulties. Some families had only one pair of breeches; boys could attend school only when it was their day to wear the trousers. This was significant for, as the Reverend Gurney told the Committee, he took young people into school 'as soon as ever the boys have got breeches; we do not consult their age, but their size'.

A later Parliamentary report (the Newcastle Report of 1861) was more definite in its conclusions. It approved the evidence of the Reverend James Fraser, who doubted 'whether it would be desirable, with a view to the real interests of the peasant boy, to keep him at school till he was 14 or 15 years of age ... We must make up our minds to see the last of him, as far as the day school is concerned, at 10 or 11 ... I have no brighter view of the future, or the possibilities of an English elementary education, floating before my eyes than this.'[15]

The Taunton Report of 1868 pursued this question of ideal school-leaving age. It suggested a First, Second and Third Grade education, with different leaving ages. The Report found, fortunately, that these distinctions corresponded roughly with 'the gradations of society' and that the needs of the Third Class (small farmers, small tradesmen, superior artisans) were for their children to be taught 'very good reading, very good writing, very good arithmetic'. Unsurprisingly, the Report added that 'those who can afford to pay more for their children's education will also, as a general rule, continue that education for a longer time'.

In 1870, W E Forster (Vice-President of the Education Department) was one of the first in his position to propose explicitly a link between schooling and a thriving economy. 'Upon the speedy provision of elementary education depends our industrial prosperity. It is of no use trying to give technical teaching to our artisans without elementary education ... if we leave our work-folk any longer unskilled, notwithstanding their strong sinews and determined energy, they will become over-matched in the competition of the world.'[16]

Forster's speech – and the Act which prompted it – suggest that British schooling was moving away from its religious provenance, and would in future be justified, at least partly, on grounds of economic utility. But, as we have seen, churches' hold on schooling was tenacious, and took a long time to loosen. The 1888 Report of the Royal Commission on the Elementary Education Acts concluded that 'the evidence does not warrant the conclusion that ... religious and moral training can be provided otherwise than through the medium of elementary schools'.

The post-1870 spread of elementary education led to a slow growth in 'higher grade' (post-elementary) schools. These were not what we would now recognise as secondary schools; and were designed not to be so. Many charged weekly fees, and were of course beyond the financial reach of poor parents. They benefited mainly the aspirant lower middle classes. Those more affluent – but not rich – sent their children to grammar schools, most of which continued to teach a reassuringly anachronistic curriculum. The rich of course sent their children to those 'public' schools whose classical curricula were wanly reflected further down the social scale.

By contrast, a Technical Instruction Act, passed in 1889, allowed local councils to spend money on scholarships for the poor. Then as now, many councils were not particularly interested either in helping the poor or advancing technical instruction. There was also strong opposition from those who believed that 'liberal' and technical education could not coexist. Response to the Act was uneven and, in the main, ungenerous.

But, as funding from the public purse increased, so did state and local control of schooling. Education authorities were faced with the problem of how 'to get more children into the existing schools, to get them there in a fit condition to receive instruction, and to keep them to an older age'. In many districts, bylaws were passed to make children's attendance at elementary school compulsory. Machinery of enforcement was established. In 1895 the Bryce Commission recommended a central English authority for education, adding, disingenuously, that this was not in order to control post-elementary education, nor to override local action. It was not the first or last time that central government would present increased control over schooling as freedom of choice.

Four years later, in 1899, a Board of Education was created, which did extend state control over schooling in England and Wales. In time, the Board and its successors displaced local control, though it took the best part of a century for central government to complete the debilitation of those local education authorities which had been set up at the beginning of the twentieth century.

The battle against free and comprehensive secondary education was to continue for another four decades. The 1902 Education Act had established what its departmental author described as 'Pretence-Secondary Schools' designed, he noted, to head off 'the natural local pressure in the big towns for the development of true Secondary Schools' – that is, schools which were more closely related to contemporary society, and less class-based.[17] But by the century's second decade, many politicians had come to favour vocational rather than religious education. The 1917 Report to the Departmental Committee on Juvenile Education in Relation to Employment after the War stressed 'citizenship education' in schools, rather than religious observance. However, if 'citizenship' had become more prominent, it was citizenship closely linked to membership of the national workforce. It was not enough, this report concluded, to be a 'reasonable human being': the young person must also be a 'competent worker'. 'We are clear,' the authors wrote, 'that the business of [part-time] classes is to do what they can in making a reasonable human being, and a citizen, and that, if they do this, they will help to make a competent workman also.'

The system of compulsory schooling to fourteen did not end the divisive nature of 'elementary' schools (which might have pupils from age four to fourteen) for children of the lower classes, and secondary education for most children of higher-status, or richer, families. Nor did it end the divisions in schooling between fee-charging schools for the rich, state schools (which might also charge fees) for the poorer classes, and voluntary schools, mainly for those parents whose first concern was either their children's religious condition or (as now) avoiding schools entirely supported by the state.

By the mid-nineteenth century political pressures on schools were forcing change. The proportion of religious education was very slowly being reduced in many schools, and replaced by 'basic training for industry'. At the beginning of the twentieth century, nearly half of all primary schools remained in the control of one or other church; but, by the start of World War Two, the number of such Church of England establishments had halved, with a roughly corresponding decline in schools run by other protestant sects. There was a consequent rise in state expenditure on schooling and, of course, in state intervention. State grants to post-elementary schools also rose steadily in the first decades of the twentieth century, with a similar expansion of state control over what was taught.

Twenty years later, concern about the education of future workers had a contemporary tone. In the years before World War Two, politicians and administrators fretted about state-supported schools' attachment to academic curricula. The Spens Report of 1938 noted that 'the most striking feature of the new secondary schools ... is their marked disinclination to deviate to any considerable extent from the main lines of the traditional grammar school curriculum. That conservative and imitative tendency, which is so salient a characteristic in the evolution of English political and social institutions, is particularly noticeable in this instance.'

The vocational/academic split was formalised in the previously noted Norwood Report of 1943: a document which did much to shape secondary schooling for the rest of the century. Dr Cyril Norwood 'steered his willing committee toward his own cherished objective' which was 'to preserve the domination of the grammar school and its academic values at the cost of other kinds of secondary school and of any type of education inspired by purposes related to life and work in the modern world'.[18] To this end the Norwood committee divided young people into three groups: those who 'can grasp an argument, or follow a piece of connected reasoning'; those who are able to work 'in applied science or applied art'; and a third type of pupil who deals 'more easily with concrete things than with ideas' and whose 'horizon is near and within a limited area his movement is generally slow'. Norwood's subsequent report proposed three types of school for these three types of person, who were to be identified and sorted at age eleven. In the end, only two kinds of school emerged: grammar schools for those could grasp an argument, and secondary modern schools for the slower and more concrete pupils who could not. They were destined to labour in industry.

In the early 1940s there was renewed pressure, among the good and great of Britain, for a return to religious teaching in schools – pressure which seemed, for a while, as if it might lead lower-status schools away from their mission of preparing a workforce, and back to a primary focus on gentling, civilising and indoctrinating. The postwar desire for structural change curbed that aim, though social renewal in education was limited, as ever, by pressure groups, and by the conventional wisdom of its bureaucratic architects.

That wisdom decreed, in the 1944 Education Act, a tier of secondary schools, leading on from what were now called primary schools. The secondary tier was to have Norwood's tripartite (or, in the event, dual) division; and of course Britain's fee-charging ('public') schools still stood outside the state system. By the end of World War Two, many thought, as Correlli Barnett later wrote, that the 'public school ethos' – which he describes as hierarchical, homosexual, games-playing, robust Christianity – was partly responsible for the debilitated condition of post-war Britain. Others (who proved more influential) believed that public schools were essential for the running of what has been termed England's 'oligarchy masquerading as democracy'. R A Butler, Britain's wartime Minister of Education, noted that his Prime Minister, Winston Churchill, believed that 'we must reinforce the ruling class' by reinforcing public schools, which should begin to select not only by accident of birth or wealth, but also by 'the accident of ability'. This seems not to have been Butler's view; but, here and elsewhere, Churchill prevailed.

Butler, engaged in a long-running battle to reduce religious influence in Britain's schooling, decided not to fight on two fronts. As we have seen, he missed the only moment in the twentieth century when the public schools might have been made working a part of the society around them. Anthony Howard[19] wrote of Butler, 'the time was ripe, the public mood was propitious, the opportunity was there. And yet he contrived to throw it all away.'

Having survived the threat of modernisation, the country's public schools flourished. They continued to educate most of Britain's cabinet ministers, top civil servants and judges in the half century after the 1944 Act. (Until recently, fewer Labour Ministers came from public schools but, at least to the end of the twentieth century, Labour had fewer years in government; and many fewer Ministers of whatever educational provenance.)

Within the state system, the 1944 Education Act instituted a tier of schools designed to educate children of the less affluent middle classes and to produce industry's middle managers. These were traditional grammar schools, as well as some newer, 'academically oriented' state secondary schools. Such favoured institutions imitated grammar schools in curriculum, in pupil discipline, and in ethos. Both sets of schools were intended for those who had passed a newly instituted 'eleven plus' examination. The eleven plus was, as the name implies, taken by pupils around the age of eleven. It was intended to measure that degree of innate intelligence which was unaffected by class, wealth, poverty or learning style. Those who failed the exam were assigned to technical, or 'modern', schools, to prepare for a future of being managed by those who had passed the exam. This allotment of pupils to suitable strata was described as schooling appropriate to the needs of every young person: or as 'appropriate to the needs of the child'. By fortunate chance, the arrangement fitted also with the perceived needs of contemporary industry.

Training – rather than education – of teachers was now a further cost to the British state. After World War Two a political decision was taken to establish a central body to supervise the training process. The report on which this development was based insisted that 'nothing but drastic reforms, involving the expenditure of considerable additional sums of public money, will secure what schools need, and what children and young people deserve'.[20] These 'considerable additional sums' were spent first on crash courses for training school teachers after the war and, later, on establishing new training colleges, as they were called, for a postwar generation of primary and secondary teachers. There were twenty-nine local authority colleges in 1944. By 1962 there were seventy-seven. The additional sums involved in educational expansion amounted to an approximate trebling of expenditure between 1945 and 1965.

Public financing of secondary schools, and the 1947 raising of Britain's school leaving age to fifteen, had already expanded education's cost to the state. Despite this, some argued that the country's economic needs demanded a further rise in the school-leaving age. In a break with the past, such arguments were often now couched specifically in terms of human capital. The Crowther Report of 1959 saw education 'as a vital part of the nation's capital investment'. In allowing young people to leave school at fifteen, 'the odds are weighted against the national interest'. Showing unusual interest in both educational equity and economic change, the report concluded that 'more time and care must be spent on education and training ... it is not only at the top but almost to the bottom of the pyramid that the scientific revolution of our times needs to be reflected in a longer educational process'.

The 'scientific revolution' was not the only reason for keeping pupils longer at school. (Nor were schools anywhere near the forefront of that revolution.) In postwar decades, despite a number of changes, a main purpose of schooling was still the civilising of poor and rebellious young. The material advance of 'British working-class youth' should, in the circumspect language of the time, be accompanied by an 'equivalent cultural advance'.[21] A practical way of organising such cultural advance might have been changing the school system to ensure that working-class youth was offered a less class-biased and impoverished form of education. A Public Schools Commission did, in 1970, make such recommendations. They were not implemented.

More state funding was, however, made available, in 1971, for the fee-charging schools favoured by affluent parents. In the same year the school-leaving age in the state system was to have been raised to sixteen. That change was delayed, due to its expense.

Other areas of schooling were absorbing more of the state's revenues. Despite the decline in the number of 'church schools', politicians paid an increasing amount to church-run, but now 'controlled', schools, of various types. But with higher funding of religious schools came stricter educational discipline. For some churches (notably Roman Catholic) this was a price too high. Others questioned the whole idea of state funding for church-run schools and argued for an American-style separation of church and state, or at least of state-run institutions such as schools. These arguments had less than no visible effect. In an increasingly irreligious nation, the 1944 Education Act had made religious instruction and collective worship a necessary (in the sense of mandatory) part of schools' syllabus.

In the decades following the 1944 Act doubt was cast on the proposition that humans were born either to labour or to rule, and that schooling should match those immutable fates. The idea of one type of school for all (or almost all) young people gained favour. Mr Crosland, who became Secretary of State for Education in 1965, enthusiastically supported comprehensive schooling. The British school system, Crosland believed, 'had been primarily geared to educating the middle classes. Working-class children, with rare exception, were faced with overcrowding, a shortage of teachers, deteriorating buildings, and were segregated into different schools. Nature assures that an elite is always rising and asserting itself in a democracy. But the state should do its utmost ... to make it possible for those without money or position or a literate family background to have equal access to the opportunity that a decent education bestows'.[22] But Crosland's ministerial tenure looks, in retrospect, like equity's high tide. From the 1970s, opponents of equal educational opportunity – in both of Britain's main political parties – have held most of the cards.

Of course opposition to comprehensive schooling did not start in the 1970s. It was opposed both before and after its implementation. The comprehensive reform was accused of dumbing down a school system which had hitherto been (at least in part) intellectually respectable. It was alleged that comprehensive schools lowered standards; pupils left school illiterate and innumerate. Furthermore, these schools introduced frivolous and non-traditional subjects to their curricula.

Some of the criticisms of comprehensives were justified. But subsequent, or parallel, proposals for reform of state schooling in Britain were intended to undermine, not improve, the comprehensive system. Kenneth Baker – the most active Education Minister in the 1979-1992 Thatcher era – has said that the real target of his sweeping school legislation (notably the 1988 Education Act) was the comprehensive system of schooling itself. 'I would,' he now admits, 'have liked to bring back selection.'[23] Since that might have been controversial among those who still believed in equality of educational opportunity, Mrs Thatcher's Conservative government decided to erode the comprehensive system by stealth. A series of anti-egalitarian measures were, then and later, marketed under such innocuous labels as 'maintaining standards' or 'increasing parental choice'.

Since 1997 a Labour administration has covertly continued to reduce equality of educational opportunity, first by continuing its predecessors' policies of classifying schools by 'league tables' and, secondly, by creating a hierarchy of school types, clearly antithetical to the comprehensive principle; and finally by expanding the number of religious (or 'faith') schools – which are by definition selective – and creating a small, but expensive, tier of 'city academies'. These, while principally financed by the state, are commonly run by rich eccentrics often wishing to proselytise some unscientific, but God-given, ideology, of which creationism is the best known.

Looking back from the early twenty-first century, we see a steady growth in public expenditure on education, with only occasional retrenchment. The initial £20,000 education grant of 1833 rose to over three per cent of the UK gross national product in 1950; and had doubled again by 1972. In 1977, seven per cent of GNP was spent on education: over £7 billion.[24] By 2002-2003 that figure had risen (in unadjusted figures) to around £54 billion, of which the largest proportion (around £34 billion) went to schools. In part, this expenditure was due to increased economic expectation. 'A common theme underlying the educational reforms [of the 1980s and 1990s] ... was that they treated public education as an instrument of economic policy. The assumption was that the reforms would lead to a more highly skilled workforce qualified at a lower cost per person, and that this would improve national productivity and make the country better able to perform in the global marketplace'.[25] Whether this has been the case is (as we shall see) open to question.

Inevitably, with increased state expenditure came increased central control of school systems. In the last three decades of the twentieth century Britain has had Conservative and Labour administrations which talked decentralisation, and energetically practised centralisation. In the context of English and Welsh school systems, that has meant (among other things) a centrally dictated 'national curriculum'. This sharply reduced the influence of local education authorities, which had formerly been responsible for curricula, and correspondingly expanded the influence and control of central government. In 2005 Britain's Prime Minister announced plans to ensure that 'schools are no longer tentacles of the state, but instead one of the central institutions of the local community' with 'greater curriculum freedom'.[26] Since this ostensibly attractive proposal is directly opposed to the Labour government's centralising ethos, and since Mr Blair is, at the time of writing, increasingly preoccupied with parallel realities, this proposed liberation from central control has had a muted reception from those who genuinely wish for a freer, more innovative and egalitarian school system. In essence, Britain's problem, an adjudicator of admissions has said, 'is not that schools are rigging their intake to get the best students, or that middle-class parents are using their clout to get into the best schools, though both are true. It is that there are just too few good schools to go round'.[27]

Over the past century, the British school system has failed to meet most economic expectations; as did others abroad. 'The dissatisfaction felt by many Western governments with the performance of their public schooling system toward the end of the last century partly reflected a concern that existing and future economic and social challenges were not being adequately responded to by that system. From the 1970s it was believed in much of Europe and North America that slowdowns in economic growth and losses in international competitiveness were partly the result of failures in schooling systems.'[28]

These 'failures' were addressed, if not cured, by late-twentieth-century neo-liberal reforms. In what seems to have been a further effort both to control and destabilise the comprehensive school system, Britain's 1979-1997 Conservative administration initiated a regime – noted above – of targets and tests, school league tables, and 'assisted places' (in fee-charging schools) for poor but academic children. Those measures arguably improved some aspects of industrially oriented schooling (notably numeracy-and-literacy) while being in most other ways retrogressive. The subsequent, post-1997, Labour administration retained many of these innovations, on the grounds that they 'raised standards', and, in some loosely defined way, improved comprehensive schooling.

As of 2005, some school-system-defined standards have indeed been raised. More general educational improvement has not been demonstrated. At the same time, there has been growing (and so far justified) scepticism among some critics that 'sustained economic growth', even if achieved by educational and by other means, 'would automatically generate sufficient "trickle-down" effects to promote social inclusion and prevent widening income inequality'.[29]

So, returning to this chapter's original question, what to do politicians think they are paying for when they allocate state funding for schools? In recent years the circumspect answer is likely to be 'a good education for all young people'. The reality, of course, is more complex.

Since the state first supported schools many politicians have seen one of their aims as civilising the young – particularly the young of poor families – and, more simply, keeping them off the streets; or, in depressed times, out of the labour market. For some, this is still one of schooling's more useful functions.

A second purpose has been, in sociological jargon, 'reproducing society' or, in Mr Churchill's simpler and more limited view, renewal of the ruling class. In Britain a thriving group of fee-charging schools has, to great extent, taken care of the latter, though occasional muttering about inequity has led, in the last half century, to minor adjustments in the intake of public schools, or of the 'good universities' to which public schools have traditionally assured entry.

A third end is to maintain schools as places for child-minding. Britain's economy, at least since the 1940s, has depended on the labour of women, as well as men. With either one or two parents, this commonly means that no adult will be home during the day; the family will depend on school to keep children safe and, in the best of all worlds, to educate them. As noted, there are plans to increase the opening hours of schools to allow parents more time for paid work.

A fourth – and arguably dominant – purpose has been the training of a national workforce; a training which assumes that most young people will, in future, work in industry. For at least the past half century this has been, for most politicians who could influence schooling, the principal return on the state's now substantial investment. The aim was succinctly expressed in 1995 by the then Department for Education and Employment, which believed its mission was 'to support economic growth and improve the nation's competitiveness and quality of life by raising standards of educational achievement and by promoting an efficient and flexible labour market.'[30] Quality of life was not the first of those desiderata.

There are problems here. There is still considerable opposition to what is seen as a technicist training in schools. Those who are agnostic on this issue have other questions. They ask, are schools generally doing a good job of training, or educating, young people for life and work in the early years of the twenty-first century? Do politicians – or indeed teachers – have the expertise needed to get this right? How would we know whether or not they are getting it right? And – if they are not – what can be done?

The following chapters of the book are concerned with those questions.

[1] Aldrich 1982
[2] Lawson and Silver 1973
[3] Carpentier 2003
[4] *The Economist* 1848, quoted in Chancellor 1970
[5] Booth 1858
[6] Barnett 1988
[7] Carpentier 2003
[8] This figure was reduced in later years by the introduction of the Revised Code.
[9] Steer (London, undated)
[10] Simon 1974
[11] *Daily Mail* 23.6.1927, quoted in Simon 1974
[12] Simon 1974
[13] Ibid
[14] Quoted in Maclure 1973
[15] Ibid
[16] Ibid
[17] Eaglesham 1956
[18] Barnett 1988
[19] Howard 1987
[20] The McNair Report (London 1944)
[21] Fyvel 1961
[22] Crosland 1982
[23] Kenneth Baker, quoted in Davies 2000
[24] Fenwick and McBride 1981
[25] Young 1998
[26] *The Guardian* 20 October 2005
[27] Philip Hunter, schools' admission chief adjudicator, quoted in *The Guardian* 18 October 2005
[28] Adnett and Davies 2000
[29] Ibid
[30] DFEE press release 2.10.95

CHAPTER 5

HOW SCHOOLS TEACH

'There is really no learning without doing. There is the appearance of learning without doing when we ask children to memorise stuff. But adults know they learn best on the job, from experience, by trying things out, Children learn best that way too. If there is nothing actually to do in a subject area we want to teach children, it may be the case that there really isn't anything children ought to learn.'
  Roger Schank

'I remembered only one thing from my schooldays: the implicit message that all problems in the world had already been solved; that the answers were to be found in the head of the teacher or, more likely, at the back of his textbook; my task being to transfer the answers to my head.'
  Charles Handy

We have no record of teaching methods in Britain's first recorded schools, but we can make an educated guess that the dominant way of working was didactic: there would have been a teacher talking to (or at) a group of pupils. We can make that guess because this is the way that most schools work, and have worked for centuries, if not millennia. And that modus operandi makes sense, if we assume that one person has a stock of knowledge that should be transmitted to others who don't have it. Thus we have a remarkably long-standing tradition in schooling: a teacher who transfers (or tries to transfer) information to a larger number of usually younger people who are termed 'pupils', 'students' or 'learners'. As shorthand, we have called this the didactic paradigm. Its components – teachers, pupils, classrooms, chairs, tables, and chalkboards – make up a technology that has changed remarkably little over time. The two significant scholastic innovations – printed textbooks and computers – have not markedly altered the paradigm. Rather, they have been co-opted to become a functional part of it (see chapter 20).

Against this picture of a timeless way of working is now set an image of a British school system in creative flux. Over the past half-century our schools have been subject to a accelerating flow of new (and often short-lived) initiatives: selection, testing of 'general intelligence', tripartite school strata, dual secondary strata (grammar and secondary modern), middle schools, comprehensivisation, beacon schools, CTCs, academies, mixed-ability teaching, tracking, intra-class streaming, newly devised tests and examinations, teacher assessments, 'independent' inspections of schools, advisers, inspectors, teaching assistants, privatised school assessment, privatised education authorities, literacy and numeracy hours, various vocational qualifications (GNVQs, AVQs, 'modern apprenticeships'), school league tables, and so on. The *Economist* summarises this restless political reworking of the English school system over the past eight years as 'eleven white and green papers [legislation or legislative proposals], serial changes to the national curriculum, reforms of old qualifications and the introduction of new ones, beefing up the schools inspectorate and performance league tables, new ways to expand some schools and close others, creating academies and dumping the Tories' scheme for directly funded schools. [The government] has also spent freely: state education has risen from 4.7% of GDP to 5.5% today.'[1] It is not clear, however, that this extra spending has produced any quantifiable benefit (see chapter 8).

The government's initiatives have been typically haphazard in conception and, often, at risk of early extinction. Education Action Zones are a case in point. In 1999 they were welcomed into the world of English education by Mr Blair, who predicted that they would 'change attitudes and approaches in order to seek solutions to long standing problems, working with businesses and other partners'. They did none of these things. Not long afterward, unmourned, they were quietly buried.

Such febrile and often ephemeral activity changes some of what happens in some schools, in some classrooms, some of the time. Most schools – the submerged majority – remain effectively untouched. They are altered (often for the worse) only by the well-meaning system-wide directives of central government. What is clear, through all this, is that the didactic paradigm remains dominant in most of our schools. There are many exceptions but research shows that, across the school system, in different settings and with different job descriptions, teachers still spend most of their time transmitting information – or setting exercises on that information – in the hope that pupils will retain some of it long enough to reproduce at examination time.

It is worth reminding ourselves how unusual our schools are; how unusual it is to have a modus operandi which remains substantially unchanged over centuries. If we accept the Kondratiev theory of long cycles of technological change, the didactic paradigm has lasted through (at least) five Kondratievs: the water-powered mechanisation of industry; the steam-powered mechanisation of industry and transport; the electrification of industry, transport and the home; the motorisation of transport and the era of mass production; and the computerisation of advanced economies.[2] Few other enterprises have remained essentially unchanged over a similar timespan. Such persistence demands both comparison and explanation. Why has schools' way of working outlasted those of other institutions?

First, we need to see if there are other modus operandi – other technologies – as persistent as the didactic paradigm in schooling. Agriculture is a possibility: it still goes through the same nominal cycles – ploughing, sowing, harvesting, processing – as it did in the sixth century when Britain's schools were first recorded. But with powered machinery, biologically modified seeds, computerisation and factory processing, agricultural technology has changed so radically that it is hard to argue for unbroken continuity. The change in the percentage of agricultural workers (from over 80% of the active population in the seventeenth century to, at a generous estimate, less than 5% now) emphasises the qualitative nature of the change. (The number of teachers has, of course, increased markedly in that time.)

Commercial enterprises have nothing like schools' longevity. Most change, or renew, their core business relatively frequently. The average half-life of large companies 'was 75 years during the twentieth century; for small companies most studies suggest a half-life in single figures'.[3] It has been argued[4] that the Swedish enterprise Stora is the oldest firm 'which has had the character of a publicly owned company from its very beginnings' in 1288. But Stora's core business has changed: it started life as a copper mine and is now a paper, packaging and timber conglomerate. The same is true of John Brooke and Sons, reputedly Britain's oldest family enterprise. Brooke started life in the sixteenth century. It was then a textile maker. Now its core business has altered: its mills have become a business park. Clearly the technology of a copper mine is very different from that of a paper and packaging firm; as is that of a textile mill from a business park.

If we take British education as a publicly available service it bears comparison with other public services, such as medicine and transport, and, perhaps, the church. (All of these may, of course, work for profit, as do some schools.) But neither medicine nor transport has a modus operandi unchanged, or largely unchanged, over centuries. We have taken the sixth century AD as the date of the first recorded British schools. At that time, of course, medicine had none of the technology – anaesthesia, pharmaceuticals, sterilisation, radiography – now central to its practice. Transport was either by foot or by animal power. Perhaps only with the Roman Catholic church can we argue that a core business has changed as little in that time as it has in our school system.

We might ask why schools have a near unique degree of stasis in their central practice. Or we could turn the question around and ask why other ways of working have died sooner. To that Mokyr[5] would answer that some technologies have been eliminated by war: the idea of war's fostering benign innovation is, he writes, 'a curiously Eurocentric notion ...for the rest of the world, war was an unmitigated scourge'. But war, or its legacy, has not always been a scourge for schools. Prussia's school system was spawned by war; and the aftermath of World War Two brought an unprecedented degree of change to Britain's schools. R A Butler's 1944 Education Act was 'a mighty creation' which, Mr Butler himself hoped, would 'be as much social as educational' and would have the effect 'of welding us all into one nation ... instead of two nations, as Disraeli talked about'.[6]

The postwar pressure for change was so strong that Butler could probably have found support for altering schools' didactic practice, and, by appealing directly to the public, might have carried through his wish to integrate England's fee-charging schools into the state system. Writing of this lost opportunity, Timmins[7] notes that 'there would never again be a moment when [it] would be at all feasible' to eliminate 'the class and opportunity-based divisions that have so marked Britain's version of the public/private split'. It was a split which strengthened the country's conservative educational sector and slowed the pace of social and scientific change. From the mid-nineteenth century, 'English public schools opened their doors to members of the new elite, but painstakingly avoided providing them with the kind of practical education that would enable them to threaten the technological status quo.'[8]

Mokyr further argues that some technologies have been buried by political change, and more by competition: someone has simply found a better way of doing things. There have been many suggestions as to why that has not happened with our schools. One is that most schools are, at least nominally, free at the point of use, which eliminates competition. There is no profit to be made by undercutting a free service. But there is – in England more than elsewhere in Europe – a fee-charging school sector, equally wedded to the didactic paradigm. (There has also been a small number of fee-charging schools – Dartington, for instance – which rejected didactic teaching. Few of them have lasted and none has permanently altered the dominant instructional pattern within the British school system.) So the issue of cost seems not be explanatory here.

Another possible explanation for schools' stasis is clients' lack of power. Schools' clients are, by definition, of school age. They lack the authority, or financial leverage, which may come later. Often pupils do not even make decisions about which school they will attend; nor can they easily change schools if their parents' first choice is not working well. There may be little incentive for change in an enterprise whose clients have no power to make their wishes felt. Many schools assume that their pupils are content, but are careful not to check by asking.

There are other reasons for persistence of the didactic paradigm. The first is the hermetic and self-assessing nature of school systems, discussed more fully in chapter 7. Any organisation which is the sole arbiter of its own performance is unlikely to find compelling need for significant change.

A second reason is convenience. From teachers' – and schools' – viewpoint, didactic teaching is the method of choice. It has generated a huge literature but, at its heart, it is an appealingly simple method, which teachers have been trained in. It works well, only if we assume that learning is a necessary consequence of teaching. Sadly, this is not the case.

If the conditions are right, traditional teaching works for such basic skills as reading and simple numeracy. But real learning comes more from what learners do than what teachers do. If we want schools to educate, as well as train, we need to shift our focus from teaching to learning. We need to call into question schools' time-honoured attachment to the didactic paradigm.

We should not underestimate the difficulty of doing that. Even a limited shift of focus from teaching to learning means a fundamental change in the work of both teachers and students; in the notion of a one-size-fits-all curriculum; in the use of new technologies; and also in the hierarchical structure of schools. Then there are the pressure groups to deal with. Affluent parents, teachers, schools of education, conservative politicians and business groups are all, as groups, inclined to resist change in schools (see section V). That vested interest in stasis means that no real development in our school system is likely to come about unless changes in the national economy generate sufficient political pressure for a paradigm shift in schooling.

[1] *Economist* 22.10.05
[2] Freeman and Louca 2001
[3] *Economist* 18.12.04
[4] De Geus 2002
[5] Mokyr 1990
[6] Barnett 1988
[7] Timmins 1995
[8] Ibid

CHAPTER 6

WHAT SCHOOLS TEACH AND WHAT THEY DON'T TEACH

'School hit me like a ton of bricks. I wasn't prepared for gender obsession, race and class complexities, or the new-to-me notions of war, male leadership and a god who mysteriously resembled the ruling class.'
    Gloria Steinem

'Obviously, a power elite will not enjoy putting in place and practicing a pedagogical form or expression that adds to the social contradictions which reveal the power of the elite classes.'
    Paulo Freire

The staples of mass schooling don't change much. For over a century schools have trained young people in the basic skills of a future workforce: reading-writing-arithmetic. For a time, girls were trained in skills appropriate to home-maker, servant or mother. That changed gradually after World War Two, as women became part of the industrial workforce. Then as now, it was assumed that future managers or professionals learned what they needed outside or beyond the state school system.

In Victorian England, however, 'the school day' became problematic, though not for the reasons we might expect. Training in what are now called 'basic skills' may have satisfied the business community but, for the wider public, it no longer seemed enough – even for mass schooling – to fill the day with reading-writing-arithmetic-religion-and-respect. Some of those who ran schools came to believe that poor children should be taught other useful or moral accomplishments. Thus were born the ancestors of what are now centrally mandated school curricula, filled with subjects which have the same names as disciplines in the world outside school: 'history', 'geography', 'biology', 'chemistry', 'mathematics', and so on. But, as Goodson remarks, what is surprising is not the novelty of contemporary curricula, but their similarity to the curricula of higher elementary schools a century earlier (this despite the revolutionary social and economic changes of the intervening years). In 1904 the state's 'Secondary Regulations' laid down that 'the [school] course should provide for instruction in the English Language and Literature; at least one Language, other than English; Geography; History; Mathematics; Science and Drawing; with due provision for Manual Work and Physical Exercise, and in a girls' school, for Housewifery'.[1]

The idea that the school day should be divided into separately taught subjects was widely accepted a century ago. It is now taken so much for granted that we find it hard to imagine a different organisation of secondary schooling – though for most of us what we need to do in life does not fit into subject divisions. But, once accepted as scholastically legitimate, school subjects rapidly establish their own culture, traditions, examination rituals and tenuous links with higher education (though school subjects have commonly been inward-looking and, intellectually, have drawn little from contemporary academia).

This is confusing because, though subject names are the same as those in the world outside school, practice is often different. School biology is not what working biologists do. School mathematics is not what mathematicians do. In general, school subjects are in a category of 'school knowledge' which has only a distant and tangential relationship with knowledge in the world outside. Those who doubt this should ask a historian, a cook, a biologist, a carpenter, or a physicist, how their work relates to what is taught in school. As the physicist Richard Feynman said, of the school textbooks he was asked to review, 'how anybody can learn science from these books, I don't know, because it's not science'.[2]

A tenuous relationship with the world outside does not mean that school knowledge is simple, or unsophisticated. Huge amounts of time and effort have gone into refining it – into producing what has been called 'curriculum as fact': a conception which 'with its underlying view of knowledge as external to knowers, both teachers and students, and embodied in syllabi and textbooks, is widely held and has profound implications for our conceptions of teaching and learning.'[3]

Curriculum as fact and 'curriculum as central mandate' focus especially on what administrators call 'basic education'. As we have seen, particular stress is still laid on reading-and-writing – 'literacy' as it is now officially known. Some have high hopes of literacy. Among them was the late Walter Ong, who believed that reading, like writing, 'was a consciousness-raising and humanising technology' which can 'enrich the human psyche, enlarge the human spirit, set it free, [and] intensify its interior life'.[4] Had Father Ong spent more time outside his library, or the printery in which he once worked, he might have qualified this view. Perfectly printed newspapers systematically spread mendacity, or act in America, it has been said, as the White House stenography pool. Then there are books which numb the senses, and a press full of nicely printed advertisements designed to separate the credulous from their cash.

As with other technologies, the value of reading and writing depends on who is using them for what. We have argued elsewhere that literacy is rarely neutral. Commonly it is related to power and influence: certain types of literacy confer status, and point to power. Others do not.

In the early twenty-first century – in a time of constant propagandising and well-funded policies of 'information dominance' – it seems that reading and writing subtract from the sum of human wisdom as often as they increase it. But, for our school system, basic literacy has the virtue of being easily testable. Either you can decipher printed symbols, or you cannot.

'Literacy' is not the only area of school life to suffer from the current British (and American) fashion for low-level testing and targeting, and national control. When school knowledge is reduced to easily measurable quanta, real knowledge suffers, as it does when its content is centrally prescribed by politicians. Local control of curricula may have been an imperfect system but it was, in many ways, preferable to control from Whitehall. Now, 'if a group of teachers began to examine critically and reformulate their current practice, there would be two likely outcomes. Either they would immediately come up against external constraints from the Governing Body or Local Authority' – or now of the central educational enforcement agencies like Ofsted – 'or in their attempts to implement alternatives, they would in practice, be taken outside the context of the classroom and into discussions with local employers and parents.'[5]

Central control of knowledge – as practised in England and Wales over the past decades – has meant a general rationalisation and simplification of what is taught. Recent advances in science and mathematics, for instance, are not easily made accessible in the classroom (or easily examined) and so do not find their way into most schools. To take a an example from the natural sciences: in England, only a quarter of physics teachers have a degree in their subject, and many of those who have a qualification do not (perhaps cannot) help their students to learn about the discoveries and rethinking which revolutionised physics, and changed our lives, in the twentieth century. Nor do they teach about the effects of those changes – effects which continue to transform physical sciences in the twenty-first century.

Few people become theoretical physicists: for the rest of us, the excitement of physics is its translation into new, sometimes transformational, technologies – most of which depend on the physical discoveries of the twentieth century. As Kaku[6] says 'the track record of physics has been formidable: we have been intimately involved with introducing a host of pivotal inventions (TV, radio, radar, X-rays, the transistor, the computer, the laser, the atomic bomb), decoding the DNA molecule, opening new dimensions in probing the human body with PET, MRI and CAT scans, and even designing the internet and the world wide web.' Yet in most schools the timetable's archaic subject divisions work against teachers' transmitting the real excitement of physics, for physics 'as a science subject' is likely to be separated from design and technology classes, which might illuminate transitions from theory to practice.

Given England's system of streaming pupils it is, in many cases, unlikely that a pupil taking an 'academic' subject will also take a more 'practical' one. And, if both are available, they are likely to be taught at different times, in different places, by different people: all of which makes it hard to convey the continuing relevance of physics. Unsurprisingly, this branch of science is in quite rapid decline as a school subject.

Much the same is true for the life sciences. Arguably these are now usurping the world-transformative role of physics – but, if they are, the news has not reached many schools. Today's pupils will probably leave without understanding the potential, or threat, of post-genomic biology, biotechnology, transgenics, cloning, gene substitution, gender determination, and the wider field of genetic engineering. The science behind those changes, and their social and ethical implications, will not have been on the syllabus of most schools. Something similar is true of the humanities. If students want to follow new developments in the visual arts, in writing, in music and in film, they will likely do it outside school.

Our testing regime impoverishes classrooms that were already – and have been for centuries – intellectually closed and information-poor. 'Legitimate knowledge' has traditionally entered the classroom in two forms: first, what is in the teacher's mind, and secondly what is in whatever textbooks or computers may be in the room. Follow, for a moment, the foregoing example of biology. In recent decades the discipline has been transformed. Last century the distinguished biologist J B S Haldane suggested it would take till the middle of the twenty-first century to decode the human genome. In fact, the decoding was complete by 2003. Computing power changed the process of genome decoding and revolutionised biology. But most of our school teachers were trained before this biogenetic revolution. In many cases, they cannot adequately cover it in class. Nor – given the pressures on schools – do teachers have time, or funding, to retrain.[7] This leaves textbooks as the main alternative classroom source of legitimate knowledge. But, as we know, textbooks in their various forms are themselves problematic. They are unlikely to be written by leading scientists, who have more interesting things to do with their time. Texts are edited by people whose subject knowledge is, in the nature of the case, likely to be shallow. (If it were not, they would be doing something else.) Cost pressures mean that texts are not fully tested, either for quality of information or for quality of learning design (see chapter 21). Then there is the development, printing and distribution cycle which, for science texts, from start to finish, probably takes three years; sometimes more. By the time they reach the classroom, most textbooks are out of date. The web, of course, has a different publishing cycle, but is not yet a practical alternative to texts in schools.

In recent decades other questions have been raised around the problem of what science should be taught in school. In the past half-century (often building on discoveries in the early twentieth century) many disciplines and intellectual fields have been revolutionised: among them physics, astrophysics, nanotechnology, biology, communication and information theory, economics. This raises real questions for our school system. Can it keep pace with these changes? Should it try, or should these developments come into the capacious category of things schools don't teach? And if – for economic or other reasons – we decide that schools should try to keep pace with new developments, how is that to be done?

Consider now another difficult area for schools: the treatment of new technologies in the classroom. For example, MIT's Technology Review for October 2003 lists what it takes to be the year's 'hundred top young innovators'. Among other issues, members of this group are dealing with insect vision for unmanned reconnaissance planes; tools for assembling and analysing genomes; anthropomorphic robots; architectures to build practical molecular computers; three-dimensional integrated circuits; chip-integration of photonics and electronics; GPS tractor control systems; sound spotlights for concerts; voice-over-IP; assistance for innovative entrepreneurs in emerging nations; faster and cheaper brain-imaging machines; new drug combinations to treat cancer and rheumatoid arthritis; software to alleviate air congestion; fuel cell technologies; nanotubes to speed optical signalling; writing algorithms to ease traffic jams; assembling nanowires to build nanocomputers; devising time-release polymers to eliminate multiple drug injections; creating qubits for quantum computing; making higher-density hard drives with nanomaterials; and fabricating organic semiconductors. Does your local school teach any of these techniques or technologies? Probably not. Does it teach about any of them? Does it encourage pupils to explore these fields? Possibly not. Does that matter? Perhaps not – if we are educating young people for an industrial age. If we are hoping to educate them for a twenty-first-century knowledge-based economy, then yes, it may matter.

As times change, technologies change, and economies change, yet our school system lags some way behind, concentrating on the teaching and testing of 'school knowledge'. (At the time of writing there is an official move to 'teach young people emotions' – as in how to feel 'angry' or 'hurt' or 'loved' – but this emotional initiative is unlikely to last, while the teaching and testing of school knowledge undoubtedly will.)

Though there is little evidence that most school knowledge is generally useful in life beyond school, it does have more limited uses. School knowledge serves as gatekeeper. Some young people do well with it. They learn to read fluently, and write neatly. They remember facts – whether or not the facts are worth remembering – and write legible answers when questioned about them. These are the school's 'academic pupils'. It is a title bestowed without irony. They will be scholastically promoted and, parents hope, given access to a relatively scarce and class-biased resource: the upper levels of higher education. (In this respect, affluent parents' beliefs are, generally, justified. The UK Minister for Higher Education, speaking in 2002, said that only 15% of entrants to what she called 'top universities' came from families in the lower half of the UK income range. Thus 'more than 85% of those who go to our top universities come from the top three income groups'.[8])

In this context, the user-value of 'top universities' lies not so much in their teaching as in the networks of contacts made there. These are networks which, parents also believe, increase their children's subsequent chances of well-paid work, and a comfortable life. Such selectivity in the school system ensures the support of that part of the middle class that cannot afford the surer route to worldly success offered by fee-charging schools. State schools are, therefore, organised so that middle-class children will manage to negotiate the obstacle course of school knowledge. Working class and poorer children are less well equipped for this task, and are more likely to fail. Leaving school, they are of course directed to less lucrative and less interesting work. A corollary is that university-entrance examinations are central to all that secondary schools do. They influence all of a school's other activities. Most English schools are, effectively, run for the benefit of their A-level ('university entrance') pupils. If A-levels are taken elsewhere – at a tertiary college, for instance – preparation for that university-entrance stage still shapes secondary schools' practice.

Sorting young people cannot be seen to be arbitrary. To demonstrate a level playing field, promotion in state schools is based on quality-assessed tests and examinations. School tests, like school knowledge itself, is print-centric, and favours children from homes which value bookish, rather than practical, skills. That means middle-class homes where parents, as well as having books, can afford out-of-school tutoring if their children (despite domestic advantages) are not doing well in school exams. The United States – usually a little ahead of the UK in these matters – has refined these strategies of class and income division as the social and educational sorting mechanism becomes more effective. 'Wealthier and more ambitious parents are choosing highly regarded private schools or good public schools ['public' here meaning public] in tony suburban communities where other students are likely to exert a positive influence, trouble-makers can be easily extruded, and slower learners quietly isolated... Or such parents choose publicly funded 'charter' schools with more leeway than public schools about whom to admit or expel. In most states, charters have little room explicitly to exclude or expel, but they can craft their offerings in such a way as to deter less desired students, for example by failing to offer services for children with learning disabilities, or admitting children only from the surrounding upscale neighbourhood.'[9] State funding of schools run by those who have a non-educational message to convey is a path both the UK and the US are following. However, if we take into account Britain's traditional financial concessions to fee-charging ('public') schools, we might argue that the UK has been a pioneer.

Since the inauguration of a Labour government in 1997, selection in British schools has been covert. In the United States, under right-wing governments, selection is becoming more open. In North Carolina, for example, schools are now compelled to institute 'pathways' – an early-selection mechanism which steers students into courses leading respectively to a 'four year college or university; a community or technical college; or directly into the job market'.[10] Other states are close behind. 'Tracking' is now common: young people are effectively selected for specific futures – which may be higher education or manual labour – at an age when they cannot be expected to know what future they want, or would be good at. Given the present outlook of both red and blue political parties, it seems likely that such early selection, under new names, will spread through US schools.

The American federal government has less influence over schools than does Whitehall; but it does have means of persuasion, and there is open admiration in Washington for British testing-and-targeting regimes. In both countries school systems are in intellectual retreat. Not having learned from educational history, they are, it seems, doomed to repeat it.

This rather pessimistic summary appears to conflict with official rhetoric in the UK. In 2002, the Prime Minister spoke of his 'passionate belief in equality of opportunity' and declared that 'our commitment to education also springs from our understanding of the modern world, and of the challenge facing Britain'.[11] Mr Blair is not known as a man who lets facts interfere with his theories. If he were, he might feel a need to align his engaging rhetoric with the finding that Britain's population is, on most measurable indices, increasingly unequal; that this inequality is growing; that schools, in terms of resources and reputation are also increasingly unequal; and – as we have argued – they continue to support an industrially-oriented education in a 'modern world' which is, in the UK, post-industrial.

With this inter-school inequality goes a wide division between academic and vocational scholastic strata. From the second half of the twentieth century to the present there have been repeated attempts, in Britain, to raise 'vocational subjects' to status equivalent with their more abstract academic counterparts. None has succeeded. Though attitudes have changed somewhat in the last quarter-century, Britain's educational system – in particular, its public schools – is still at heart 'the same institution that first promoted a negative view of the life of business and industry'[12] and, in practice, a negative view of vocational classes.

Debates about the academic-vocational balance of schooling may never be finally settled; and perhaps should not be. But there is another issue, more rarely discussed, to do with academic subjects. What meaning do these 'unrelated' subjects have, for those compelled to take them? Consider this excerpt from the national curriculum for England and Wales in 2005. Under the heading 'science' teachers are told that their pupils 'should be taught to ... use a wide range of scientific, technical and mathematical language, symbols and conventions, including SI units, balanced chemical equations and standard form to communicate ideas and develop an argument'. For science teachers this doubtless makes perfect sense. They have served years of apprenticeship; they are familiar with scientific, technical and mathematical language, symbols and conventions, SI units and balanced chemical equations. For pupils, on the other hand, these matters often make no sense at all; they simply do not understand (and often are not helped to understand) why they are learning these things. Many teachers do not feel it necessary to set such work in context, or to show them as a way of solving real problems. They – the teachers – 'understand science' or, at least, they understand school science; they have been dealing with it for years; they take it for granted and commonly see no need to confront its unrelatedness. They see no need to set science in the context of pupils' lives, or of life outside school, or to give good reasons for learning what the curriculum demands.

To say 'I teach physics' implies 'a body of knowledge to be transferred from the teacher who has it to the pupil who has not, whether by rote and test, or enquiries and assignment'.[13] We are now a long way from the ideals of the 1970s American Curriculum Movement – beliefs that leading scientists should be involved in the construction of science curricula; that 'intellectual activity anywhere is the same, whether at the frontier of knowledge or in a third-grade classroom'; and that 'any subject can be taught effectively in some intellectually honest form to any child at any stage of development'.[14] Now, for the most part, we teach what administrators believe should be taught, in the way they believe it should be taught. And that is, of course, a very different approach to education.

If there are disciplines which schools find it difficult to deal with, there are others they choose to avoid. Among these are the knowledge that pupils bring to the classroom and a critical understanding of the society we live in. There is a long scholastic tradition of avoiding such contemporary issues, and issues which concern young people. Williams notes that 'politics – in the wide sense of discussing the quality and direction of [students'] living – was excluded from [Mechanics'] Institutes, as it was to remain largely excluded from the whole of nineteenth century education'.[15] And not just nineteenth-century education. We earlier noted that the 1943 Norwood Report, which did a great deal to shape Britain's post-primary education in the second half of the twentieth century, vigorously rejected the idea of relevance. Sir Cyril Norwood – who dominated the reporting group – felt that schools should, instead, continue to concern themselves with Platonic and Christian verities.

Other decision-makers have more immediate concerns about studies of contemporary life. To be useful, such work must (at least some of the time) be a critical account of the powerful; dealing with powerful institutions, or powerful people is, after all, a large part of any life, and may determine its direction. Consider the kinds of power and authority many of us encounter: banks, benefit agencies, employers, overseers, bureaucrats, landlords, managers, mortgage lenders, taxation authorities, insurers, social workers, surveillance agencies, politicians, credit-rating companies, administrators, teachers, retailers and wholesalers, planners, police. Then there are issues which affect us locally but which are, in the widest sense, political: drugs, crime, health, housing, poverty, inequality; and globally: wars, climate change, fuel costs, offshoring of work, automation, networking, shortage of energy and raw materials, Asian industrialisation, global inequity and globalised economies. These too we need to understand if we are to have any say in shaping our lives, or our society.

Critical consideration of such people, agencies and issues might be more useful than most other things which fill the school day. For, as Raymond Williams said, 'we cannot in our society call any educational system adequate if it leaves any large number of people at a level of general knowledge and culture below that required by a participating democracy'.[16] But there is a difficulty. For politicians to authorise within schools a critical consideration of society would mean agreeing to critical consideration not only of their powerful supporters, but of themselves and their own activity. Clearly it is easier and safer to find reasons for excluding such critiques from state schools.

Unsurprisingly, that is what politicians commonly do. This is a dilemma for administrations like Britain's post-1997 Labour government which has been genuinely concerned about what it sees as young people's apathy when it comes to democratic procedures and public life. Yet members of the Labour administration have not honestly confronted the connection between educational complaisance and young people's cynicism. In place of critical scrutiny schools, explicitly or implicitly, convey the impression that those who have power and money are benevolently devoted to those who have less of both; a proposition which is, at best, arguable – and which clearly does not convince all pupils.

In the past, as we might expect, the regulation of school knowledge was more visible; control was imposed more openly than now. Of all school subjects, Chancellor remarks, 'history is perhaps most obviously a vehicle for the opinions of the teacher and of the section of society which he [or perhaps she] represents'.[17] The purpose of history teaching, according to a nineteenth-century expert whom she quotes, is 'to impart correct historical knowledge and at the same time to convey beautiful lessons of morality' with the aim, wrote another authority, of exciting 'in the minds of children a spirit of loyalty to the king and attachment to the monarchical form of government'.[18]

Continuing this reassuring account of the rich man in his castle and the poor man at the gate, nineteenth-century schoolbooks informed the children of the poor that poverty was their fault; or at least the fault of their feckless parents. We know, wrote a bishop, 'that too many people are living in great wretchedness, and we hear them complain against the government; but we see plainly enough that the government has no share in causing their misfortunes, but that they are frequently brought on by themselves... drunken and careless people are generally in a state of poverty.'[19]

Such openly edifying teaching continued, with minor modification, until the mid-twentieth century. School history was 'cast in broadly self-congratulatory and heroic, high political mould. Emphasis was placed upon the role of Britain as a peacemaker in India and other colonised countries, and as an opponent of tyrants from Napoleon to Hitler. Good government was exemplified by Westminster, the "mother of parliaments"; Britain's role as leader in the industrial revolution, confirmed by the Great Exhibition of 1851, was seen as proof of the nation's technical and entrepreneurial skills. Missionaries like Wilberforce, Shaftesbury and Livingstone were hailed for having carried the Christian message into the darkest corners both of England and of the Empire.'[20]

These days we are more subtle in reassuring pupils that all is well with the world (unlike France which, in 2005, passed a law obliging schools to 'recognize in particular the positive character of the French overseas presence, notably in North Africa'[21]). Overt argument for the nationalistic teaching of British history (or any other subject) is now rare. The Education Minister John Patten, who held office from 1992 to 1994, is a recent exception to the rule. For him, 'to have national pride should be seen as a virtue not a vice. That is why,' he wrote, 'the Prime Minister [Mrs Thatcher] and I are determined to see British history at the heart of history teaching in our schools.'[22] Mr Patten amplified these themes in a further speech in which he insisted that 'all children must understand such key concepts as empire, monarch, crown, church, nobility, peasantry... Public education systems contribute to a willingness of persons to define themselves as citizens, to make personal sacrifices for the community and to accept legitimate decisions of public officials.'[23] Clearly Mr Patten's outlook could not accommodate the notion of critical scrutiny; nor did the courses he promoted include anything of that nature. Instead, the Minister advocated an engagingly named school history course, 'Crowns, Parliaments and Peoples 1500 to 1750'. The peoples of the title were to be British or – since the Mr Patten did not favour Celts – English.

This was, in recent years, a high point of nationalistic education. But even in times of patriotic fervour, British schools still dealt with some vital questions; though only when the life had been wrung out of them. Schools might consider racial issues, let us say, or war, or social discontent, but only as past history (slavery; the World Wars; the French revolution): not as matters to be coped with in our own lives. Desiccated bodies of information still edge their way into classrooms when the embalming process is complete. We drive forward, as McLuhan remarked, peering in the rear-vision mirror. Pupils sense that. As we shall see, they respond in different, mainly negative, ways.

In this context, Hargreaves notes that 'since Aristotle [education] has been accepted as an inherently political concept that raises questions about the sort of society we live in, how it has come to take its present form, the strengths and weaknesses of current political structures, and how improvements might be made... Active citizens are as political as they are moral; moral sensibility derives in part from political understanding; political apathy spawns moral apathy.'[24] Although more difficult to provide, it is elements of a critical education that 'achieve these aims of understanding, enquiry and participation'. Cullingford, agreeing that critical education is difficult to achieve, argues that it is nonetheless necessary. 'On the one hand,' he writes, 'we expect children to have developed enough social literacy to make political judgments by the age of eighteen [when, in the UK, they are allowed to vote]. On the other hand, we avoid giving them the means of acquiring such knowledge and analytical skills.'[25]

We have seen that, for politicians in charge of schooling, this is a dilemma. They may be concerned about apathy in young people – about their 'disengagement from the public sphere' – but they do not wish to encourage in schools the sort of critical education which, while engaging pupils, might raise awkward questions about authority and power. One way out of the dilemma is to raise the spectre of indoctrination. The Crick Report (described below) notes that, in the context of critical citizenship education, 'parents and the public generally may be worried about the possibility of bias and indoctrination'.[26]

This is a curious statement, given schools' long history of moral, religious or political indoctrination of pupils; but churchmen, politicians and administrators are nonetheless skilled in using fears of indoctrination to neuter attempts at critical education in schools. As we have seen, members of Britain's 1979–1997 Conservative administration vociferously opposed 'political' or 'contentious' education. Keith Joseph, a minister for education under Mrs Thatcher, was vigilant in seeking out what he saw as political bias. He 'scrutinised the syllabuses of every [school] subject, and sought amendment to those that displeased him'.[27] He went on to proscribe 'partisan teaching about political matters' – 'partisan' here meaning views he did not share – and to ensure that headteachers must 'have regard to police representations about curriculum matters' – whatever that might mean.[28]

Joseph's ministerial successor, Kenneth Baker, took the covert control of what schools teach a stage further with his Educational Reform Act of 1988. This Act 'introduced plans for a national curriculum that covered virtually everything that was taught to students during the compulsory period of schooling. It complemented the programmes of study which were to be stipulated by such a curriculum with plans for the establishment of detailed "levels of attainment" ' that students should reach, and with universal systems of testing, for students aged 7, 11 and 14, to ensure the performance of the whole system'.[29]

Baker's most explicit act of school censorship came in the same year when, through Section 28 of the 1988 Local Government Act, he forbade schools' promotion of homosexuality.[30] No one was sure what 'promotion' meant in this context (or whether any teacher had been doing whatever it was). Schools therefore took the Queen Victoria option, and pretended that same-sex relationships did not exist. This may well have been the outcome the government intended. In these ways Baker instilled 'great caution among educators. Schools had to beware of questioning received ideas. Councils had to think twice before turning their attention to newly-recognised areas of discrimination. Around the new network of "positive" state powers developed a negative climate of banning and deterrence.'[31]

Censorship is not of course the prerogative of any political party. At the time of writing Britain's Labour administration has proposed legislating a new offence of 'glorifying terrorism' which, if carried into law, would significantly affect what schools could or could not teach. Those drafting this potentially oppressive legislation had problems deciding, for instance, whether celebrating resistance to the Nazi occupation of France is (in terms of terrorist glorification) equivalent to supporting those who resist the present occupation of Iraq. Such semantic puzzles make the legislation problematic.

Control of school knowledge does not mean the excision of all contemporary issues. In schools, some are now dealt with under the heading of 'citizenship education'. Citizenship classes have been made mandatory in all state secondary schools and, at the time of writing, are being extended to primary schools. (To take one example from the primary arena, a 'citizenship resource sheet' for five-to-seven-year-olds lists the attributes of the Good Young Citizen. He 'smiles a lot; helps others if they fall; waits his turn; lets others borrow his things; always tries his best; doesn't push when lining up; is careful with his work; and doesn't upset other children if he is feeling annoyed'. It is unclear what this list will do for the model child. But it's certainly a way of persuading other, less perfect, young citizens to fill his trainers with glue.)

In the UK, compulsory citizenship courses were the brainchild, in the 1990s, of Mr Blunkett, then an instinctively authoritarian Education Minister. Mr Blunkett's view was that 'we must infiltrate children's minds if we are to have a society worth growing up in.' When in office the Minister's brief was led by the need to explain 'the nature and practices of participation in democracy'.[32] The brief went on to recommend 'the teaching of civics, participative democracy and citizenship, and may be taken to include some understanding of democratic practices and institutions, including parties, pressure groups and voluntary bodies, and the relationship of formal political activity with civic society in the context of the UK, Europe and the wider world...'[33] Despite this briefing's reference to civics, the main author of the official 1998 report on citizenship, Professor Bernard Crick, did not intend to establish a new generation of civics classes, whether or not the Minister saw 'citizenship education' in that light.[34]

Citizenship teaching is, in practice, descended from 'civics education' in schools. Civics was (and at times still is) a way of acclimatising young people to their social system. In the United States – where civics and citizenship curricula were refined –

this meant introducing pupils to the benefits of American federal and democratic government, and to its formal mechanisms: for example, the legislative, executive and judicial branches of government. In the UK, the Crick Report laid down a range of learning outcomes (pp 50-54 for Key Stages 3-4) which, for most teachers, could be covered only through case studies and practices that each incorporated a fair number of them. For example, it is possible (though very difficult) to imagine a comprehensive case study which helped learners to 'understand the significant aspects of topical and contemporary issues and events; understand, at a basic level, the law and the legal system in relation to areas such as the family, consumers, the law at work and in relation to the environment; understand about different sources and types of law, including statute, judge-made law, and European law (including ECHR); know about the different ways in which the law is enforced, the role of the police, crime and punishment and penal reform as a personal and social issue; also understand the meaning of terms such as rule of law, civil law, criminal law, civil rights, natural justice; to know about the different ways in which MPs can be elected and the Government held accountable through parliament to the electorate, including the importance of voting, public opinion, opinion polls, the role of the media, lobbying, pressure groups and different forms of protest; the different electoral systems and understand the reasons for the differences; also understand the meaning of terms such as proportional representation, referendum, federalism, monarchy.'[35]

Whatever the original intention of current citizenship education, much of the guidance for the citizenship curriculum takes for granted our present social infrastructure, and system of governance. Learners may be invited to discuss aspects of social and political life, but not seriously to question them. Opportunities for questioning in depth are commonly reserved for significant but more distant problems, like the future of the Amazonian rain forest. To take a current example, in the wake of suicide bombings in 2005 in London, there have been suggestions of using education (which in this context probably means citizenship classes in schools) to combat the alienation of young British Muslims. If this were to have any chance of success schools would have to address the contemporary question of British, US, Russian or Israeli military wounding and killing Muslims in Palestine, Afghanistan, Chechnya and Iraq. Whether or not those actions are justified would, clearly, be a matter for classroom debate; but in most schools that debate does not happen for these issues are 'too political'. But while such controversial topics are absent from schools, the project of using education to combat alienation will not get far.

In their citizenship blueprint Professor Crick and his colleagues suggested that 'schools need to consider how far their ethos, organisation and daily practices are consistent with the aim and purpose of citizenship education, and affirm and extend the development of pupils into active citizens'.[36] But conventional teaching about parliamentary democracy in schools (as the Crick Report recommends) faces difficulties. One is that telling young people about 'our democratic practices and institutions' seems not to engage them. There is a danger that 'increased levels of citizenship education' will merely create 'a kind of illusion of being informed …

not a guarantee of active citizenship'.[37] Research conducted for the BBC in 2004 on 'television for citizenship' 'revealed that five new shows commissioned in a wide-ranging review of its political output have not succeeded in boosting the proportion of younger viewers'.[38] In fact, they seem to have driven young viewers away. In schools 'it is important to recognise how comparatively minor a role schools seem to play in the political education of our children at the moment. Teachers come low [in fact, last] on the list of those the young rely on for information about important issues facing Britain; the media, though distrusted by many young people, and family and friends are the primary sources. Voting intentions are still largely inherited from parents, forty years after Butler and Stokes first suggested it was so; but these days, that includes inheriting the intention not to vote, a corrosive development... Only one pupil in eight is sure that he or she would vote in a general election tomorrow if old enough.'[39] A parallel investigation found that, when asked to describe politicians in three words, the most common terms young people used 'were "old", "posh" and "liars"'.[40]

Another difficulty with the uncritical teaching of democracy is that schools themselves are notably undemocratic. The National Curriculum strand of 'developing skills of participation and responsible action' is, in practice, difficult to apply in most schools. School systems are notably hierarchical, with top-down management. Pupils do not elect their teachers, or their school administration, or any other effective part of the school system. Nor do they commonly have any significant say in the wider issues of what they are taught, or how they are assessed. Conventional school citizenship courses recommend democratic practices which, alert learners will note, are not applied in their immediate environment.

Nor is 'active involvement' always approved by schools. The DfES Citizenship website[41] has recommended 'creating links between pupils' learning in the classroom and activities that take place ... in the wider community and the wider world'. Yet when thousands of young people created such links between their learning and the UK's unprovoked invasion of Iraq in 2002, the school system did not welcome this very active, though generally oppositional, involvement.

The conventional approach to citizenship education does not pause long on such dilemmas. Its underlying aim is acclimatisation to the wider society, sometimes in forms more ideal than actual. Learners, here and elsewhere, are often aware of this gap between ideal and actuality: 'I mean I'm not saying we live in a bad society, or anything, but I mean, you know, things are not perfect, so ... [we need] a more balanced view of society than we actually get'.[42]

Away from his report on citizenship education, Professor Crick has suggested that education should focus on citizenship and politics 'as participative and controversial matters'.[43] However, throughout the Crick Report – and in much of schools' subsequent citizenship education – it is implied that 'the nature and practices of participative democracy' are fixed entities, which can be studied like any other unchanging artefact. Clearly this is not so. There are many systems described as democratic, and our most familiar democracy (that of the UK) has changed significantly as economies and power distribution have changed. 'Arguably, a main concern of citizenship education should be the type of democracy, and type of economy, in which, over the next decades, young people will live', and 'the globalisation of production and consumption led by information technology'.[44] Yet these issues are seldom considered, either in citizenship's founding charter, or in current practice. In part, that may be because going beyond the status quo and its strengths is seen as educationally controversial, or risky for teachers.

CENSORSHIP, OR SELF-CENSORSHIP?

How are we to analyse teachers' response to this imposed and generally anodyne education, with its subtle undertones of censorship? Clearly there was control of schools' knowledge in the late twentieth century, as there is in the twenty-first. Teachers do not imagine it. But the mechanisms of control are diffuse – which does not make them less real – and sanctions vague. Of the clauses in the 1988 Education Act that proscribed 'partisan' teaching, it has been said that they were redundant, since apparently they were never used. 'Thus the argument can be made that the [political] right's initiatives are not really relevant to what goes on in schools.'[45] What would have happened to a teacher, when Section 28 was being promoted, who initiated an honest classroom discussion of same-sex relationships? At the state level, probably nothing much. But it may be that 'the reason [such] clauses have not been activated is because they have not needed to be ... The press and the political right have made the figure of the aggrieved parent a power in the land. Local authorities have maintained a watch on "controversial" issues, and circulated schools with the text of legislation on the matter. Teachers, in a similar process of self-censorship, tend to be more cautious than they once were in relating what they teach on issues seen as "political".'[46] So, returning to our imagined teacher who discussed same-sex relationships, the state might not act but, at school level, conservative parents might well complain, causing the school's administration to tag the teacher as 'unreliable'. Her promotion prospects would be harmed.

For most teachers, though, the issue does not even arise. There are half a dozen good reasons for not entering 'contentious' or 'political' territory. These issues 'are not on the curriculum'. And there are other, more potent reasons for schools not to deal with live issues. In current conventional wisdom, teachers should be scrupulously neutral; teachers should not 'take a political stance' in the classroom; teachers 'do not have the expertise' to deal with contemporary and controversial issues; and anyway – the clincher – why go looking for trouble? Why stick your neck out when you don't have to? Why not concentrate on the safe stuff, and keep out of trouble?

Why indeed? Teachers now censor themselves and save governments the trouble. Schools' teaching about contemporary life remains, as it has commonly been, a locus of well-meaning evasion. For school systems, in England and elsewhere, lessons on 'society', and controversial areas of science, politics and the arts, are now (as they traditionally have been) a territory of benign propaganda. Seen from the classroom, our society may have its faults, but those in power will, with the support of decent citizens, put things right. This optimistic depiction is unsurprising, since those who pay the bills – in this case, governments – understandably choose their own versions of reality. Here as elsewhere, the winners write the history books.

In these polite fictions, schools generally collude. Underlying much education is a sincere belief that, if you tell pupils all is well – in citizenship classes or elsewhere – they will believe it, and will grow to be good citizens of the idealised democracy they have learned about. There is, though, a central problem with this panglossian account of society. It is not only untrue; it is manifestly untrue. Though the news may not have reached schools, politicians are likely to be more interested in personal power than in the common good. Businessmen are known to exploit their workers. Entrepreneurs do not always consider customers' welfare when profit is at stake. Religious leaders may be bigots or chauvinists. The influential good and the great may live and write in some parallel universe. Too many young black men are imprisoned. News media are often racist, mendacious and malignant. Public money is squandered, or spent secretly on projects we would reject, if we knew what we were paying for. Capitalism may be linked with democracy and consumer choice – but it is also linked with endemic inequality, environmental degradation, ruthless globalisation, and the impoverishment of weaker countries. Most of this seems to pass unnoticed by school administrators, though not always by pupils.

Avoiding the complexity and darkness of contemporary life brings to mind Bernard MacLaverty's description of the Irish troubles: it's like having an elephant in the living room, he said: something we don't talk about, but so enormous that it can't be ignored; something we finally got used to. In the same way, we are all accustomed to schools' failure to offer an even-handed account of contemporary life. It's a considerable failure, but one we don't talk about, and have learned to ignore.

In summary, then, there is a long list of social, scientific and political topics that schools do not, or cannot, deal with. In their place we have omission, distortion or, at worst, bland denial. That might – just might – be justified if it did in fact turn pupils into model citizens. But it does not. Its effect is quite different: it fosters cynicism. (According to Mori, a UK research agency, only 39% of 18–24-year-olds voted in Britain's 2001 general election – 20 percentage points below the figure for older adults, which was itself the lowest British voter turnout since universal suffrage began.) But if we have led young people to believe our rulers will solve all our problems, why should they get involved in public affairs? That, we might say, is 'induced apathy'. It will continue, and will spread. 'Disengagement in youth is a good indicator of disengagement later on... People won't just grow out of it. They get into a habit of disengagement.'[47]

This is not specifically a problem for British school systems: it stretches across the world. American classrooms also proclaim the virtues of the US political process and, as in the UK, the message appears to convince fewer people as the years pass. 'Americans in the mid-sixties were strikingly confident in the benevolence and responsiveness of their political institutions...Three in four said that you could "trust the government in Washington to do what is right all or most of the time"…Such views nowadays seem antiquated or naïve. In virtually every case the proportions agreeing or disagreeing with such ideas essentially have been reversed. In the 1990s roughly three in four Americans didn't trust the government to do what is right most of the time.'[48] More generally it can be said that 'there is nothing in present proposals for education for the global economy that would provide the general population with the knowledge and skills to exercise political power.'[49]

The issue, in this country and others, is set where knowledge, truth and learning intersect. Why, we must ask, are honest answers to such questions seen as being outside the competence of school systems? The questions of contemporary life are surely more important than, say, the date Napoleon invaded Spain, or the temperature at which copper melts. We can look up the answers to those. But we cannot look up definitive answers to the questions which vitally affect us – those to which we urgently need answers, and which have no easy answers. Commonly we cannot even find the information on which to base answers – at least not in the places, like the mass media, where we might expect to look. Most of the mass media are uninterested in the non-celebrity world, or under political control, or are concerned with maximising profits while relaying the views of their corporate masters. For students an interesting task is to see whether they can publish, on the web, a blog, a news sheet, a forum or a journal more lively, honest and accurate than the media offered by our corporations. Given the chance, most can.

As the media move away from critical reflection, education might be expected to take that role. But if contemporary and contentious themes are excluded from the classroom, that does not augur well for our common and precarious future.

---

[1] Quoted in Goodson 1988
[2] Feynman 1985
[3] Young 1998
[4] Ong 1982
[5] Young 1998
[6] Kaku 1998
[7] The (few) teachers equipped to deal competently with the post-genomic biogenetics are, in most cases, unable to deal adequately with the social and ethical issues raised almost weekly by this scientific revolution
[8] Margaret Hodge, reported in *The Guardian*, 14.1.2002
[9] Reich 2000
[10] *Rethinking Schools* 17(2) Winter 2002/2003
[11] The Prime Minister's speech to the tenth annual conference of the Technology Colleges Trust, 26 November 2002. www.pm.gov.uk/output.page 6678.asp
[12] Wiener 1992
[13] Ibid
[14] Bruner 1963
[15] Williams 1961
[16] Ibid
[17] Chancellor 1970
[18] Ibid
[19] Davys 1822

[20] Aldrich, R (1989) 'Class and gender in the study and teaching of history in England in the twentieth century' *Historical Studies in Education*, Vol. 1, No. 1, p. 121

[21] *USA Today* 21.10.05. The French newspaper *Liberation* helpfully republished 'drawings from *France Overseas*, an illustrated colonial Atlas of 1931 that showed "before" and "after" drawings, one a sketch of Africans cooking and eating another human being, the second a school house on a well-manicured street with a French flag flying overhead'.

[22] Department for Education Press Release 70/94, 1994

[23] John Patten, television broadcast, BBC1, 24 March 1994

[24] Hargreaves, D (2001) *Mosaic of Learning Demos*

[25] Cullingford 1992

[26] The Crick Report p. 8

[27] Jones 1989

[28] Ibid

[29] Ibid

[30] The post-1997 Labour government opposed (and eventually repealed) Section 28, but its control of school knowledge is as tight as that of its predecessors

[31] Jones 1989

[32] Education for Citizenship and the Teaching of Democracy in Schools (henceforward 'the Crick Report') London: DfES 1998

[33] Ibid

[34] Personal communication from Professor Bernard Crick

[35] The Crick Report

[36] Ibid

[37] Buckingham 1999

[38] *Independent* 12.5.04

[39] 'Young People's Attitudes to Politics' Nestlé Family Monitor 16, July 2003

[40] A young person's agenda for democracy – one year on: a report from the Youth Voting Network Youth Voting Network 2003

[41] www.dfes.gov.uk/citizenship/

[42] US teenager, quoted in Buckingham (2000)

[43] Crick 1999

[44] Selwyn 2004

[45] Ibid

[46] Ibid

[47] Matthew Taylor, IPPR, quoted in *The Guardian* 29.8.02

[48] Putnam 2000

[49] Spring 1998

CHAPTER 7

SCHOOLS AS SELF-ASSESSING SYSTEMS

'Whether they were used for placing people within the mass production systems of the industrial economy, or for certifying an apprentice's competence within the craft system of the pre-industrial economy, or for unlocking access to university education, traditional forms of assessment were predicated on the assumption that the range of skills or competences that citizens or workers would need to demonstrate was narrow and durable.'
    Paul Skidmore

'Who, we may ask, has had the greatest impact on American education in this century? If you are thinking of John Dewey or any other education philosopher, I must say you are quite wrong. The greatest impact has been made by quiet men in grey suits in a suburb of New York City called Princeton, New Jersey. There, they developed and promoted the technology known as the standardized test, such as IQ tests, the SATs and the GREs. Their tests redefined what we mean by learning, and have resulted in our reorganizing the curriculum to accommodate the tests.'
    Neil Postman

State schools are unusual in that almost every measure of their effectiveness comes from within the school system, or from those who control it. That is to say, assessment measures are created and maintained by people who run the system, are paid by it, or who directly depend on it. Effective independent evaluation is almost non-existent, while endogenous testing proliferates. (It has been estimated that, across Britain's primary and secondary state schools, some 35 million test papers are now set and marked in the course of a school year – a figure which translated into teachers' and pupils' time, gives an idea of how much of the school year is not spent teaching or learning.)

Exams, tests, league tables (in Britain), teacher appraisals, school assessments – all are internal to the system. They risk overwhelming it: some exam papers are sent to India for marking, others have been marked by the secretarial staff of English exam boards. Decisions on what schools should teach; on the measures which judge pupils' performance; on the assessment of teachers and of individual schools; on the school system's overall performance – these too are predicated on assumptions from within education's closed community. The system decides not only what should be taught but also decides on how well pupils have internalised that content, and how well (in the short term) they recall it. In turn, schools are judged on their pupils' success or failure in meeting the system's criteria. At the next level, teachers are judged on 'how well they teach' – judged not by those who are taught, or by those who will live and work with the teachers' pupils, but on how well the teachers themselves conform to the education system's rules. The wider school system is judged principally on an amalgamation of league tables: on whether the annual percentage of examination passes is rising or falling. It is a system of accountability described by Baroness O'Neill as one that 'can do two bad things: it can damage assessment and fundamentally damage education'.[1]

Independent assessment – whether by the market or by other means – encourages change. A business which sells unpopular products will be deserted by its customers: the market is an independent, often harsh, assessor. A hospital which kills more people than it cures will lack patients, if they have any choice in the matter. (Nor is it a consolation to tell suffering patients that there are good hospitals in other cities, though this technique is commonly used to excuse bad schools.) Schools can persistently offer bad education and still have a new cohort of clients each year, since there is no independent assessment of what constitutes a good or a bad education and since, for many people, there is no accessible alternative.

Over the past decades in Britain (or parts of Britain) we have seen the creation of various quangos – quasi-governmental organisations – charged with regulating the school system: the Qualifications and Curriculum Authority, the Teacher Training Agency, the General Teaching Council, and others. None is independent of the education system and all – being unelected and having some power over schools, teachers and pupils – raise the question *quis custodiet ipsos custodes*? Who polices the police? If these official bodies get things wrong (as all organisations sometimes do) who will put them right?

The most influential of these British quangos is the ostensibly independent Ofsted (Office for Standards in Education). Ofsted is charged with evaluation of British state schools and, though more moderate in recent years, it seems to have taken its original inspiration from that earlier Office which was charged with stamping out heresy. (Heresy for Ofsted is child-centred education.) Ofsted does not operate on behalf of schools' staff and clients (pupils, ex-pupils, parents, teachers, employers and so on), but on behalf of its political paymasters – within limits set by them and (which may be the same thing) within taken-for-granted assumptions about teaching, curricula, and learning. Within these parameters Ofsted's aspirations have ranged between the destructive aims of a chief inspector who did not believe in the comprehensive state schooling he was appointed to regulate[2] and a liberal apologia for increasingly unequal educational opportunity, under the catch-all guise of 'raising standards'. (Schools which are forcibly closed do not have low, or indeed any, standards.) If we seek independent assessment of schooling, we should not look to Ofsted.

Politicians at times tell us that school systems' self-assessment is standard practice. It is not. On the contrary, it is highly unusual for any commercial or social system to be self-assessing for so long a period and, hence, to have so little need to be dissatisfied with its performance, or so little incentive to improve its basic way of working. Over centuries, the didactic method has come to seem a fact of nature. Around it has developed what Davis calls a consensus trance. We take it as the way that schools must be, though of course that is not the case. Schools are human creations. However they are now, they might be otherwise.

There are those, like Headley Beare,[3] who argue that schools, despite their appearance of stasis, are in fact changing significantly. But the argument turns out not to be empirical, but rather a series of ways in which schools *might* change; the sort of idealistic wish list educators have been drawing up since education began. In reality it is hard to see significant alterations in schools' way of working: the many scholastic changes are, almost invariably, at the periphery of schools' practice, not at the centre.

School systems, being self-assessing are, almost by definition, closed. Like other closed systems, they take little from the world outside, and are little influenced by it – which accounts for the oddly parochial nature of educational dialogue. At most times the only effective outside influence on school systems comes from the politicians who control them. As we have seen, most politicians have two main aims for schooling: civilising the young, and training them to be, in the near future, a productive workforce. But, whatever one thinks of these aims, there is a caveat. Politicians are not very good at putting them into effect. We now need workers trained (and educated) very differently from those of the industrial era, but politicians and educational administrators seem to have no clear idea of how that might be done. And this too is characteristic of closed systems: they respond lethargically, and often imprudently, to changes in the world around them.

HOW MIGHT INDEPENDENT ASSESSMENT WORK?

So how might school systems be judged otherwise than by themselves? How might we go beyond self-auditing? In theory, there are several ways. Pupils, or ex-pupils, might be asked whether what they had learned was useful; or was what they wanted to learn. Employers – rather than business lobbyists – could be asked whether school had given their employees an ideal preparation for work they are doing, or might do. We have little information on what employers think of school qualifications. 'Limited facility with calculus; the ability to analyse strains of irony in *As You Like It*; an excellent knowledge of riverine sedimentation; and a thoughtful analysis of the reasons for the Franco-Prussian war'... does this equip a school-leaver to join a team designing and marketing the next generation of mobile phones?

Entrepreneurs too could be asked whether school leavers have the innovative and practical qualities enterprises need. Parents – notably those who were not pushing for 'good universities' – could be asked whether schools were serving their children as well as they might. Those who deal with coming economic change could be asked whether schools were now preparing pupils adequately for the next half century of their working lives. Indeed this type of assessment could be left entirely to those outside, rather than within, the school system. 'Schools believe they have the job of assessment as part of their natural role [but] assessment is not the job of schools. Products ought to be assessed by the buyer of those products, not the producer. Let schools do the best job they can, and then let the buyer

71

beware. Schools must concentrate on learning and teaching, not on testing and comparing.'[4]

That of course is unlikely to happen for, while schools assess their pupils, and themselves, there will be little pressure for radical change. Nor is there any real competitive pressure to find new and better ways of encouraging learning in schools. The post-1997 Labour government (and more specifically the Prime Minister's office) has continued its predecessors' policy of privatising the state system, under the flag of increased competition and parental choice, which is discussed more fully in chapter 8.

Competition from private for-profits and non-profits sounds as if it might be what an ossified and monopolistic school system needs – and so it is, until we think through what it means in practice. Understandably any privatised part of the system (whether profit-making or not) will go for 'good results'. That means, in effect, going for what politicians now demand of state schools: an emphasis on training; easily testable routines; concentration on students likely to deliver academic success; open or covert removal of pupils likely to lower the school's examination success rate; easily marked tests; easily ranked school standings.

We might like to believe that these privatised parts of the school system would innovate by concentrating on developing school-leavers who will be curious, critical and interested in learning. So far, that has been a vain hope – at least in the case of schooling for the majority. Of course there are differences from school to school but, in terms of teaching and learning, distinctions are likely to be superficial while most teaching remains didactic, subject-based and evaluated from within a closed school system. By continuing the principle of a self-assessing (though partially privatised) system, the British government is likely to get the worst of both worlds: widening the 80:20 divide, worsening schools in poor areas, and diverting to private hands funds which might have improved them.

---

[1] Onora O'Neill, principal of Newnham College, Cambridge, quoted in *The Guardian* 25.10.05
[2] Chris Woodhead, the first head of Ofsted, opened his incumbency by announcing that 15,000 teachers in England and Wales were incompetent. Like the late Senator McCarthy speaking of Communists in the US State Department, Mr Woodhead was unable to say who the culprits were, or how he assessed their competence. Mr Woodhead is also on record as wanting 'pragmatic education policies, implemented with crisp Arthur Andersen efficiency'. To be fair, the comment was made before Arthur Andersen was found guilty of illegally shredding incriminating documents related to its highly dubious accounting practices. Though later cleared, the firm collapsed in a notably un-crisp welter of lawsuits and recrimination
[3] Beare 2001
[4] Schank 2004

CHAPTER 8

EQUITY; OPPORTUNITY

'The hereditary curse upon English education is its organisation upon lines of social class.'
    R H Tawney

'We cannot afford to waste the talent of any child, write off the potential of any young person, discard the abilities of any adult.'
    Gordon Brown

Since the start of mass schooling Britain has always had dual-track educational arrangements. Traditionally, as we have seen, a minority got a good education; though the good part may not have begun till schooling ended. The majority had an education which was not only inferior, but was meant to be inferior. The ruling classes were aware of the danger that the educated man (men were the main concern) 'forgetting the humility that belonged to his condition, was contriving to raise himself out of his proper place'.[1] The fear was not misplaced. As we have seen, a handful of radicals – Tom Paine among others – were led from grammar school literacy to the reading of dissenting literature. Later, the Chartists, arch-enemies of the established order, took the same subversive path.

There was, besides, no real need to educate the masses above their station. The basic skill of reading moral and religious texts, sufficient to prepare the mass of industrial workers, was unlikely to lead to a radical, or even critical, outlook. We have made an educated guess that this minimally schooled cohort was around eighty per cent of the total population. The rest – the other twenty per cent or so – were and are destined to be administrators, officers, managers, directors, politicians and professionals. (The constituents of each group will change a little over time, but the proportions seem to stay about the same.)

The schooling of the favoured twenty per cent was a path to a select post-compulsory education, ideally at a 'good university', a military college or, latterly, at a good business school. That, in turn, should lead to a well paid job or (which is likely to be the same thing) a position of influence.

Something similar happens in the United States. Reich notes that America's school system at mid-century fitted nicely 'into the prevailing structure of high volume production within which its young products were to be employed. American schools mirrored the national economy, with a standard assembly line curriculum divided neatly into subjects, taught in predictable units of time, arranged sequentially by grade, and controlled by standardised tests intended to weed out defective units and return them for reworking.'[2] More recently, Reich adds 'some people who called themselves "educational reformers" [have] suggested that the standard curriculum should become even more uniform across the nation and that standardised tests should be still more determinative of what was poured into young heads as they moved along the school conveyor belt. (Of course standardised tests remained, as before, a highly accurate method for measuring little more than the ability of children to take standardised tests.)... Remarkably often in American life, when the need for change is most urgent, the demands grow more insistent that we go "back to basics".'[3]

America, which on independence so enthusiastically rejected much of its British heritage, seemed to have rejected also the old world's class-based educational provision. If that was ever true, it is not now. 'These days the biggest determinant of how far you go in life is how far you go in education. The gap in income between the college-educated and the non-college-educated rose from 31% in 1979 to 66% in 1997. But access to college is increasingly determined by social class... The obvious way to deal with this is to use the education system to guarantee a level playing field. Improve educational opportunities for the poorest Americans, make sure that nobody is turned away from university on grounds of financial need, and you will progressively weaken the link between background and educational success.'[4] The problem is that, as in Britain, 'the schools the poorest Americans attend have been getting worse rather than better'.[5] Over past decades the US has become progressively more unequal and the affluent are increasingly skilled at entrenching advantages, educational and otherwise. Reich notes that 'while the vast majority of American children are still subjected to a standardised education designed for a standardised economy, a small fraction are not... Fully seventeen per cent of American seventeen-year-olds are functionally illiterate. Some American children receive almost no education, and many more get a poor one. But some American children – no more than fifteen to twenty per cent – are being perfectly prepared for a lifetime of symbolic-analytic work.'[6] In short, America's educated classes 'still do a superb job of consolidating and transmitting their privileges.'[7]

As in Britain, then, there is in America a well-educated, self-perpetuating elite. But, surprisingly, there was in Britain, in the second half of the twentieth century, an anti-elitist counter-current. Some politicians, of the party formerly known as Labour, favoured a system of comprehensive secondary education which would educate all pupils – apart perhaps from children of the rich – in the same neighbourhood secondary schools. Across the electorate, in the postwar years, that was a generally popular policy, though it was not extensively implemented until the 1960s. In that decade Anthony Crosland, who became Secretary of State for Education in 1965, enthusiastically supported comprehensive schooling and, at the same time, provoked a barrage of criticism from educational conservatives.

Some of the criticisms were justified. There are real problems with a system of universal comprehensive schooling; a number of these are considered later in this book. But there are also problems with a system that fails to offer equal educational opportunity to all, and they are more far-reaching than the faults of the comprehensive system. Yet, in recent decades, most politicians – both Labour and

Conservative – have preferred the long-standing British tradition of unequal educational opportunity. Since the then Prime Minister's 'great debate on education' in 1976, politicians have taken every opportunity to undermine genuinely comprehensive schooling, rather than address its difficulties. But, since comprehensive schooling is still popular with the majority of parents, the undermining must be done by stealth. Anti-comprehensive measures are now marketed under user-friendly, hard-to-argue-with labels, like 'raising standards' or 'increasing parental choice'.

'Parental choice' is an interesting one. In its present form, the notion was born of mid-to-late-twentieth century right-wing critiques of state schooling. These, in turn, had their intellectual origins in two sets of theories: neo-liberal and neo-conservative. (There were, and are, substantial areas of overlap between the two.) The more intellectually respectable neo-liberal critique accused state school systems of being monopolistic and, thus, of lacking 'market qualities'. This position was energetically advanced by the neo-liberal American economist Milton Friedman.[8] Friedman repeated his supply-side arguments, with admirable persistence, but little intellectual advance, for decades after their first formulation in the fifties. He was later joined by other conservative economists and right-wing think-tank members, in Chicago, London, Santiago and elsewhere.

From the early 1980s to the present, conservative (and mainly Anglo-American) politicians have found libertarian, pro-choice arguments a useful intellectual cloak for an array of policies designed to promote not only selective schooling, but also universal market primacy, diminution of trade union power, 'reducing the state', lower rates of income tax, and other means of transferring money from the relatively poor to the relatively rich. Throughout this period the Friedmanite case for reform of schooling was part of the neo-liberal package, and widely promoted in conservative political circles. In Britain, these included most of the post-1997 New Labour leadership.

In brief summary, the neo-liberal argument around schooling ran like this. If parents have to send their children to the state school in their local catchment area, and if state schools are part of national system, that makes each school effectively a geographically-limited monopoly, which is in turn a constituent of a wider national educational monopoly. To use a term popularised by Mr Blair's staff, each school in such a system is thus likely to be a bog-standard, but unavoidable, educational facility. Parents who cannot afford to opt out of the state system are therefore denied choice. Lacking competition, schools have no incentive to innovate, or to improve their service, since they are assured of a constantly renewed, young and captive clientele. The available choices for parents (rather than children) have been summarised by Hirschman[9] as 'exit, voice and loyalty': leave an unsatisfactory school; use political channels to improve things; or keep your head down and stay. Right-wing critics of schooling are not enthusiastic about either the second or third options. Hirschman quotes Friedman's argument in favour of schooling vouchers: 'Parents could express their views about schools directly, by withdrawing their children from one school and sending them to another, to a much greater extent than is now possible. In general they can now take this step only by changing their place of residence. For the rest they can express their views only through cumbrous political channels.'[10]

Education vouchers introduce a market mechanism to schooling. For neo-liberals it is axiomatic that the market will cure most problems, in school systems and elsewhere. The market was, and for them is, the optimal and preferred mechanism for all resource allocation. In an educational context, these economists and their political associates advocated market transactions in which parents freely chose the state-subsidised (public or private) schooling they wished their children to have. In some cases, parents might choose not to school their children: in a libertarian state the buyer, after all, will decide; or will decide for his or her children. However, some neo-liberals, and most conservatives, additionally believed that the state has an economic need for an educated or trained workforce with habits of industry. Therefore provision and quality of mass schooling could not be left entirely to market forces. The most common way of squaring this theoretical circle has been to propose school systems partly run by, or partly financed and quality-assessed by, the state, but open to the competition of private enterprise. Parents might be given the 'schooling vouchers' noted above and could then choose freely among state-supported or privately provided scholastic offerings. Others would do as some have always done, paying to buy a more prestigious class of schooling for their children than that offered by the state. Now these wealthier parents would have additional financial assistance, to the value of their vouchers (and of course would continue to benefit from the tax breaks which fee-charging schools in Britain have come to expect[11]).

Those arguments appealed to the British administrations led by Mrs Thatcher and Mr Major between 1979 and 1997. The seventeen Education Acts passed under these administrations 'fundamentally changed the way in which education is provided. What was a service largely based on co-operation and broad consensus [was] changed to one based upon individualistic striving and competition between schools. The keyword used to justify these changes has been "choice".'[12] Policies descended from neo-liberal theories were advertised as increasing parental choice and, in ways which were not closely defined, as improving standards of schooling. The motivation for most of these reforms to state school systems 'was ideological rather than evidential'.[13] No hard evidence was presented to support the choice-and-standards platform. No serious international comparative studies were undertaken, though visits were made to then-radical-right administrations, like that of the 1980s New Zealand Labour party and General Pinochet's military government in Chile. On the theoretical side British neo-liberals argued vociferously against compatriots like R H Tawney who had earlier 'theorised a new positive connection between economic efficiency and equality'[14]

Given that state school systems are closed, technologically ossified and monopolistic, introducing a market and competition seems entirely desirable. Since 1987 market elements have been introduced to British schooling, usually under the guise of parental choice. Markets were, as noted, then taken to be a desirable innovation in this and almost any other state-financed setting, with the partial exceptions of the armed forces and the police, neither of which are usually free to work for the highest bidder.

Had there been a less strong ideological motivation, more attention might have been paid to the practical problems of introducing a free market to school systems. In any ideally free market, prosperous buyers have of course unfettered choice between a range of goods. Within each category each item will have a more-or-less similar function. If I want a chair, for example, I can physically or virtually visit a number of furniture shops, which will offer me various chairs. All of them do much the same thing – you can sit on them – but they will differ in design, durability, availability and price. Buyers choose what they deem to be the best-value chairs; those which best suit their needs. In theory, their makers should flourish, while their less competitive chair-vendors will wither.

A moment's reflection shows us that the world is not quite like this. Advertising, lobbying, legislation, targeted corruption, ignorance or gullibility can distort free markets for chairs or schools. Modern versions of snake oil are still being sold. Further, schools are not like chairs, and will not be in any foreseeable future. In an ideal market there is no outside or official interference with the buyer-seller transaction. With mass schooling, there is, and always has been, a high level of religious or governmental interference, which has increased during the Thatcher-Blair era of 'quasi-markets'. (Again, tighter state control of schools, and school knowledge, has been for ideological rather than evidential reasons, though presented otherwise.)

In an ideal market, sellers are free at any moment to adjust the cost of their goods. This is not the case with schools. The cost of providing mass schooling is not easily or freely adjusted. Nor is there free choice for buyers. For most families there are likely to be few age-related schools – sometimes only one – within reasonable travelling distance for their children. Further the ideal buyer of market theory is fully informed about every item he or she may wish to purchase. In education, though, there are few ideally informed buyers. 'Schools are too complex to portray their quality effectively to parents and pupils. Most parents make infrequent, but closely spaced, schooling decisions and the consequences of those decisions are only revealed, if at all, in the long term.'[15]

For those interested in theoretical formulations, economists of education describe parental choice like this. 'Amongst the opportunity costs that will influence educational decisions are search costs in gathering relevant information [about schools]; transport costs involved in getting a child to an out-of-neighbourhood school; the cost of foregone income through supporting a child in education beyond sixteen [and often before that age]; and tuition costs in the form of parental and pupil time, private tutors, and books. For a given level of schooling, these costs will be a higher proportion of the income of parents with lower incomes. Where capital markets are imperfect it therefore follows that there may be an unequal ability to finance these costs'.[16] In other words, and unsurprisingly, poor families have less choice of schooling in either a state-financed or free market, fee-charging system.

Decisions about schooling are further complicated by the pet-food principle referred to earlier: as a rule, the chooser is not the user.[17] It is also hard to predict the benefits of schooling, either social or economic. Again, in technical terms, 'the estimation of expected investment benefits is particularly problematic for parents and students.' Parents have difficulty in predicting 'what kind of schooling and the mix of investment outcomes will best suit their child. *This will be particularly so where, say, the impact of the "new economy" is rapidly changing the structure of educational premiums*'[18] (emphasis added).

Given these factors, it is not a simple matter for those purchasing or selecting schooling to choose which is right for their children, even if market principles obtain, and there are several schools available and accessible. Most of the valuable qualities of schools are not easily measurable, and may not be obvious to a briefly visiting parent. To make parental choice simpler, 'official school league tables' were introduced in England during the Thatcher years. Since these ranked schools primarily on pupils' success, mainly in written examinations, they favoured academic advantage groups, as schools have always done. (If word-based examinations were replaced with tests of accomplishment in singing, let us say, or speed of sprinting, we would of course have quite different advantage groups. Doubtless we would also have vigorous protests from obese and tone-deaf youngsters, and from their parents.)

Ranking by academic league tables naturally directs parents' attention to the academic dimension of schooling: that is, the dimension measurable by standard tests. This ignores what may be a school's most valuable qualities – care for young people; a degree of mutual respect between pupils and staff; the fostering of idealism; internationalism; tolerance; width of subject choice; capacity to deal with contemporary life; a range of learning styles. League tables also set pupils against teachers (as did the nineteenth-century system of payment by results) and school against school. While that may be the intention – this is, after all, what markets do – it clearly does nothing to improve learning.

Despite a general rhetoric of open access to British state schools, there has been a steady increase, over the past three decades, in selection of pupils. At the time of writing faith schools may select on religious affiliation (using church attendance records, recommendations from priests, mullahs, or primary head teachers) and on parental interviews. Foundation and voluntary aided schools are free to set selection criteria as long as they comply with schools' admission code of practice; academies may set their own admissions criteria 'in line with the accepted code of practice', and can select 10% of pupils on 'aptitude'; specialist schools can select 10% of pupils on aptitude in the school's chosen specialism; grammar schools can select on academic ability from across local authority areas (and may legally access prospective pupils' examination results ahead of neighbouring comprehensives); and most public [fee-charging] schools select in any way they wish, including parents' ability to pay the school's fees.[19]

'Parental choice' means in practice that middle-class parents who cannot afford public schools will find ways (up to, and including, moving house) to send their children to state schools which get good results in public examinations. These strategies are not, of course, new. 'The British educational system,' Walford notes, 'has always been inequitable. Those with sufficient financial capital have always been able to purchase elite education for their children in the private sector or by buying homes near to high-status state-maintained schools. Those with cultural capital but insufficient finance have been able to "work the state system" to ensure their children received the best available. The whole of the education system has been riven by divisions according to class, gender and ethnicity, and those children from the most disadvantaged families have usually received the poorest educational experience.'[20] What is new in Britain is the institution of those league tables which are supposed to make it easier to locate 'good schools'. As their 'academic' and middle-class intake increases (and as they find ways of defenestrating non-academic pupils) schools improve their results in academic examinations, and are financially rewarded. 'Very efficiently, the current system identifies those schools which are struggling. It then robs those schools of their brightest pupils, and thus of their funds, guaranteeing that their struggle becomes more desperate. The fact that these schools almost without exception are struggling in the first place because they are sited in poor areas with an intake of disadvantaged children means that these extra burdens are placed almost unfailingly on schools that serve the poor. The converse is also true: those that serve affluent neighbourhoods prosper. And so the school system divides along class lines.'[21] Parents who are less good at working the system (or who have fewer resources, or time for the school run) send their children to the nearest school, which may not be one of those favoured by the middle-classes and their academic children. In this way, throughout the system, inequality increases.

A 2005 study by Britain's Sutton Trust argued that 'the reasons for the under-representation of children from poorer backgrounds at top state schools are undoubtedly complex. It is clear, though, that the admissions system is not operating equitably and is in need of review, and that more needs to be done to raise standards earlier down the educational chain. The unevenness of the state school system serves to exacerbate existing inequalities, and we see its consequences in the under-representation of those from lower social classes and poorer areas in higher education, particularly at the leading universities.'[22]

Middle-class parents often say that they avoid schools with a lower class intake because their more favoured children cannot learn in the company of others who do not wish to learn. And they are right. But it's not just middle-class children who feel that way. *Nobody* learns well in the company of others who simply refuse to learn – and who probably prevent others from learning. But there is a remedy. If pupils refuse to learn *even in areas of interest*, then clearly they should not be in school. They should leave, with an educational credit which allows later re-entry to post-compulsory education if they change their minds about education (and many people do, for different reasons, change their minds about learning).

At the time of writing, Britain's Conservative Party has not matched the Labour government's ability to impose school selection by stealth; nor do they feel the same need, since the Party is more openly tolerant of unequal opportunity. But there was, and is, a problem. Understandably, the Tories wish to skew the British school system to favour its middle-class and lower-middle-class aspirational heartland. The Conservative Party has also, traditionally, been the party of business[23] but is pulled in different directions by its various constituencies: corporate, parental, neo-liberal and patriotic. It has been difficult to reconcile

79

education 'as a key to the global economy' with education as an 'institution for the preservation of the national state'.[24] Pushing schools toward more academic and selective policies pleased affluent parents, but worked against the interests of post-industrial business. In the early years of the new century, the Conservatives are still trying to resolve their educational dilemma.

But if Conservative policies are puzzling, those of the subsequent Labour government are more so. Education was Labour's much publicised first priority, when it came to office in 1997. The Party seemed to have sustained its belief in equitable provision as an aim for the country's state school system. Yet Labour retained most of its predecessor's provisions which, as we have seen, were designed to make schooling less equitable. This was partly due to the fact that post-1997 Labour's first Education Minister and first Prime Minister were both instinctively conservative and both apparently unaware of the different ways in which we learn, as well as the relationship of learning to Britain's post-industrial economy.

Doubtless there were other reasons for aggravating inequity, which will take time to sort out. We may find that, in schooling, New Labour is a true heir to its Conservative predecessors, and that its undeclared aim is an increasingly inequitable, selective, and partly-privatised school system. After more than two terms of Labour government, policy directions are now becoming clear. But their motivation is not. What is clear is that, under Labour, into the new century, systemic inequality in English schooling has continued to grow.[25]

Here, then, is schooling's dilemma. A monopolistic, hermetic, self-assessing school system (which we now have) is in many ways unsatisfactory. As we will see (chapter 15) it has a poor record of encouraging innovation and – insulated from the world outside – commonly fails to offer an education which properly prepares young people for life and work beyond school.

The trouble is, the Conservative solution – a free market in schooling – may be no better, and could be worse. Fee-charging schools may (as David Hursh shows in chapters 10 and 11) be educationally inventive. But this is unusual. Certainly it is unusual in Britain. The record shows that unregulated free markets and fee charging schools tend to follow their own understandable logic. They focus on the most profitable markets – affluent families – in the most rewarding places, notably the richer parts of thriving cities or rural counties; and opt for the simplest core business, which is training young people to pass standardised exams. Experience suggests a business model built around scholastic discipline, didactic teaching and academic achievement. That makes good commercial sense. It is what any chief financial officer would recommend. What it will not produce is an affordable, equitable and educationally progressive national school system, which prepares all young people for the life and work ahead of them, and which supports a fast-changing national economy. What it will do is increase our school system's national inequality of provision.

Inequality, in school systems and in society at large, raises a perennial question: do schools reproduce our visibly inegalitarian society? (At least it is a perennial question for sociologists, who ponder the matter, and compile books about it.)

Writing of Britain, Ball, for example, asserts that 'the implementation of market reforms in education [was] essentially a class strategy which [had] as one of its major effects the reproduction of relative social class (and ethnic) advantages and disadvantages'.[26]

In practice, the idea of social reproduction is simple enough. As noted, rich parents send their children to expensive schools which other parents can't afford. From these schools most young people move into highly rewarded work, and into social networks of influence. These are, if you like, advantage groups. We have seen that poor parents may have no choice but to send their children to local schools which – if they lack 'academic' middle-class pupils – will be officially classed as 'poor' or 'failing' schools, since that is in practice the definition of a failing school. Within schools, the converse of advantage groups are, of course, disadvantage groups. To these are assigned 'unacademic' pupils: commonly, the children of poor parents. Disadvantage groups may lead to pupils being certified as 'technical'. Any qualifications they earn will be those often derided or disregarded by employers. (For example, Britain's National Vocational Qualifications – NVQs – were dismissed by many employers, and known on the street as 'no value qualifications'. Kids are nothing if not realistic about such things.)

In sociological theory – and often in life – young people move from poor schools into poorly paid work, if they are employed at all. Sorting young people into these more- and less-favoured groups is, clearly, a main social function of school systems; but it is not one that should be dressed up as equality of opportunity, or enhancement of life chances.

There is a related theory, even more daunting for those who believe in education. This argues that what schools actually do makes no real difference to pupils' future working lives. What interests employers is parents, and what their choice of school for their children says about the family. Parents who choose certain types of school advertise themselves as 'desirable families', and their children as desirable employees. All the school does is to act as an 'organisation of stratification' which signals to employers these familial assumptions. In other words, 'investments in schooling have little direct influence on productivity' – or, indeed, on education – 'but instead provide signals of ability, or preferred personal characteristics, to potential employers.'[27] In this sense, schooling signals whether or not a candidate comes from an 'employable family' or one the employer sees as either 'less employable' or 'unemployable'. A main activity of schools, in stratification theory, is to teach and certify students 'in particular status cultures which consist of values, preferences, vocabulary and sociability rather than technical job skills... increases in absolute levels of educational attainment merely induce higher educational entry tariffs to be applied to "good jobs", perpetuating social inequalities.'[28]

It does seem possible, then, to say, if we don't look closely at the complexities, that our present school systems do reproduce society; or that society is reproduced in its school systems. But, even now, educational divisions are not completely watertight. An 'academic' child from a poor home may thrive if she is fortunate enough to find a school which will encourage her. Children from affluent homes may fail to clear school's academic hurdles and, without extensive private coaching, may fall from the social network which would have helped them in later life. Or there may be arrangements which transfer 'academically gifted' poor children to schools for the affluent. These, though, are exceptions to the rule, and do nothing significant to increase equality of opportunity. Nor do they change the fact that parents in each generation try to reproduce, or improve on, their own education, if they have found that education socially or economically advantageous.

As Americans are discovering, in the land of opportunity an educated elite perpetuates itself, and puts a deliberate distance between itself and the rest of the less successful population. The United States 'is becoming a stratified society based on education: a meritocracy...Historically, America's education system has been the main avenue for upward mobility. Mass secondary education supplied the workforce of the world's most successful industrial economy in the late 19th century; mass university education did the same for the period of American economic dominance after the second world war.'[29] But now what had been engines of social mobility risk becoming brakes. 'At secondary-school level, American education is financed largely by local property taxes. Naturally, places with big houses paying larger property taxes have schools with more resources. At university level, the rise in the cost of education has taken Ivy League universities out of the reach of most middle-class and poor families. The median income of families with children at Harvard is, at the time of writing, around $US150,000. The wealthy have always dominated elite schools, but their representation is rising. Between 1976 and 1995, according to one study, students from the richest quarter of the population increased their share of places at America's elite universities from 39% to 50%.'[30] The widening gap between the well educated and the rest may be as reassuring to the elite as it is daunting to the rest. As Gore Vidal has said, it is not enough that some succeed. Others must fail, and must be seen to fail. Anglo-American education ensures that they do, and are.

There are other, and less obvious, aspects of social reproduction through education. These have to do with knowledge. 'School knowledge' tends to confirm the social and political order. As we have seen, this message was clearer in Victorian schools, where children were instructed that they should 'order themselves lowly and reverently' before their many betters, including 'the land owners, the mine owners, the factory owners, the Squire, the Vicar, and all who provide employment' (see chapter 3). Poor children were instructed to repeat after the teacher 'I should not try to change my lot in life', which, in the circumstances, was probably realistic advice.

Though manifestly inegalitarian, education may have been functional for the nineteenth century; in the twenty-first we need to level the playing field. This is not simply because we all deserve equality of educational opportunity – though of course that *is* what we deserve. But equity also makes economic sense. The 2005 World Development Report argues that 'there may be various short-run, policy-level tradeoffs between equity and efficiency. These are well recognized and extensively documented' but 'the (often implicit) cost-benefit calculus that policymakers use to assess the merits of various policies too often ignores the long-term, hard-to-measure but real benefits of greater equity.'[31] Among those benefits is the possibility of opening up a hitherto untapped pool of inventiveness and innovation among the children of the poor, while acknowledging that 'greater equity implies more efficient economic functioning, reduced conflict, greater trust, and better institutions, with dynamic benefits for investment and growth. To the extent that such benefits are ignored, policymakers may end up choosing too little equity.'[32]

A PRIVATISED FUTURE

Late in 2005 the UK government published a White Paper (foreshadowing legislation) with the beguiling title 'Higher Standards, Better Schools for All'. This paper – manifestly the Prime Minister's, though channelled through his current Secretary for Education and Skills – proposes that 'schools will have greater independence and freedoms to innovate and run their own affairs through bodies such as a self governing trust'.[33] That, in itself, sounds like a valuable advance; but the small print suggests a different agenda. Assuming that Mr Blair's motivation is primarily political, rather than educational, we must ask, first, who benefits and, secondly, what is in it for the Prime Minister? The answer to the first question is, of course, that group of ambitious middle-class parents profiled in chapter 17. The answer to the second question is – a further move toward academic selection of school pupils and, thus, regress toward traditional teaching and a grammar school ethos for schools, at least in more affluent areas. Mr Blair has said that he wishes to be 'more radical' and, in these measures, he is likely to be supported by the Conservative opposition, who see his proposals as a logical extension of those put forward by Mrs Thatcher. The Prime Minister may need opposition assistance to force legislation, in its present form, through the House of Commons.

As with earlier systemic changes, the 2005 reforms have been introduced under the banner of parent power – in this case, the authority to control schools and to replace those who currently have that task. This immediately raises questions, since parents, collectively, have never demanded such power. Contemporary polls suggest that 'fewer than one in three people think schools have improved since Labour came to power despite record investment totalling £39bn since 1997',[34] but that very few parents questioned believe that 'choice' (as the government now uses the word) is the central issue. Every wide-sample survey of parents suggests that, for most, their priority is a good school within a reasonable distance of the family home.

'Parental choice' has been, for two decades, a useful fig leaf for an increasingly selective and unequal school system, and in 2005-6, that seems again to be the case. Democratically elected local education authorities in England are, under current proposals, to lose control of schooling, changing role from 'providers' to 'commissioners'. They will be expected to commission schooling from businesses, interest and faith groups (which means that churches will once more expand their influence over the school system). In practice, the Prime Minister is proposing to privatise – or largely privatise – the nation's state school system.

The suggested reforms will 'promote fair admissions' through testing children and 'banding' them as bright, less bright, and not bright; and then asking (but not compelling) schools to take some pupils from each band. Further, in current selection processes, statistical inference indicates that 'the results of about one third of the children will be determined by chance'.[35] As many people have pointed out, if the government were seriously interested in 'fair admissions' to schools it would formalise the process of chance by legislating for random selection of pupils; a lottery, in fact. But, since fairness is currently a slogan rather than a priority, lotteries do not fit with government thinking.

The proposed reforms will 'increase parental choice' by giving parents 'the opportunity to set up new schools, with support from the local authority'; a process which is estimated to take between four or five years, so parents are advised to initiate it (if this is legally allowed) before their children start school, and thus before it is clear that present schools are unsatisfactory for those children.

The journalist Alice Miles investigated how parents might in practice commission a new school in the moderately affluent London suburb of Kingston. First, she writes, 'you get a proposal together for a new Trust school, backed by like-minded parents, and an educational foundation or voluntary organisation. Then you go to your LEA [local education authority], which must provide "consultancy support" to help you to develop a concrete proposal. If the LEA then rejects the proposal, parents can appeal to the [yet-to-be-appointed] Adjudicator, and if the Adjudicator rejects it they can appeal to the [yet-to-be-appointed] Schools Commissioner, who will make a recommendation to the then Secretary of State. If [he or she] OKs it, the LEA has to find some land . . . not exactly straightforward in an area such as Kingston.' The proposed regulations for parents setting up schools give 'a useful insight into the bureaucracy that parents will face. The "Information to be contained in published proposals" begins: "(1) This regulation prescribes for the purposes of section 28(3)(a), section 29(3)(a), paragraph 5(2)(a) of Schedule 7 (where the proposals relate to a mainstream school) and paragraph 5(1)(a) of Schedule 23, the information which proposals published under section 28 or 29, paragraph 5 of Schedule 7 or paragraph 5 of Schedule 23 must contain." Will any parents have the time and dedication to fight their way through the morass?'[36]

As well as extending privatisation of the English school system, the 2005-2006 legislation will 'encourage popular schools to enlarge', at the expense of other schools, which will decline or, in some cases, will close. Popular schools will be 'encouraged (not compelled) to allocate places randomly or admit balanced numbers of children of differing abilities'.[37] Nick Davies has seen this Darwinian process at first hand.[38] He studied two Sheffield schools, Abbeydale (which was then failing) and Silverdale, which was not. 'Here is the truth.' he writes, 'which almost every teacher knows, and almost every politician denies: a school system which becomes as socially polarised as Britain's is guaranteed to generate failure... The early damage was done by a combination of cuts and 'parental choice', polarising school catchment areas by house price. But the market has other means of attack, and now, with each year that goes by, the polarisation grows. The key to this is that when [school] children move, they take the funding with them. The successful school becomes richer; the struggling school becomes poorer... The market has one more weapon with which to bludgeon the weak and wounded – academic cleansing. Some head teachers are so anxious for their schools to shine in the league tables that they get rid of students who are likely to perform badly in exams... On the other end of the cleansing is a struggling school which has vacancies, and cannot refuse to take a displaced child.'

Further, management is a weak point of almost all school systems – though of course worse in some than in others. But enlarging even well-managed schools risks threatening the 'quality' which made them popular in the first place. A great deal of evidence suggests that, on almost every indicator, large schools perform worse than smaller schools.[39] Therefore, provision should be made for the painful process of shrinking enlarged schools. The initially appealing idea of 'rewarding the best' – or most popular – works well in a free market, where firms make packaged items: after all, we can order goods as easily from Boulder as from Birmingham. But children are not packaged goods, easily dispatched to distant places. It's difficult for politicians to admit, and even more difficult to achieve, but families need local schools – *good* local schools.

There is an unlikely, but interesting, comparison to be made with Britain's rail network which, rather like the nation's school system, is meant to offer equal treatment to clients in any part of the country: that is, from any station you should be able to get to any other, at a cost per mile roughly comparable with costs elsewhere. The railways, 'the most important invention of the industrial revolution', were, in Victorian times, the country's largest industry,[40] employing 648,000 people. By the end of the twentieth century, however, the rail network was nationalised, widely criticised, run-down, undercapitalised, and unreliable. The Conservative government of the 1990s (and its committed civil servants) believed that 'improvement in customer service could only come about if there were competition'.[41] As a result the then-nationalised British Rail was fattened for sale, and in 1995 pieces of the network began to be sold, rather hastily, to different bidders. Ministers 'were too concerned with ensuring that the whole edifice was broken up and sold in time for the 1997 election to bother much about the short-term financial effects or the long-term robustness of the structure they were creating'.[42]

The stated targets for the late-twentieth-century rail structure were rather similar to the targets for the school system under the 2005 reforms. The railways would offer improved customer service and – since the competition of private rail companies would drive down costs – the network would be cheaper to run, and no longer a significant cost to the state. In practice customer service and train punctuality deteriorated sharply, due to the difficulties of running a previously unified rail system which had been suddenly fragmented into a hundred entities, and to the fact that most British Rail employees who knew how to run a railway were replaced by staff of the new owners, who did not.

A decade later customer service and punctuality have improved, largely due to unpublicised efforts to re-unify vital parts of the rail network. What has not improved is cost. The state subsidy to rail – which was meant to dwindle to insignificance – is, a decade after privatisation, in real terms a good deal higher than it was to the state-owned network. (It is hard to find exact subsidy figures since a somewhat embarrassed Treasury disguises them in various ways.) Further, the companies which run bits of the railway tend to behave not like competitive capitalists, but more like parts of government, assuming that, in the last resort, they will be saved from any threatening bankruptcy, or unmanageable debt. In this reassuring position, the rail companies have steadily raised fares by amounts above the rate of inflation, making Britain's rail network one of the world's most expensive.

As a monopoly-breaker, rail privatisation signally failed. A passenger might hear that there was a marginally more efficient rail company two hundred miles away; and its trains might even go where she wanted to go. But, since it would not start from her local station, that would be no help; indeed might add to her discontent. It is very unlikely that perfect competition will obtain: that two competing trains will leave at the same time, for the same destination, from the same station. Similarly with schools. If we built a free-enterprise school next door to every state school this (though extravagant in land use and, except in the Highlands, difficult to do) might offer genuine competition. But not even the most convinced free-marketeer thinks that likely to happen.

Competition in a school system is not strictly analogous with the disastrous privatisation of the British rail network, but (if we have any belief in learning from history) we need to be sure that we are indeed moving toward a brighter scholastic tomorrow. Fragmenting the English school system will, it is promised, give the yet-to-be-established 'trust schools' freedom over their running and over curricula, which (as noted) seems undeniably to be an advance. But we must ask whether this freedom is real and, if so, what are its limits? We are told that the proposed trust schools will not be free to select all their pupils. What of school knowledge? We know that Mr Blair has no objection to schools' teaching creationism or intelligent design; but could they decide, let us say, that numeracy was no longer necessary in an age of electronic calculation? Could evangelical schools denounce religions they disapprove of (in other words, most of them; but, problematically, involving an area of formerly free speech which Mr Blair's government proposes to legislate against)? Could they critique government policies like this legislation against 'religious hatred', or the blanket prohibition against 'glorifying terrorism' – or even the starting of illegal wars and the use therein of chemical weapons? If a schools trust is run by, for example, Microsoft, will the pupils be encouraged to discuss the disbenefits of monopoly?

The issue of equality of opportunity raises other questions. A network – whether in transport or education – which aims to offer equal service to all clients must be centrally planned. This certainly does not mean that it should be centrally micro-managed; nor does it preclude a high degree of autonomy for parts of the network and a high degree of trust in those who work within the network. But absence of any central control means that not all clients will receive equal service; and, as with railways, it may mean that – by any independent measure – the entire network functions badly.

At the heart of the matter is the question of whether or not competition will improve a national school system. Since we have argued that the English state school system is now over-regulated and backward looking, offering schools to businesses and other groups – priests and imams, for instance – might appear to be positive and liberating.

But what does competition mean in the context of compulsory education? What will the foreshadowed trusts compete for? Almost certainly – even with non-profits – the answer is 'the easiest and least expensive results': in management jargon, low-hanging fruit. Which means achievement in standardised tests, and a focus on training tasks, while finding ways of making redundant those pupils who do not fit the standard achievement pattern, and who will therefore look bad on the school's balance sheet. In fact, this is not so different from the ways in which most schools are now directed to operate. Unfortunately, though, it is a method which benefits neither the majority of learners, nor the country. The result, as Wolmar said of rail privatisation, is likely to be an unsympathetic amalgam of ideology and avarice. Britain's Deputy Prime Minister has said that his party's currently proposed reforms 'will create a two-tier school system',[43] but this is not the case. England has always had a two-tier school system. The foreshadowed reforms will do no more than widen and consolidate it. For a system which does not work well, we are proposing a remedy which, while superficially attractive, will probably make matters worse.

The legislation proposed in 2005-2006 seems likely, if put into effect, to increase parental choice by reducing the number of available and accessible local school places, since, according to government announcements, 'failing schools' (which are many people's local schools) will 'be ruthlessly closed'. Even Mr Blair seems to sense that this is an idiosyncratic definition of choice. He has therefore suggested compensating families who lose places at their local school (or lose the school altogether) by offering subsidised transport to school 'so that poorer parents who choose to send their children to distant schools will be eligible'.[44]

Ministerial briefings have suggested a system in England like the American yellow school buses, to take young people (or some young people) to schools far from home. Leaving aside educational considerations, this is an odd proposal when oil supplies are rapidly declining, and Britain is, once again, becoming an oil importer. As Kunstler says of America's school buses 'think of a school bus fleet as a mass transportation system that runs only twice a day for people under eighteen, and you may grasp the profligacy of the system'.[45] That is a difficult proposal to defend at a time of increasing fuel scarcity and cost.

For the UK, as for other countries, there are contentious policy decisions ahead. For many of the reasons noted above (among them the inevitable sclerosis of closed, self-assessing institutions) state school systems are not working well. Yet the easy answers – hand schooling over to private enterprise, to religious organisations and to charities while the government culls what it labels 'failing' comprehensives – is not a solution. At least it will not be a solution until we find a way of persuading businesses and evangelicals to offer, to all pupils, across the country, schools which dwell in the present century, and which foster a wish and an ability to learn and innovate. That is something we have not yet learned to do.

[1] Booth 1858
[2] Reich 1992
[3] Ibid
[4] *Economist* 9.6.2005
[5] Ibid
[6] Reich 1992
[7] *Economist* 9.6.2005
[8] Friedman 1953
[9] Hirschman 1977
[10] Friedman 1962
[11] Britain's fee-charging schools have recently wanted more than tax breaks. It was reported in 2005 that fifty of the nation's leading public schools have not only year on year increased their fees above the rate of inflation, but have also allegedly breached competition law by forming a cartel – which, according to Britain's competition regulator, has resulted in parents 'being charged higher fees than would otherwise have been the case'. The public schools, in an understandably affronted response, have replied that they never realised laws applied to them. (Reported in *The Economist* 12.11.2005)
[12] Walford 1994
[13] Adnett and Davies (2002)
[14] Aldrich, Crook and Watson 2000
[15] Ibid
[16] Adnett and Davies 2002
[17] There are, of course, parents who pay attention to their children's school preference. But the proportion of young people who choose their own school, from among several possibilities, is small.
[18] Adnett and Davies 2002
[19] See Taylor, M, *The Guardian* 10.10.05
[20] Walford 1994
[21] Davies 2000
[22] 'Rates of eligibility for free school meals at the top State Schools' The Sutton Trust 2005 [since only children of poorer families are eligible for free school meals this is commonly used as one indicator of a school's social intake]
[23] There may have been a cooling of this relationship from the late 1990s, but it will doubtless be repaired.
[24] Aldrich, Crook and Watson 2000
[25] David Bell, the chief inspector of schools [in England and Wales], said: "Since 1996, the socio-economic attainment gap has widened in secondary schools. We must look again, urgently, at how to close the gap in achievement between youngsters in the most deprived areas and elsewhere." ePolitix.com 21.11.2003
[26] Ball 1993
[27] Adnett and Davies 2000
[28] Ibid
[29] *Economist* 14.7.2005
[30] Ibid
[31] 2006 World development report, World Bank, Washington 2006
[32] Ibid
[33] DfES Schools white paper' http://www.dfes.gov.uk/highlights/article06.shtml
[34] Guardian/ICM poll, *The Guardian*, 25.10.05
[35] Gavyn Davies in *The Guardian* 10.11.05
[36] Alice Thomas *The Times* 29.10.05
[37] *Economist* 22.10.05

[38] Davies 2000
[39] For a passionate and practical exposition of this view, see Littky 2004
[40] Wolmar 2005
[41] Ibid
[42] Ibid
[43] *Yorkshire Post* 26.10.05
[44] *Economist* 22.10.05
[45] Kunstler 2005

III THE US SCHOOL SYSTEM

EDUCATION AS A CONTESTED TERRAIN:
THE RELATIONSHIP BETWEEN EDUCATION, WORK AND THE STATE

The history of primary and secondary education in the US has many parallels with that of England and Wales, from the expansion of public (state) schooling throughout the twentieth century, to increasing regimentation during the last decade. In this chapter I will first situate the last century of education reform in US within the context of the contested and changing economic system and the debates over the purpose of schooling. After providing a historical overview, I will argue that the shift from Keynesian economic policies to neoliberal policies is resulting in increasing educational inequality and preparing fewer students than before with the ability to think critically. In particular, I will focus on the possibilities and problems in developing schools for the twenty-first century where students can think beyond congealed curriculum categories and learn from all the resources available to them both in and outside the classroom and from persons directly and via technology. I will describe how New York state education policy makers have continually undermined efforts by educators to implement innovative curriculum and pedagogy, including the efforts of a small group of public schools that have proven successful. In the following two chapters I will examine the education policies of the city of Chicago and of the federal government and show how these policies undermine the kind of innovations we are calling for. However, in examining the difficulties educators continue to face, I will describe some of the innovations carried out by educators in schools with which I have worked.

While some members of the public may desire an education for the twenty-first century, such innovations have always been contested. As I will show, the US has had, and continues to have, a two-tier system in which White students coming from economically privileged families are much more likely to experience a challenging and thoughtful curriculum and working class students and students of colour receive an education that prepares them for, in the past, manual jobs and, currently, retail and service jobs. While the passage of Brown v. Board of Education in 1954 resulted in schools becoming less segregated[1] beginning in 1991 the Supreme Court began undermining desegregation efforts, restoring what Kozol calls "apartheid schooling."[2]

Not only are schools becoming increasingly segregated, but Kozol also describes how the programs in urban schools are becoming highly regimented and standardized. Kozol focuses, in particular, on "Success for All," which, a century later, builds on the managerial efficiency movement initiated by Frederick Winslow Taylor in the early 1900s. Kozol rightly points out that the kind of regimentation and simplification characteristic of "Success for All," while seen as appropriate for "urban schools" (in the US a euphemism for schools largely composed of poor students of colour), similar programs would never be implemented in middle-class schools.

That "Success for All" and similar programs prevail in urban schools suggests that employers may not, as often stated in policy statements, desire highly skilled students who engage in critical thinking. In fact, when surveyed, corporate executives often express a desire not for more creative and innovative workers but for workers who do what they are told and show up on time.[3] Therefore, developing schools for the twenty-first century will require not only changes in our schools but creating educational and corporate institutions in which all students and employees are assisted in becoming life-long learners engaged in democratic decision making.

Throughout the twentieth and into the twenty-first century, education in the US has been a contested terrain, with some arguing for schools as places to prepare students for the workplace as it currently exists, and others for a democratic society in which the workplace is transformed. For some, writes historian Fones-Wolf,[4] schools have been seen as a "means of socializing workers for the factory, and as a way of promoting social and political stability." In contrast, progressives have promoted education to develop the social conditions and intelligence to enable citizens to make social and vocational decisions that support their own and their community's welfare.

Kliebard,[5] in his history of the American curriculum, details the disputes at the beginning of the century between those promoting "socializing for the factory," which he terms "scientific efficiency", and those arguing for progressive change, such as George Counts and John Dewey, whom he terms "social reconstructionists."

In the early 1900s, "productivity expert" Frederick Winslow Taylor promoted scientific efficiency as a way of increasing working productivity. Many curriculum theorists and education policy makers quickly adopted Taylor's principles and techniques as a way of improving educational productivity.[6] For example, David Snedden, a powerful state commissioner from Massachusetts, argued that schools should aid the economy to function as efficiently as possible by sorting and training students for their "probable destinies" in the workforce. The efficiency movement emphasized hierarchical decision making, with experts conceptualizing educational goals, curriculum, and pedagogy to be carried out by teachers. Teachers, according to Snedden, would be required to be neutral, "disinterested" presenters of the opinions of the majority or, if unable to do so, should withdraw from teaching. Under social efficiency, teachers are to prepare students to be productive workers within the status quo.

Dewey, in response, did not desire to make students' interests subservient to those of business. He argued instead for the development of such intelligence, ingenuity and capacity as shall make workers, as far as possible, masters of their own industrial fate.

The kind of vocational education in which I am interested is not one which will "adapt" workers to the existing industrial regime...but one which will alter the existing industrial system and ultimately transform it.[7]

During the Depression of the 1930s, the capitalist crisis invigorated the debate over education. George Counts, in his 1932 speech, "Dare the School Build a New Social Order?,"[8] explicitly challenged teachers to develop a democratic, socialist society. His call came at a time when many were questioning whether capitalism was tenable. In the journal The Social Frontier (1934-1939), reconstructionists such as Dewey, Counts, Charles Beard, and Harold Rugg called for reforming the economic system to serve the needs of people. Rugg believed that society required a "thoroughgoing social reconstruction..." and that "there is no social institution known to the mind of man that can encompass that problem except education."[9]

Teachers, argues Counts, working with a curriculum that promoted a critical study of contemporary economic, social, and political problems could "remake the world."[10] To this end, Rugg, seeing the curriculum as central to what could be accomplished, developed a series of social studies textbooks that rather than presenting the United States as a flawless democratic beacon for the world, focused on social issues and problems.[11]

Of course, the ideas and activities of the social reconstructionists were vigorously opposed. Conservative educators and corporate leaders denounced the reconstructionists and the critical emphasis in education. During the Depression, the US Chamber of Commerce led a campaign to reduce school taxes and slash school budgets. Leaders of the "National Association of Manufacturers and the Chamber of Commerce joined the [American] Legion in charging that collectivists were indoctrinating students through [Rugg's textbooks] and reducing the younger generation's trust in the free enterprise system."[12] Organizations, supported by the Daughters of the Colonial Wars and Bertie Forbes of Forbes magazine, successfully forced the removal of Ruggs' texts from the schools.

After the Depression, the National Association of Manufacturers teamed with the National Education Association (then primarily an organization of school administrators, now an organization for teachers) to promote corporate interests in schools. For example, at a jointly sponsored 1945 conference, schools were urged to "indoctrinate the students with the American way of life" and teach that "the American system of free enterprise has done more for human comforts than any other system,"[13] thus revealing that they were not against indoctrination, as long as corporations and those in power did the indoctrinating. Their efforts aimed to rid the schools of any criticisms of the US economic system and to prepare students through teaching and tracking for their "appropriate" place in the workforce. After the war ended, women were to leave their paid work and to return home, thus ending the career of "Rosie the Riveter."

After World War II, the mild support for an expanded welfare state, including support through the G.I. Bill for returning veterans, "roused the ire of all but the most moderate business leaders...[who] disliked the liberal agenda and feared that the New Deal traditions associated with the labour movement and the Democratic

Party continued to appeal to the American workers."[14] When programs such as the G.I. Bill and social security could not be blocked, they were amended or implemented in a way which disproportionately benefited Whites over people of colour. For example, a disproportionate number of Black and Latino soldiers were not able to take advantage of funding for a university education under the G.I. Bill because they were more likely to have dropped out of secondary school or been dishonourably discharged from the military. Home mortgages were unavailable to people of colour because suburban housing tracts were often legally segregated and banks engaged in red-lining, designating whole areas off-limits to people of colour.[15] And, finally, Southern politicians demanded that social security (pension) laws exclude those employed as agricultural or domestic household workers, jobs typically filled by African-Americans.[16] While citizens in England and other European countries experienced an expanded welfare state, corporate and political leaders in the US aimed to limit social benefits as much as possible.

When the US emerged from World War II as a world leader relatively unscathed by the war, reformers increasingly tied education and worker productivity not only to corporate efficiency but also to economic and military competition with other countries. When the Soviet Union launched Sputnik in 1957, political leaders feared that the US was falling behind the Soviet Union both militarily and educationally, particularly in math and science. Sputnik spurred the federal government to pass the National Defense Education Act, which began:

> The Congress hereby finds and declares that the security of the nation requires the fullest development of the mental resources and technical skills of its young men and women...The defense of this Nation depends upon the mastery of modern techniques developed from complex scientific principles.[17]

The act focused on curriculum reform in math, science and foreign languages. As Kliebard notes, most of the funding was funnelled through the National Science Foundation, established in 1950 as part of the executive branch of government, and funding went to university researchers. The Act marked the beginning of federal efforts to influence the curriculum, a development that has become more pronounced over time.

The mid 1950s were also the coming of age of the civil rights movement, with most notably, the 1954 Supreme Court Decision Brown v. Board of Education outlawing school segregation as separate and unequal, and the 1955 Montgomery Bus Boycott, precipitated by Rosa Parks, ending segregated buses. While the 50s are often described as quiescent, they, in fact, marked the beginning of not only the civil rights but other movements for economic and social equality, including gender and welfare rights. Moreover, even within the constraints of restrictive laws, such as the Taft-Hartley Act, workers gained strength and increasingly fought for and achieved better working conditions.

While desegregation was fiercely resisted, many schools and school districts and some residential areas became integrated. Integration contributed to increasing educational achievement by Hispanic and Black students from the 1960s until the

1990s. For example, the National Assessment of Education Progress (NAEP), conducted by the National Center for Educational Statistics and the best, if still flawed, assessment of student learning in the US, shows that from the 1970s into the 1990s, Black and Hispanics substantially reduced the achievement gap with White students.[18] While over the last two decades many on the political right have criticized the educational structures that existed previous to the recent accountability reforms, the data show that under the old reforms the achievement gap was closing. It is only under the current reforms, that ostensibly aim to close the gap, to "leave no child behind," that the gap is widening.

In 1983, the Reagan administration sponsored and released the report *A Nation at Risk*, which was highly critical of American public education. The report claimed, without providing evidence, that the "average achievement of high school students on most standardized tests is now lower than 26 years ago when Sputnik was launched."[19] Moreover, education was blamed for the Reagan induced economic recession and the nation's supposed failure to compete economically with other countries. *A Nation at Risk* began:

> Our Nation is at risk. Our once unchallenged preeminence in commerce, industry, science and technological innovation is being overtaken by competitors throughout the world...The educational foundations of our society are presently being eroded by a rising tide of mediocrity that threatens our very future as an Nation and a people.[20]

Since *A Nation at Risk*, schooling in the US has undergone numerous reform waves, most led not by educators but by corporate executives and governmental leaders. Initial reforms focused on developing and implementing standards but these soon transformed into efforts to hold schools, teachers, and students accountable through high-stakes testing. Some states, such as Texas, Florida and New York, imposed requirements that students pass several standardized tests in order to graduate from high school. However, it was the No Child Left Behind Act,[21] passed in 2001, in which the federal government imposed high-stakes testing on students throughout the country.

While students face increased testing, schools are becoming re-segregated. The advances in integration and academic achievement for students of colour from the late 1950s through 1980s began to unravel in the 1990s. As mentioned above, numerous Supreme Court decisions outlawed almost all the methods through which urban schools could desegregate. Many urban school districts are currently composed of 80-90 percent Black and Hispanic students. Some schools within districts have less than one percent White students.[22] Consequently, while the achievement gap between White students and students of colour narrowed following Brown v. Board of Education, with re-segregation and the introduction of testing and accountability measures, the gap has widened. "There was a tremendous amount of gap narrowing in the '70s and '80s but somewhere around 1990, the gap-narrowing stopped,'" according to Craig Jerald of the Education Trust.[23]

In order to evaluate whether and how the US will have schools for the twenty-first century, we need to understand how educational policy has been affected by changes in political and economic policies from the 1950s to the present. In the immediate decades after World War II, both the US and England implemented social democratic policies that emphasized an expanding role for the government in ensuring economic growth and social services, including an educational system that educated all students through secondary school and provided relatively inexpensive public post-secondary education. However, with the elections of Reagan and Thatcher, both the US and England began to shift their country's economics and social policy away from a social-democratic Keynesianism towards a neo-liberal approach. Understanding these changes helps explain the forces that work for and against having classrooms in which students engage in asking complex real world issues using resources that take them beyond the school.

SHIFTING POLICIES: THE RISE OF NEOLIBERALISM AND THE END OF THE WELFARE STATE

Since the end of World War II, the social and economic policies of both the US and the UK (and much of the rest of the world) have shifted from the Keynesian welfare state to the neo-liberal post-welfare state. This shift has been well described by many[24] and while I cannot do justice to the issues in a chapter, I will provide a brief description of the social and economic changes. Furthermore, I will argue that the current educational policies arise out of the need for governments to retain legitimacy by appearing to be doing something about the increasing economic inequality, to support capital accumulation through the reduction of taxes and the education of workers, and, particularly for neo-conservatives, in response to the social unrest of the 1960s and 70s, to regain social control.[25]

At the risk of greatly oversimplifying, neoliberal policies arose as a corporate and political response to the previous Keynesian economic accommodation that existed to different degrees in Europe and North America after World War II. In contrast to the years preceding the war, an unusual level of agreement between corporations and workers marked the first two decades after the war. During this period, in exchange for improving wages, workers consented to capital's right not only to control the workplace but also to allow capitalist control of investment and growth, primarily through the growth of multinational corporations. At the same time workers, women, and people of colour struggled for and were able to extend their personal and political rights for education, housing, health, workplace safety and to vote.[26] In part fuelled by workers' growing wages, the post-war period was marked by unusually rapid and stable economic growth. However, as workers earned and spent more, businesses' net rate of profit fell by more than fifty percent between 1965 and 1974.[27] Profits fell primarily because cost pressures from labour could not be passed on to consumers in the increasingly competitive and open world economy.[28]

In order to restore higher rates of profit, corporate and political leaders promoted neo-liberal policies that emphasize "the deregulation of the economy, trade liberalization, the dismantling of the public sector [such as education, health, and social welfare], and the predominance of the financial sector of the economy over production and commerce."[29] Tabb wrote that neo-liberalism stresses

the privatization of the public provision of goods and services—moving their provision from the public sector to the private—along with deregulating how private producers can behave, giving greater scope to the single-minded pursuit of profit and showing significantly less regard for the need to limit social costs or for redistribution based on nonmarket criteria. The aim of neoliberalism is to put into question all collective structures capable of obstructing the logic of the pure market.[30]

For neo-liberals, the market is both a democratic and efficient solution. Whitty, Power and Halpin,[31] Robertson,[32] and others[33] have described how the US, Great Britain and its former colonies have embraced markets and choice as a means of improving education. Whitty *et al* analyzed the changing educational system in five countries and concluded, 'within the range of political rationales, it is the neo-liberal alternative which dominates, as does a particular emphasis on market mechanisms.'[34] They describe how proponents of market reforms argue that they will lead to more efficient and effective schools. Similarly, Robertson notes, 'Much of the choice/markets agenda has been shaped by the criticism of schools as inefficient bureaucracies that are unresponsive either to community or individual interests.' Schools, and particularly teachers, are unresponsive, write the critics, because they know parents cannot take their children elsewhere. Therefore, proponents of choice and markets argue, 'efficiency and equity in education could only be addressed through "choice" and where family or individuals were constructed as the customers of educational services.'[35] Increasing the range of parents' choice over their children's schools and funding schools based on the number of students that they attract introduces a competitive market approach to the allocation of resources.

Thrupp and Willmott note that by 'the mid-1990s, Gewirtz and colleagues wrote that the market solution (to just about everything) currently holds politicians around the world in its thrall…Schools in England are now set within the whole paraphernalia of a market system.'[36] Market promoters decry 'state intervention because it is held that administrative and bureaucratic structures are inherently inferior to markets as a means of allocating resources.' Instead, resources are allocated through 'spontaneous exchanges between individuals.'[37] Markets, they assume, permit individuals choice based on the available data and to choose well. However, as Thrupp and Willmott point out, all markets, ranging from international trade, to local farmers' markets, to school choice depend on the state for regulation.[38] In education, such regulation exists in the form of the standardized testing and reporting (whether as "school report cards" in New York or "league tables" in England) and bureaucratic structures in which preferences are recorded and selections made.

Furthermore, the shift towards promoting corporate over social welfare redefines the relationship between the individual and society. Under Keynesian welfare policies, social justice required decreasing inequality through social programs and a redistribution of resources and power.[39] Under neoliberal post-welfare policies, inequality is a result of individuals' inadequacy, which is to be remedied not by increasing dependency through social welfare but by requiring that individuals strive to become productive members of the workforce. Neo-liberal governments take less responsibility for the welfare of the individual; the individual becomes responsible for him or herself. The goal for neo-liberal societies is to create the competitive, instrumentally rational individual who can compete in the marketplace.[40]

Because employability and economic productivity becomes central, education becomes less concerned with developing the well-rounded liberally educated person and more concerned with developing the skills required to become an economically productive member of society. Robertson describes the changing mandate as requiring "educational systems, through creating appropriately skilled and entrepreneurial citizens and workers able to generate new and added economic values, will enable nations to be responsive to changing conditions within the international marketplace."[41]

Neo-liberal governments, therefore, desire to reduce funding for education while at the same time reorganizing education to fit the needs of the economy. Because the public might object to cuts in social spending and increasing economic inequality, neo-liberal policy makers have skilfully packaged the reforms to make it appear that they are promoting equality. As I will describe, they use discourses emphasizing increasing education fairness, such as "requiring all students to achieve high standards as measured by objective tests," and opportunity, such as "leaving no child behind."

Another way in which neo-liberal governments are able to retain their legitimacy is by blaming schools for the essential injustices and contradictions of capitalism, while they preserve inequalities through other policies (such as taxation and social spending reductions).[42] For example, in the UK, Prime Minister Callaghan, in his 1976 speech at Ruskin College, laid out the framework for the debates that were to follow. One of his fundamental themes 'was the notion that the education system was not providing industry and the economy with what it required in terms of a skilled and well-educated workforce.'[43] Similarly, as stated earlier, in the US the authors of *A Nation at Risk* (1983) connected education to the economy by explicitly blaming schools for the Reagan- induced economic recession of the early 1980s[44] and for the US falling behind other countries economically.[45] These reports shift the blame for increasing economic inequality away from the decisions made by corporations and politicians and on to the educational system, what Apple calls "exporting the blame." Moreover, because they have framed schools as the root of the problem, by proposing reforms they appear to be doing something about the social problems. To cite Apple again, 'governments must be seen to be doing something…Reforming education is not only widely acceptable and relatively unthreatening, but just as crucially, its success or failure will not be obvious in the short term.' [46]

Focusing on educational reform not only diverts attention away from the negative implications of other policies, but also transforms the way in which we understand the relationship between the individual and society. The individual becomes central, with society and the community less important. Consequently, by shifting responsibility for individual welfare away from society as a whole to the individual, fewer expect society to provide an adequate education.

This individualism is also reflected in the way in which education is organized. In the past, when students attended the schools in their own community, they and their parents had a common stake with other parents over the quality of the school, including, in the US, voting on local school taxes. Schools in the US have had a long history of local control, with families committed to making schools work because the school was the community school. Children would attend the same schools as their siblings and their families would become involved in the welfare of the school. Parents were likely to come to know other parents in their neighbourhood and discuss curricular and pedagogical concerns.

However, with school choice, as promoted in the US by the No Child Left Behind Act (NCLB) (2001) and in England with open enrolments, parents are encouraged to transfer their children from school to school, therefore undermining their allegiance to the local school and the incentive to engage in public discourse regarding the nature and purpose of schooling. Because, as I will describe, the reforms focus on turning schools into competitive markets in which students apply to the school they want to attend, children and their parents no longer have shared interests with other students and families and, instead, become competitors for the available openings.

Lastly, not only have governments blamed schools for economic inequality, they propose that a system of standards, testing, and choice will increase educational efficiency and improve education for all. Moreover, because neo-liberal doctrine aims to reduce the size of the state and conservative doctrine claims to desire to intervene less in individual's private lives, they have been careful not to directly intervene in the everyday practices of schools. Consequently, the state has devised a system in which they can govern schools from afar through policies promoting testing, accountability and choice, what Ball describes as 'steering from a distance.' [47]

As I will describe, rather than moving education in the direction of the reforms advocated in this book, the emphasis on high-stakes standardized testing, competition, and markets is more likely to drive all but the wealthiest schools to focus on teaching the basic skills rather than complex, interdisciplinary learning.

EDUCATION FOR THE TWENTY-FIRST CENTURY: THE RISE OF HIGH-STAKES
TESTING AND THE ATTACK ON NEW YORK'S PERFORMANCE STANDARDS
CONSORTIUM SCHOOLS

Over the last decade, the relationships between local schools, state governments
(i.e. New York, California, etc.) and the federal government have been radically
transformed. As I described above, until recently the federal government has had
little influence over curriculum and pedagogy, with school districts free to adopt or
reject curriculum reforms such as those created under the National Defense
Education Act after the launching of Sputnik. Unlike England, which has a national
curriculum, no national curriculum formally exists in the US and school districts
determine what curriculum will be instituted in their schools. (However, a few
publishers produce the majority of textbooks and because publishers want to sell as
many texts possible, they are, not surprisingly, uniform, inoffensive and bland.)

Since there is no national curriculum, with authority for developing curricula and
tests restricted to individual states, states, previous to the passage of NCLB, varied
in developing mandated curricula and standardized tests. Most states had no
statewide-standardized exams while others, such as Texas, New York, and Florida,
began using, within the last two decades, standardized exams as a graduation
requirement. However, under NCLB all states are now required to develop
standards and to give annual standardized tests in math, reading, and science over a
span of seven grades. In states such as New York, the combination of federal and
state testing requirements results in students facing a minimum of thirty-three
standardized exams during their school career. Moreover, while states such as New
York have no *de jure* state curricula, the standardized testing requirements result in
a *de facto* state curriculum as teachers prepare students for the tests by focusing on
what they think will be tested.

In the remainder of this chapter I will describe how high-stakes standardized
testing in New York has harmed innovative successful schools like those that
composed the Performance Standards Consortium (hereafter the 'Consortium
schools') and lowered rather than raised standards for students. I will begin by
describing some of the characteristics of the Consortium schools and the efforts by
the State Education Department to restrain innovation in the schools. I will also
show how efforts to implement innovative, interdisciplinary curriculum are
undermined and made almost impossible by the rigid state requirements.

In New York, the Commissioner of Education and the New York State Regents,
who are appointed by the State Assembly, govern all the state's education
institutions: whether private or public, from birth through adulthood. The
Chancellor is appointed as Chair of the Regents.

For most of the last century, the Regents have permitted secondary schools to
award students either the Regents diploma, achieved by passing a set minimum
number of Regents subject area exams and courses, or a local diploma, determined
by local school districts' governing boards. Consequently, during that time, New
York public schools, like most schools in the US, offered different curricula for
different students and track or stream students depending on their "probable

futures." Typically, university bound students enrolled in the ostensibly more difficult Regents courses, and students not planning on attending university enrolled in the easier local courses. In urban districts, from 30-70 percent of student graduated and a majority of them received local diplomas.

However, some urban schools decided against the two-track system and, instead, developed an innovative, rigorous non-Regents program for all students. These schools often developed an innovative integrated curriculum, like that advocated by the authors of this book, in which students were not assessed through standardized exams but by exhibits, portfolios, and performances. In the 1990s, twenty-eight of the schools formed the Performance Standards Consortium. I have served on the board that oversees the schools and on the community board for School Without Walls, the Consortium School in Rochester. As I will describe, the New York State Education Department explicitly required that they eliminate their innovative curriculum and, instead, focus on preparing students for the statewide standardized Regents exams. Examining this conflict reveals how little the state values innovative challenging interdisciplinary curriculum, particularly for its urban students.

The most well known of the Consortium schools is Central Park East in New York City, founded in 1974 as a primary school, later becoming a secondary school with its first graduating class in 1991. Its founder, principal, and best known advocate has been Deborah Meier,[48] author of The power of their ideas: Lessons for America from a small school in Harlem (1995), which describes many of the underlying principles of not only Central Park East but other Consortium Schools.

Central Park East and the other Consortium Schools have been, by any measure, inordinately successful. While the characteristics of their student population has been roughly equivalent to other schools in New York City, the percentage of students graduating from high school and later university has been much higher. About 90 percent of ninth-grade students graduate four years later and about 90 percent of those continue on to university. In comparison, approximately 35 percent of NYC ninth-grade students graduate from high school.

While each of the Consortium Schools is unique, they share certain characteristics. They are all small compared to the typical urban secondary school. Most have a few hundred students, while many secondary schools in the US have several thousand students. The Consortium Schools also endorse the view that most urban schools, in trying to ensure that students pass the Regents exams, focus on "covering' the material that is likely to be on the test, therefore sacrificing depth and complexity for breadth. Instead, schools like Central Park East offer primarily two courses – one on the humanities and one on sciences and math – each lasting about two hours and co-taught by two teachers. The structure makes its possible for the teachers to teach 40 students during a day, rather than the 150 students per day in the typical secondary school. Not surprisingly, the teachers and students come to know one another well.

At the Urban Academy (also in New York City), rather than providing every teacher with a separate office, the office is a classroom where the dozen teachers each have a desk and the students have their lockers. What the teachers lose in

103

privacy, they gain by having multiple opportunities to informally meet with students, and to check with other teachers about a student's progress or collaborate with teachers and students on a project.

The courses themselves typically focus on one or more "essential questions," that is, questions to which there is not an agreed upon answer and requires students to use a variety of resources. For example, in the first year that I became acquainted with Central Park East, the question for the year was: What is a revolution? This led students to analyze political, industrial, and cultural revolutions and to ask open-ended questions, such as, "was either Malcolm X or Martin Luther King a revolutionary?" By focusing on one question for an extended period of time, students are pushed to develop what the school calls five major "intellectual habits": Concern for evidence (how do you know that?), viewpoint (who said that and why?), cause and effect (what led to it and what else happened?), hypothesizing (what if, supposing that) and, most importantly, who cares?[49]

Some of the Consortium Schools require students to carry out a year-long senior project. At Rochester's School Without Walls, seniors are required to propose a project, carry it out, and then defend their project in a committee meeting in much the same way that doctoral students carry out and defend dissertations. One student, for whom I served as the "community representative" on his committee, developed a video documentary on Hilton, a rural community near Rochester. He began by taking courses on documentary film-making at local universities and then researched the history of Hilton, focusing in part on the 1970s fire that destroyed the village centre. He interviewed some of the residents involved in fighting the fire and collected film and photos from those at the fire, including video taken by television reporters. He then edited his film, provided the narrative, and composed and played the background music. Many residents attended the premier of his 90-minute video, which he subsequently donated to the town historian. The film enabled him to obtain a position with Ken Burns, one of the best known documentary film-makers in the US. The student decided that the best path to a career in film was not through a university but by producing independent films: he is currently an independent film-maker in New York City. While his project is obviously atypical, it points out the possibility of what secondary students can do if given the time and the resources to pursue an in-depth, sophisticated project.

While neither Central Park East, the Urban Academy, nor School Without Walls have a particular academic theme (other than strong academic preparation), several other schools in New York City have specific themes and partner with various institutions to achieve them. One school I visited, The School for the Physical City, aims to "prepare and empower city youth to take care of and take charge of the city." The school collaborates with several other organizations, including "Cooper Union, a private, tuition-free arts, architecture and engineering college geared toward the children of working people," and Outward Bound, which has an expeditionary character-building program.[50]

Mike Rose, in *Possible lives: The promise of public education in America* (1995), interviewed the principal of the School for the Physical City, who described how a small school with an innovative, integrated curriculum allowed him to think differently about learning. The principal describes the transition from focusing on exams to focusing on learning. He stated that he did not think he had "ever thought as clearly about what learning is. The big leap is between teachers learning in order to teach and then teachers knowing enough about learning in order to teach what they know."[51]

Yet, in 1996 the newly appointed New York Commissioner of Education, Richard Mills, began implementing a requirement that every student in the state would only graduate from secondary school if they passed five Regents exams: in math, science, English, US history and global studies. While on the surface this might seem reasonable – in fact, the Commissioner repeatedly asserted just how reasonable it was – for innovative schools like the Consortium Schools, the requirement would severely undermine their ability to engage students in in-depth, interdisciplinary projects. Furthermore, the testing requirement undermined student academic success at all schools and increased the achievement gap between wealthier and poor students.

RAISING OR LOWERING STANDARDS? NEW YORK'S HIGH-STAKES TESTING

As with all the reforms initiated by either states or the federal government since *A Nation at Risk*, New York State education officials promoted testing, accountability, markets, and choice by arguing that within an increasingly competitive global economy, such reforms were necessary to ensure that all students and the nation succeed. Moreover, they linked the discourse of the necessity of increasing educational and economic productivity with the discourses of decreasing educational inequality and improving assessment objectivity, a strategy also used by the proponents of No Child Left Behind.

Beginning in the 1990s the New York State Board of Regents and the Commissioner of Education radically overhauled the education system by implementing standards and standardized testing, making graduation contingent on passing five statewide standardized exams, and requiring secondary students to enrol in only the state-regulated Regents courses, therefore eliminating locally developed courses as a route to graduation. The reforms have substantially narrowed the curriculum and reduced innovation, including temporarily eliminating the successful programs at the Consortium Schools.

While new testing requirements were being developed, the state also passed legislation promoting the establishment of up to 100 charter schools, schools usually administered by for-profit educational corporations, which would take students and funds from the public schools.

The state's educational policy makers, including the past Chancellor of Education Carl Hayden and the present Commissioner of Education Richard Mills, justify the testing and accountability regime on the grounds that standards and standardized testing are the only way to ensure that all students, including students of colour and those living in poverty, have an opportunity to learn. They argue that it is these same students who, because of the end of industrialization and the rise of globalization, can no longer be permitted to fail. All students must succeed educationally to ensure that the individual and the nation succeed economically.

Carl Hayden, the New York Chancellor of Education from 1996-2002, reflects these views in a letter:

> The requirement that every child be brought to a Regents level of performance is revolutionary. It is a powerful lever for education equity. It is changing for the better the life prospects of millions of young people, particularly poor and minority children who in the past would have been relegated to a low standards path. Too often, these children emerged from school without the skills and knowledge needed for success in an increasingly complex economy [52]

Furthermore, Chancellor Hayden and Commissioner Mills argue that the curriculum standards were objectively determined and that standardized tests provide a valid and reliable means of assessing student learning. Such objective methods are required, they state, because teachers and administrators cannot be trusted to assess student learning objectively and accurately. Therefore, teacher-generated assessment protocols and instruments, such as those used by the Consortium Schools, are dismissed within this discourse as subjective and unreliable. Testing proponents imply that to adopt other means of assessment results automatically in a lowering of standards, as can be seen in Chancellor Hayden's response to the possibility of retaining the kinds of performance assessments used by the Consortium Schools:

> There is an even greater danger. The least rigorous, the least valid, the least reliable approved alternative [assessment] is then available to any school. Which schools will be first in the race to the lowest common denominator? Those having the most trouble bringing all children to a Regents level of performance. Those keen to reacquire the low standard option lost when the RCT [Regents Competency Test for the previously existing non-Regents track] and the local diploma were abolished. Those that never believed that all children can reach high standards. Were this to occur, it is all too apparent that poor and minority children would disproportionately bear the burden of diminished expectations. [53]

However, the reforms have not resulted in more objective assessments. Almost every recent standardized exam given in New York State has been criticized for having poorly constructed, misleading, or erroneous questions, or for using a grading scale that either overstates or understates students' learning. Critics argue that an exam's degree of difficulty has varied depending on whether the State Education Department wants to increase the graduation rate, and therefore makes the exam easier, or wants to appear rigorous and tough, and therefore makes the exam more difficult. The pass rate for the exam can be increased or decreased simply by adjusting the cut score, turning a low percentage of correct answers into a pass or a high percentage of correct answers into a failure. In exams that students are likely to take as part of their graduation requirement, the State Education Department makes it easier for students to pass by lowering the cut score. This occurred, for example, in a recent 'Living Environments' exam, where students only needed to answer 39% of the questions correctly to earn a passing grade of 55%.[54] Conversely, the exams for the advanced, non-required courses, such as Physics and Chemistry, have been made more difficult. In a recent Physics exam, 39% of students failed, in order, critics charge, to make Regents testing appear more rigorous. However, because primarily academically successful middle-class students take Physics, the students and their parents were able to politically pressure the State Education Department to change the scoring.[55]

Furthermore, sometimes an unusually low or high failure rate may not be intentional but the result of incompetence. The June 2003 Regents Math A exam (the test students are most likely to take to meet the Regents' math requirement) was so poorly constructed that the test scores had to be discarded. Only 37% of the students passed statewide.[56] At Rochester's Wilson Magnet High School, a school ranked forty-ninth in the nation by Newsweek, all 300 students who took the exam failed.[57]

The State Education Department has also been criticized for how it constructs the test questions. For example, a recent English exam received national censure for removing from literary passages references "to race, religion, ethnicity, sex, nudity, alcohol, even the mildest profanity and just about anything that might offend someone for some reason."[58] Examples of changes included deleting all references to Judaism in an excerpt from a work by Isaac Singer, and the racial references in Anne Dillard's description of the insights she gained when, as a child, she visited a library in the Black section of town.

Many of the authors whose passages were changed were outraged that such changes occurred without their permission and substantially changed the meaning of the texts. Others pointed out the absurdity of having students answer questions that often referred to deleted portions of the text and objected that students might become confused if they were already familiar with the passage and were now confronted with the passage in which the meaning had been changed.

Moreover, educational inequality has increased as a result of the reforms. Quantitative evidence from New York State suggests that high stakes testing has harmed educational achievement. First, fewer students, especially students of colour and students with disabilities, are completing high school. From 1998 to 2000, the number of students dropping out increased by 17%. A recent report for the Harvard Center for Civil Rights concluded that New York State now has the lowest graduation rate of any state for African-American (35%) and Latino/a (31%) students.[59] In New York City only 38% of all students graduate on time, the fifth worst of the 100 largest cities in the nation.[60] According to another recent study, New York's graduation rate ranks forty-fifth in the nation.[61] The tests have also negatively affected English language learners, who were the highest diploma-earning minority in 1996 and the highest dropout minority in 2002.[62] Lastly, dropouts among students with disabilities have increased from 7200 in 1996 to 9200 in 2001.

In addition, while one of the State Department of Education's rationales for requiring Regents exams—eliminating the dual system where some students were tracked into courses with lower expectations—made sense, tracking has re-emerged through other means. In the past, students advantaged by class or race were more likely to be in the Regents track while students of colour and/or living in poverty were more likely to enrol in the typically less challenging local diploma. However, in most schools unequal tracking continued as those who had taken Regents courses in the past now enrol in Honors and Advanced Placement courses and the Regents courses were made easier so that the students now enrolled in them would be able to pass. The Consortium Schools, which neither tracked students nor had low expectations, would have to enrol students in the less-challenging Regents courses.

In June 2005, the New York State legislature, in response to demands from parents and educators, pressured the Regents and Commissioner to lower the number of Regents exams Consortium School students would need to pass to graduate from five to two (one each in math and English). However, students in all the remaining schools in the state must still pass five Regents exams in order to graduate.

New York State's high stakes testing has resulted in increasing inequality between advantaged and disadvantaged students. Similar high-stakes testing "reforms" have been implemented in some dozen other states and, complemented by the requirements of No Child Left Behind, result in simplified curriculum taught via teacher-directed pedagogy.[63] High-stakes testing and accountability has lowered standards.

---

[1] Orfield, G. and Eaton, S. (1996)

[2] Kozol, J. (2005)

[3] Berliner and Biddle (1995), p. 89

[4] Fones-Wolf (1994) p. 190

[5] Kliebard (1986)

[6] See, for example, F.W. Taylor (1911)

[7] Dewey (May 5, 1915)

[8] Counts, G. (1932)

[9] Rugg (1923). See also the inaugural issue of The Social Frontier: A Journal of Educational Criticism and Reconstruction, Oct. 1934, with George Counts as editor.

[10] Counts (1932)

[11] Rugg (1929-1932)

[12] Fones-Wolfe (1994), pp 190-191

[13] Ibid., p. 7, quoting businessman J.C. Yeomans.

[14] Ibid, p. 7

[15] Brodkin (1995)

[16] Katznelson (2005)

[17] National Defense Act of 1958, cited in Kliebard, p. 266

[18] Berliner and Biddle (1995)

[19] A Nation at Risk (1983), p 8

[20] Ibid, p. 5.
[21] No Child Left Behind (2001)
[22] Kozol, p. 8-9
[23] Cited in Kozol, p. 381
[24] Gerwitz (2002)
[25] Ibid, p. 10-11
[26] Bowles and Gintis (1986) pp. 57-59
[27] Parenti (1999) p. 118
[28] Bowles and Gintis, p. 60
[29] Vilas (1996)
[30] Tabb (2002), p. 7
[31] Whitty, Power and Halpin (1998)
[32] Robertson (2000)
[33] Hatcher (2003)
[34] Whitty, Power and Halpin (1998)
[35] Robertson (2000) p. 174
[36] Thrupp & Willmott (2003) p. 13
[37] Ibid, p 18
[38] Sayer (1995) p. 87
[39] Levitas (1998) p. 14
[40] Peters (1994)
[41] Robertson (2000) p. 187
[42] Dale (1989)
[43] Phillips and Furlong (2001) p. 6
[44] Parenti (1999)
[45] Hursh and Apple (June 1983)
[46] Apple (1988)
[47] Ball (1994)
[48] See Meier (2005)
[49] Meier (1995) p. 41
[50] Rose (1995) p. 211.
[51] Ibid, p 213.
[52] Hayden (2001), p. 1, original emphasis
[53] Ibid. p. 2
[54] Cala (September 24, 2001)
[55] Winerip (2003)
[56] Arenson (2003)
[57] Rivera (June 19, 2003)
[58] Kleinfield (2002)
[59] Orfield et al, (2004)
[60] Winter (2004)
[61] Haney (2003)
[62] Monk et al, (2001)
[63] Amrein and Berliner (2002)

CHAPTER 10

CHICAGO: THE CREATION OF A SPATIALLY, SOCIALLY, EDUCATIONALLY AND ECONOMICALLY DUAL CITY

In the previous chapter I described the difficulty of creating schools for the twenty-first century in New York given the emphasis on high-stakes testing and accountability. Instead of developing integrated curricula focusing on real-world issues and using a range of resources, teachers focus on "covering the material" that is likely to be tested. In this chapter I will first describe changes in Chicago's educational policy and then turn to federal educational policy as represented in No Child Left Behind. Chicago's and the federal government's policies, I will show, are making it less likely that all students will participate in the kind of education we are advocating here.

Chicago, like New York, is creating a dual system in which a few students are being educated for leadership positions and most are prepared for positions in the service and retail industry or in the military. In describing Chicago's recent reforms, I rely on Pauline Lipman's[1] analysis.

Lipman situates changes in the Chicago Public Schools (CPS) within the context of an economic, political, and sociological analysis of the changing city. She relies on both older forms of historical research and recent conceptions of globalised cities from critical geography to understand Chicago's transformation from a city in which labour produced industrial and agricultural products – "the city of broad shoulders" – to one focused on financial services, real estate, and tourism. Lipman builds on the work of Castells[2] and Sassen[3] to show how Chicago's development is similar to that of other global cities that take on "a strategic role as command centres in the global economy."[4]

However, she is careful to point out that globalization does not predetermine Chicago's social and educational policies. Rather, they are an outcome of contested neo-liberal policies that privilege corporate over social welfare. She not only shows us how such policies should be and are contested, but also suggests that other city strategies and school systems are possible.

By examining various official documents, she reveals how corporate leaders worked with city and state politicians to develop policies to transform Chicago from an industrial to a financial and tourist centre. As manufacturers automated their factories, moved to more corporate-friendly states or countries, or went out of business altogether, government provided massive public subsidies to banking, retail, and real estate interests. During the 1990s city policies focused on building Chicago's Loop as a tourist and convention centre, and gentrifying the surrounding neighbourhoods.[5] While downtown composed only 15% of the city, it received 85% of the economic development funds from the city's capital budget.[6]

Transforming Chicago into a global city has transformed the labour force. The skilled labouring middle class was replaced by highly paid professionals – lawyers, finance analysts, corporate directors – and low-wage workers – immigrants, women, people of colour – to service the corporate and financial centres and the leisure and personal needs of highly paid professionals and tourists.[7]

To attract and keep the new professional class, the city government not only funded upscale housing, restaurants, and other amenities,[8] but also policies that provided a quality education to the children of the new professionals. For example, the CPS, in alliance with the city, provided additional funding so that schools located in the gentrified professional areas could offer enhanced programs, such as the International Baccalaureate (IB).

While additional public funds have transformed areas along Lake Michigan and within the Inner Loop, areas in which the poor and people of colour live face reductions in expenditures. Lipman describes how Chicago is becoming "a dual city spatially as well as socially and economically."[9]

Lipman describes how the CPS, under the mayoral-appointed head of trustees Gery Chico and his budget director Paul Vallas as chief executive officer, "installed a corporate, regulatory regime centred on high-stakes tests, standards and remediation."[10] Since 1995, she writes, "the CPS has initiated a variety of differentiated programs, schools and instructional approaches with significant implications in Chicago's current economic context."[11] One group of programs and schools prepares students for university. This includes elementary schools with programs for gifted students, secondary schools with IB programs, and secondary College Prep Regional Magnet High Schools.

In contrast, another group of schools focuses on "vocational education, restricted (basic skills) curricula, and intensified regimentation of instruction and/or control of students."[12] This includes vocational high schools and elementary schools that use scripted direct instruction, "which employs teacher-read scripts and mastery of a fixed sequence of skills."[13] Direct instruction is a behaviourist approach based on a deficit model of "economically disadvantaged" students. Education-to-Career Academies, where academic courses serve vocational goals, have been started as well as highly regimented military high schools.

Lipman maps out where the different programs have been started, showing how those that are more academically rigorous tend to be situated in, or draw students from, upper-income and/or gentrifying neighbourhoods, and those using direct instruction or preparing students for vocations or the military are situated in low-income African-American and/or Latina/o neighbourhoods. Even when programs are dispersed among neighbourhoods, such as the IB program, they serve only 30 students per high-school grade, with access to the program skewed in favour of White students.

Lipman concludes that the programs that prepare students for university serve a dual purpose:

First, they are an incentive for professional and middle-class families to live in the city, especially in areas of budding gentrification, where they provide access to a separate high-status-knowledge program ... Yet, politically, big city mayors ... cannot ignore economically and racially marginalized populations. Hence a second purpose – small, highly publicized college-prep programs and magnet high schools paint a veneer of equity and opportunity on a vastly unequal system.[14]

Rather than decreasing inequality, the new programs and schools exacerbate educational inequality and heighten economic and social dualities.

Lipman not only examines the different programs and schools that have been created, but she also provides an in-depth analysis of four elementary schools to show how the testing and accountability regime affects the everyday life of teachers and students. In the 1990s the CPS introduced, as a means of accountability, standardized testing with the publication of results by school. The test scores were used to reward and punish schools, but also to legitimate allowing those schools with high test scores to retain flexibility in achieving their goals, while those schools with low test scores (principally those primarily composed of students of colour and students living in poverty) were required to use regimented methods of instruction.

Schools that failed to perform at minimum levels on the required tests, writes Lipman:

were put on a warning list, on probation, or their leadership and staff were reconstituted by the central office. Low-test scores also carried severe consequences for students, including retention at benchmark grades three, six, and eight and mandatory summer school ... Accountability measures were backed up by new after-school and summer remedial programs ... In 1997, it [the CPS] established academic standards and curriculum frameworks to standardize the knowledge and skills to be taught in each grade.[15]

Lipman concludes her analysis by stating:

The policy regime that I have described is producing stratified knowledge, skills, dispositions, and identities for a deeply stratified society. Under the rubric of standards, the policies impose standardization and enforce language and cultural assimilation to mould the children of the increasingly linguistically and culturally diverse workforce into a most malleable and governable source of future labour. This is a system that treats people as a means to an end. The 'economizing of education' and the discourse of accounting reduce people to potential sources of capital accumulation, manipulators of knowledge for global economic expansion, or providers of the services and accessories of leisure and pleasure for the rich. Students are reduced to test scores, future slots in the labour market, prison numbers, and possible cannon fodder in military conquests. Teachers are reduced to technicians and supervisors in the education assembly line – 'objects' rather than 'subjects' of history. This system is fundamentally about the negation of human agency, despite the good intentions of individuals at all levels.[16]

Lipman's analysis shows how corporate and political interests transformed Chicago into a global city catering to the financial, real estate and tourist industries, and multinational corporations, with "urban development and gentrification, and an urban geography of centrality and marginality along lines of race, ethnicity and social class."[17] However, her study ends just before NCLB was implemented, a reform, as I will show, which is only likely to exacerbate the problems.

THE BUSH ADMINISTRATION: NCLB, MARKETS, CHOICE, AND PRIVATIZATION

President George W Bush signed into law the No Child Left Behind Act on 8 January 2002. Most of the Act's requirements immediately went into effect, including requiring states to develop standardized tests and assessment systems in order to determine whether schools are making 'adequate yearly progress' (AYP). NCLB became law because it, like the standards, testing, and accountability movement on which it builds, ostensibly aims to improve education, especially for those students who have historically been disadvantaged, including students of colour and students living in poverty. I will argue, however, that NCLB undermines efforts to decrease educational inequality, introduces neo-liberal solutions such as markets and 'choice' to education, and increases the degree to which government authorities seek to control education from a distance through increased regulation and auditing.[18]

President Bush promoted NCLB as a means of replicating at the federal level the 'success' achieved in Texas. In addition, as in New York State, the proponents of NCLB have argued that it will improve educational opportunities for all students. Rodney Paige, Secretary of Education, has described NCLB as an extension of the civil rights movement of the 1960s, building on the legacy of Martin Luther King, Jr. Paige recently stated:

> Forty-four years ago, Dr Martin Luther King, Jr. said, 'The great challenge facing the nation today is to solve segregation and discrimination and bring into full realization the ideas and dreams of our democracy'. The No Child Left Behind Act does that. The law creates the conditions of equitable access to education for all children. It brings us a step closer to the promise of our constitution. It fulfils the mandate in Brown v. Board of Education. It honours the trust parents place in our schools and teachers, with a quality education for all children, every single one.[19]

Paige, who is Black, therefore aims to position opponents to NCLB as anti-civil rights. To this discourse of equality Paige adds two other discourses, which are also prominent in the reform argument elsewhere, such as in New York State and Chicago: testing provides more objective assessments and global economic competition requires reform. What to know and where to go: A parents' guide to No Child Left Behind[20] conveys to the public the benefits of NCLB. Paige informs the reader that standardized tests provide a valid and reliable means of assessing student learning, and this approach improves on teacher-generated assessments. It informs parents that NCLB "will give them objective data" through standardized testing.[21] Further, objective data from tests are necessary because in the past "many parents have children who are getting straight As, but find out too late that their child is not prepared for college. That's just one reason why NCLB gives parents objective data about how their children are doing."[22] Teachers, it implies, have neither rigorously enforced standards nor accurately assessed students, thereby covering up their own and their students' failures. Further, test scores will be useful to parents because "parents will know how well learning is occurring in their child's class. They will know information on how their child is progressing compared to other children."[23] Because teachers, The NCLB Guide claims, have relied too often on their own assessments, test scores will also benefit them. NCLB "provides teachers with independent information about each child's strengths and weaknesses. With this knowledge, teachers can craft lessons to make sure each student meets or exceeds the standards."[24]

Under NCLB, schools must not only develop and assess students, but they must also make public the aggregated test scores for groups of students delineated by gender, race, and ethnic group, and with or without disability. Because schools may have several ethnic and racial groups, all of whom must be represented by gender and ability status, they typically have to generate and report the scores for dozens of subgroups. The test scores for each group are then compared to the state's testing requirements to determine whether the group is making AYP. If any one group fails to make AYP, the entire school is designated as failing. Sometimes, shifting one child's score from one group to another (for example, by changing a student's disability status) can mean the difference between a school's failing and passing.

Schools that fail to make AYP face significant sanctions. If schools do not make AYP for two consecutive years, they must be identified as "in need of improvement." Students in those "schools must be given the option to transfer to another public school that has not been identified for improvement"[25] with transportation provided by the failing school. By adding the option of transferring to another school, NCLB introduces markets and competition into public education.

Additional requirements are put in place for each successive year that a school fails to meet AYP goals. Schools failing for a third year must provide students with the option of obtaining "supplemental services in the community such as tutoring, after-school programs, remedial classes or summer school."[26] Tutoring and after-school programs must be provided by non- or for-profit agencies funded by the student's school. Schools failing for a fourth year must take corrective action that includes one of the following: replacing the school staff, implementing a new curriculum, "decreasing management authority at the school level, appointing an outside expert to advise the school, extending the school day or year, or reorganizing the school internally."[27] School districts failing for a fifth year must engage in:

> deferring programmatic funds or reducing administrative funds; implementing a new curriculum (with professional development); replacing personnel; establishing alternative governance arrangements; appointing a receiver or trustee to administer the district in place of the superintendent or school board; or abolishing or restructuring the school district.[28]

Further, if a school fails to make progress for five years:

> The school district must initiate plans to fundamentally restructure the school. This restructuring may include reopening the school as a charter school, replacing all or most of the school staff who are relevant to the failure to make adequate progress, or turning over the operations either to the state or to a private company with a demonstrated record of effectiveness.[29]

States paved the way for NCLB by establishing the standardized testing requirements and accountability systems that made it acceptable to deny graduation to students who failed a test and to punish schools for low test scores. NCLB increases the penalties on schools with low-test scores by decreasing the amount of funds they have available for their students as they pay for transporting former students to other schools, for private agencies to tutor their students, and for interventions in the school, such as additional administrators and professional development. Moreover, NCLB introduces markets and privatization into schools by introducing school choice, charter schools, and voucher programs.

Determining whether schools are making AYP is based on the tests that states already use; tests, if New York State is representative, that are poorly constructed and subjectively graded. However, even if the tests were well constructed and valid, the yardstick by which schools are measured – AYP – often discriminates against schools serving students of colour and students living in poverty.

The determination of whether a school is making AYP tells us little about whether a school is improving. Under NCLB, every state, with the approval of the federal Department of Education, determines, for every test, what knowledge and skills students need to demonstrate proficiency. States can, therefore, make achieving proficiency more or less difficult. However, for all states and every school, all students (regardless of ability or proficiency in the English language) are to achieve proficiency by the year 2014.

Contrary to a common-sense interpretation of AYP, schools are not evaluated on whether their test scores are improving but on whether the aggregated and disaggregated test scores exceed a minimum yearly threshold that will gradually increase over the next decade. Consequently, schools are considered to be passing as long as their scores exceed the threshold, even if their scores fall.

Similarly, schools that begin with initially low test scores may be considered failing even if they significantly improve their test scores, as long as those scores remain below the threshold. Therefore, achieving AYP may have little to do with whether a school's test scores rise or fall; achieving AYP depends only on exceeding the minimum threshold.

Because test scores strongly correlate with a student's family income, a school's score is more likely to reflect its students' average family income rather than teaching or the curriculum. Consequently, the largest percentage of failing schools in New York State is found in poor urban school districts. Almost all (83%) of the failing schools are located in the big five urban districts: New York City, Buffalo, Rochester, Syracuse, and Yonkers.[30] Most of the remaining failing schools are in smaller urban districts. The failure rate of schools in the urban districts is high, particularly at the middle-school level. In Rochester, for example, all the middle schools failed.

To NCLB's testing requirement that schools demonstrate improvement for all disaggregated groups of students on all the tests, Florida added the further draconian stipulation that no school that had been assigned a grade of a D or F by the state (per the annual rating of A through F) could meet AYP. Not surprisingly, 90% of Florida's public schools were designated as failing to meet AYP, and 100% of districts failed.[31]

That NCLB mislabels thousands of schools as failing, restricts what schools may do to improve student learning, including which curricula may be implemented, and reduces funding to so-called failing schools may indicate that the federal government is interested in replacing rather than improving public schools. In fact, influential socially conservative and neo-liberal organizations, which regularly meet with the Bush administration, aim to transform education radically through market competition, choice, and privatization.[32] Markets and privatization are supported by conservative organizations such as the Manhattan Institute for Public Policy Research, The Heritage Foundation, The Fordham Foundation, The Hoover Institution, The Education Leaders Council, and the Milton & Rose D. Friedman Foundation, which are all funded by a core group of interlocking conservative foundations, primarily the Bradley, Olin, Scaife and Castle Rock (Coors) Foundations.

These organizations are dedicated to attacking public schools and teachers with the goal of replacing public with private education. For many of them, vouchers and charter schools are the first step toward privatizing schools. For example, Milton Friedman, in *Public schools: Make them private*, advocates vouchers as a way "to transition from a government [used pejoratively by neo-liberals] to a market system," Friedman states:

Our elementary and secondary educational system needs to be radically restructured. Such a reconstruction can be achieved only by privatizing a major segment of the educational system – i.e., by enabling a private, for-profit industry to develop that will provide a wide variety of learning opportunities and offer effective competition to public schools.[33]

Others call for the immediate elimination of public education. Richard Ebeling, president of the Foundation for Economic Education, writes:

It's time, therefore, to rethink the entire idea of public schooling in America. It's time to consider whether it would be better to completely privatize the entire educational process from kindergarten through the PhD.... The tax dollars left in the hands of the citizenry would then be available for families to use directly to pay for their child's education. The free market would supply an infinitely diverse range of educational vehicles for everyone.[34]

Some privatization advocates specifically anticipate that the high number of schools designated as failing to make AYP will lead to calls for privatizing schools. Howard Fuller, founder of the pro-voucher organization Black Alliance for Educational Options (BAEO), in a 2002 interview with the National Governors Association, said: "Hopefully, in years to come the [NCLB] law will be amended to allow families to choose private schools as well as public schools."[35] The Bush administration has provided both policy and monetary support to efforts to privatize public education. The Bush administration imposed a $50 million experimental voucher program on Washington, DC over objections of residents and the US Congress, and granted $77.6 million to groups dedicated to privatization through voucher programs.[36]

Members of the Department of Education, from Secretary Paige down, frequently use public appearances to promote charter schools as the solution to public-school problems. In press conferences where Paige defended NCLB, he also speaks out for the largely unpopular charter schools.[37] At a conference I attended in spring 2004 on teaching about the relationship between the environment and health, the Department of Education's Director of Interagency Affairs began with the unexpected claim that he "knew nothing about education or science" and then devoted his talk to the virtues of charter schools.

SIMPLIFYING THE CURRICULUM, INCREASING INEQUALITY

Up until recently schools in the US were local institutions governed by a community school board overseen by the state. Over the last decade, teachers, students, and those in the local neighbourhoods have lost control over teaching and learning to corporate and political leaders in their city, in the case of Chicago, their state, and their country. Those in power have asserted that the increasingly globalised economy requires education reforms in which schools more efficiently produce productive workers. Such efficiency can only be achieved, they argue, through curriculum standards, standardized tests, sanctions for low-scoring schools, and the introduction of competitive markets and privatization.

In Chicago, as Lipman[38] shows, such reforms have resulted in the creation of a dual city, both spatially and economically, where the already advantaged White and middle-class students are prepared for university through an academically challenging curriculum and the disadvantaged Black, Latino/a, and working-class students are prepared for positions in the service sector and the military through vocational and military programs.

The introduction of high stakes standardized testing in New York State has resulted in a decline in assessment validity, the manipulation of test scores for political purposes, and an increased achievement gap between White students and students of colour, students with disabilities, and students for whom English is a second language. Further, for many students the curriculum has been narrowed and simplified as teachers increasingly teach toward the test.[39]

The Bush administration has inserted the federal government into elementary and secondary education to a degree previously inconceivable. The federal government mandates the subjects that are to be assessed through standardized exams and how often, how schools and districts are to be evaluated, what kinds of curriculum can be federally funded, how literacy can be taught, and what kinds of community groups can and cannot meet in schools. Furthermore, NCLB may be intended as the way to portray public schools as failing so that schools can be gradually privatized, initially through voucher systems and charter schools, and then by scrapping public schools altogether.

These reforms are presented as being required by the global economy and the dominance of neo-liberal policies. Such global changes, proponents argue, require reductions in public spending and the introduction of markets and privatization as means of increasing efficiency. The reforms are presented, writes Bourdieu,[40] as if there is no alternative. Dean observes that such a rationale portrays those in power as powerless to choose any other path. He writes:

> Those who use the discourse of economic globalization can simultaneously hold 'there is little (or, at least, less) [they] can do to exercise national sovereignty' and 'it is imperative to engage in comprehensive reforms of the public sector, welfare, higher [and lower] education, finance and labour market control.[41]

Together, globalization and neo-liberalism have transformed government's relationship with civil society:

> The task of the national government ... is no longer to engage in the prudential management of a self-regulating economy so as to fund benefits such as social welfare, education, national defense, etc. Rather ... the promotion of economic efficiency and competitiveness becomes the paramount goal in what amounts to a new liberal problematic of security. All other activities of government, such as those of the welfare state, higher education, or migration, must be assessed first in terms of the availability of resources and second as to whether they contribute to or inhibit economic efficiency.[42]

In the next chapter I will address two last issues that arise from educational reforms that I have analyzed in this and the previous chapter. First, I will present research that shows how the rise of high-stakes testing and accountability have narrowed and simplified the teaching and learning in the primary and secondary schools in which I and others have tried to institute an integrated, challenging curriculum focusing on the relationship between the environment and human health. Second, I will conclude by arguing that not only do we need to devise educational structures that support innovative curricula, such as those created at the Consortium Schools, but that we also need to develop schools and workplaces that promote democratic participation in a complex society.

---

[1] See Lipman (2004, 2005)
[2] Castells (1989, 1998)
[3] Sassen (1994)
[4] Lipman (2004), p. 7
[5] Ibid, p. 28
[6] Ibid p. 9
[7] Ibid, p. 7
[8] Ibid, p. 25
[9] Ibid, p. 28
[10] Ibid, p. 36
[11] Ibid, p. 48
[12] Ibid, p. 49
[13] Ibid
[14] Ibid, p. 56, original emphasis
[15] Ibid. p 36
[16] Ibid, p. 179
[17] Ibid, p. 4
[18] See Ball (1994), Rose (1999)
[19] Paige and Jackson (November 8, 2004)
[20] US Department of Education (April 2002)
[21] US Department of Education (April 2002), p. 12
[22] Ibid, p. 12
[23] Ibid, p. 9
[24] Ibid, p. 9
[25] US Department of Education (September 2002) p. 6
[26] US Department of Education (April 2002) p. 8
[27] US Department of Education (September 2002) p. 6
[28] US Department of Education (September 2002) pp. 6-7
[29] Ibid, p. 7, emphasis added
[30] New York State School Boards Association 2002
[31] Pinzur (2003)
[32] Johnson and Salle (2004)
[33] Freidman (1995), cited in Johnson & Salle (2004) p. 8
[34] Ebeling (2000), cited in Johnson & Salle (2004) p. 8
[35] Fuller, cited in Miner (2004) p. 11
[36] Bracey (2004)
[37] Shaw (2004)
[38] (2004)
[39] Martina et al, (2003)
[40] (1998)
[41] Dean (2002) p. 55
[42] Ibid, p. 54

CHAPTER 11

DEVELOPING SCHOOLS AND WORKPLACES
FOR THE TWENTY-FIRST CENTURY

We have argued that schools need to be transformed, particularly within the changing global economy. It is no longer acceptable, as in Chicago, to prepare one group of students for the university and leadership positions and another for semi-skilled positions in the service and retail industry. Furthermore, the nature of knowledge and how we access knowledge has changed. The classical subject areas of English, science, math, history, civics/social studies, and the arts no longer make sense. Outside of schools most research and thinking crosses the "subject interstices," such as biogenetics, astrophysics, and world literature. Textbooks are inadequate as a knowledge resource. What is known is quickly changing and other resources— particularly via the internet—are more current and relevant. In teaching my graduate school course on current educational issues, students read articles, many of which are online along with other resources, and use books only as an optional resource.

In this chapter, then, I will turn to describing some of my own efforts to develop curriculum in which students become democratic participants in the creation of knowledge and, therefore, develop their ability to become life-long learners. Furthermore, if we are to succeed in creating students who are motivated, critical thinkers and creators of knowledge, we need to create workplaces that also promote critical thinking and decision making... Therefore, I will conclude by suggesting that we not only need substantially to rethink the nature of schooling but also the nature of work. We cannot be satisfied with creating jobs in which employees are merely carrying out tasks designed by someone else but must rethink workplaces so that, as Dewey stated almost a century ago, workers are able to use their intelligence and ingenuity so as to be always learning.

TEACHING ABOUT THE RELATIONSHIPS BETWEEN THE
ENVIRONMENTAL AND HUMAN HEALTH: PUSHING THE BOUNDARIES

For the last five years a team of scientists and teacher educators, including myself, have been working with elementary and secondary teachers to develop and implement curricula on the relationship between the environment and human health. Funded by a grant from the National Institute of Environmental Health Sciences, our goal has been to develop an interdisciplinary curriculum in which students use technology to learn about the world beyond the classroom and to teach others about what they have learned.

Our project does not easily fit existing schools. Educators often assume that because Environmental Health has to do with the environment, it is a science course that should be taught by a science teacher. However, while assessing and understanding the risks posed by toxins in our environment requires some scientific understanding, Environmental Health includes other disciplines. Why different environmental toxins have been created and persist and pose problems primarily for impoverished communities of colour requires an historical, political, and economic analysis. Developing materials − either videos, pamphlets, and power point presentations − requires students develop skills in media technologies, writing, and, often, performance arts. Crossing interdisciplinary boundaries has been only one of the issues undermining interdisciplinary curriculum.

In addition, in the US our large secondary schools (unlike the Consortium Schools) are not structured to promote collaboration. Teachers are not provided with common planning periods, nor are they likely to teach many of the same students. Nor is there a supportive school culture in which teachers are encouraged or rewarded for working with other teachers.[1] One of the secondary social studies teachers with whom we were working stated: "We don't have time to meet with one another so we just do our own thing." Another teacher added that not only is there not time during the school day, but "there is not time after school which is limited to coaching, after-school programs, department and school meetings."

As Apple[2] observes, teachers' work is increasingly intensified, and this project becomes just one more thing they have to fit in their school day. In one school, because of budget cuts, the teaching load increased from five to six courses. A teacher in the school exclaimed: "I would always like MORE TIME! Time is a real issue."

Teaching has historically been a profession in which teachers work isolated from other teachers. Most schools are designed with classrooms that accommodate one teacher working with a class of students. Classroom are arranged in an egg carton layout, thus making it possible for teachers to close the classroom door behind them so that they can teach their lessons free from observation. Ruddick notes "education is among the last vocations where it is still legitimate to work by yourself in a space that is secure against invaders.[3] The culture of schools promotes individualism rather than cooperation. As one teacher noted: "We don't work with other teachers very often. We don't work outside our curriculum groups."

In addition to the historical constraints of school size and isolation, teachers face the more recent constraint of standardized testing. Because Environmental Health will not be assessed through any of the various standardized exams, teachers are reluctant to introduce it into any courses in which there is a standardized exam (which is almost every secondary course) out of the fear that any time devoted to Environmental Health reduces the amount of time they have to prepare students for the exam. One science teacher shared that "the Regents [statewide] exams influence which course environmental health goes into…with pressures being what they are to pass these exams and kids having as much trouble as they are passing the upper-level exams, it would be very difficult to do this in a Regents course." The difficulty comes, he notes, because "the Regents has a prescribed curricula…It makes it very difficult. You have to teach some studies in a different way if you're going to take the time to do a project like this." Another teacher added:

High school is more constraining [than in the past] because the stakes are high. Testing is so high. No teacher likes to give up any of their time. You know [teachers do not release students] for band lessons and music lessons. Five years ago, we use to have field trip after field trip. We had kids leaving this building all the time. No more.

While we have been able to introduce Environmental Health into a few local high schools, the other eight sites located around the US have all but given up on implementing Environmental Health in secondary schools. Instead, they have focused on the elementary grades in which, until NCLB, fewer standardized tests were given. But, in states like New York, state and federal testing requirements currently require 17 standardized tests between grades three and eight, which will increase to 21 in 2008. Teachers are pressured to raise students' test scores on whatever state standardized exams are required and now the yearly exams in math, reading, and science that begin in third grade. One teacher noted that "standardized testing...[is] a problem [for a particular grade] because we...teach toward the test...[we] spent three weeks cramming for the test."

Likewise, because many states' and No Child Left Behind's regulations focus on raising math and language arts scores, many states have reduced their elementary curriculum to reading, writing, and math. One Texas educator added: "They are wiping out science for kindergarten through second grade with 'Fundamentals First' There is no place for anything except reading, writing, arithmetic."

If we are to implement innovative, critical curricula in which students and teachers together create knowledge, then we need to develop school structures and cultures that promote interdisciplinary collaboration with authentic assessments. The Consortium Schools provide a model for what schools can be because at their best they encourage teacher collaboration, teachers and students learning together, and accountability toward the community through local boards composed of parents, educators, and community members.

We also need to develop structures and professional development that will support teachers to transform their pedagogical approach. In traditional classrooms, teachers can avoid making explicit the course goals and learning process because they rely on the textbook to provide that information to students. Students "know" what they are expected to learn by what is in the textbook, supplemented by teachers' lectures. The teacher checks for student understanding by asking questions in which the student is expected to respond with the "one right answer" provided by the textbook and the teacher's lectures. Since the teacher is the only one who knows the "right answer" they are seeking, I describe this pedagogical approach as "guess what the teacher is thinking." With this approach neither the students nor the teachers create new knowledge but rather reproduce the knowledge encased in the textbook and lectures.

In my own work with teachers, many find it difficult to teach in a way in which knowledge is jointly created in the classroom. Such an approach requires that teachers spend less time telling students what they should know and more time structuring learning so that they can create original knowledge with students. For example, a teacher might begin a course by developing questions with students, ideally questions with no clear answer. Grant Wiggins[4] proposes that teachers pose an "essential question," a question that is complex and for which there is no one agreed upon answer. Avram Barlowe and Herb Mack, two social studies teachers at the Urban Academy in New York City, suggest the following topics among many: "What does the Diallo verdict tell us about our society? [Diallo was a recent immigrant to the US who was shot by the New York City police when he reached into his pocket for his wallet for identification]" "Should there be laws about who can be a parent?" "Should religion and religious belief play a central role in American life?" "Is there something wrong with smoking marijuana?[5] Students then proceed to conduct research and develop an essay that they present to the class.

In developing curriculum on the relationship between the environment and human health we have used problem-based learning as an approach that encourages complex analysis and understanding. For example, one could begin by asking what policies should be developed in response to the toxic dangers posed by Hurricane Katrina striking New Orleans. The floodwaters contained toxins from industrial waste sites, household chemicals, oil refineries and, after receding, resulted in mould growth in homes. In order to answer the question of what policies should be implemented, students would need to investigate real questions such as determining how dangerous the toxins are and what, if anything, can be done about them. Students would contact local and other scientists in environmental health and use on-line resources to come up with their answers. The students would quickly gain expertise in an area that would be valuable to the community.

Given the emphasis over the last two decades on standards, high-stakes testing and accountability, and in places like Chicago, on developing a dual education system, it seems doubtful that corporate and political leaders really desire that all students engage in the twenty-first century schooling that we advocate. In fact, recent research by Moss and Tilly[6] confirms that employers desire not the "hard skills" (literacy, numeracy, computer familiarity, cognitive abilities) that they claim are missing from workers but rather soft skills, which include the ability to interact with customers, coworkers, and supervisors, ability to fit in, enthusiasm, positive work attitudes, commitment, dependability, integrity, willingness to learn, and motivation. The Moss and Tilly interviews of managers in various economic sectors revealed that except for computer literacy managers more often demanded soft skills over hard skills.

Employer surveys confirm these findings. In a Rochester City School District survey, area employers revealed that they considered the five most important attributes for employment to include: doesn't abuse substances, follows directions, reads instructions, follows safety rules, and respects others. The five least important attributes for employment included: natural sciences, calculus, computers, art, and foreign language.[7]

The desire for soft skills is also trumpeted by leading education officials. New York's current Chancellor of Education, Robert Bennett, who oversees all the state's educational institutions from birth to death, argued recently,[8] that schools need not prepare students with hard skills—they can be provided by the students' employers—but schools should develop students' soft skills. Some of the skills he cited include: "showing up on time," "working in a team with others not like you," "understanding directions and carrying them out," and "having a customer orientation."

Furthermore, the current faith in neoliberalism does not, for this author, bode well for achieving the reforms we desire. Under neoliberalism, markets guide social, economic, and educational decisions. I have criticized at length elsewhere the neoliberal faith in markets as a way to improve education.[9] The desire to transform education into a market-based system has led to the current emphasis on standardized testing and reporting, which is meant to serve as the way in which families, as education consumers, can choose their educational service. However, such an approach, as Young[10] has detailed, undermines any effort for individuals to engage in public discussions regarding their preferences with schools assessed by so-called objective test scores and not by in-depth descriptions of the kind of learning that actually occurs. Instead, preferences remain individualistic. Each individual may "engage in instrumental or strategic reasoning about the best means of realizing their preferences, but the aggregate outcome has no necessary rationality and itself has not been arrived at by a process of reasoning."[11] There is no account for the origins of the preferences and, indeed, it is unnecessary to provide a normative basis for a preference.

In contrast, Young argues for deliberative democracy, in which:

> participants in the democratic process offer proposals for how best to solve problems or meet legitimate needs, and so on, and they present arguments through which they aim to persuade others to accept their proposals. Democratic process is primarily a discussion of problems, conflicts and claims of need or interest. Through dialogue others test and challenge these proposals and arguments. Because they have not stood up to a dialogic examination, the deliberative public rejects or refines some proposals. Participants arrive at a decision not by determining what preferences have the greatest numerical support, but by determining which proposals the collective agrees are supported by the best reasons.[12]

Young's model of deliberative democracy echoes that of Dewey, who described democracy as more than a form of government, as "primarily a mode of associated living, of conjoint communicated experience."[13] For Dewey, not only schools but also all institutions—including places of employment—should be places that promote individual and social growth.

The vision we are offering is of a learning society, in which schools and other social institutions promote continuous learning. Olssen, Codd and O'Neill, in *Education policy: Globalization, citizenship and democracy*[14] build on normative ideals expressed in Dewey and Foucault to call for an "education state." They argue "democracy is embedded in the values of mutual equal respect and survival, and includes norms and practices of reciprocity, of deliberation, of dialogue, and of fair treatment of due process"[15] and that education, both in schools and the workplace, is central to achieving and maintaining democracy.

Over the past several decades we have developed models for what critical, interdisciplinary learning that examines real world issues might look like. Not only have the Consortium Schools provided insights into the direction we might move but so have other innovative programs such as the classrooms funded by the National Institute of Environmental Health Sciences and the schools that form the Coalition of Essential Schools. However, in the US, these models have been undermined by the implementation of accountability systems that include high-stakes standardized testing. Whether the US continues in the direction of high-stakes testing or attempts to build on some of the recent successful programs such as the Consortium Schools, will continue to be contested.

---

[1] Little and McLaughlin (1993)
[2] (1982)
[3] Ruddick (1991) p. 31
[4] Wiggins and McTighe (1998)
[5] Barlowe & Mack (2002)
[6] Moss & Tilly (2001)
[7] Cited in Berliner & Biddle (1995) p. 89
[8] Speech given at First International Symposium on Urban Education and Intercultural Learning, D'Youville College, Buffalo, NY, (April 30, 2005)
[9] See Hursh (2004, 2005a, 2005b)
[10] (2000)
[11] Young (2000) p. 20-21
[12] Ibid. p. 22-23
[13] Dewey (1916) p. 87
[14] (2004)
[15] Ibid. p. 276

IV RESHAPING THE SCHOOL SYSTEM: DRIVERS OF CHANGE

Scholarly activity, if viewed dispassionately, consists primarily of three elements: to create knowledge and evaluate its validity; to preserve information; and to pass it to others. Accomplishing each of these functions is based on a set of technology and economics. Together with history and politics, they lead to a set of institutions. Change the technology and economics, and the institutions must change, eventually.
Eli Noam

CHAPTER 12

CHANGING LANDSCAPES

'The effect of Gutenberg's letters would be to change the map of Europe,
considerably reduce the power of the Catholic Church, and alter the very nature
of the knowledge on which political and religious control was based. The
printing press would also help to stimulate nascent forms of capitalism and
provide the economic underpinning for a new kind of community'.
  Burke and Ornstein

'A technological revolution centred around information[is transforming] the
way we think, we produce, we consume, we trade, we manage, we communicate,
we live, we die, we make war, and we make love.'
  Manuel Castells

'The developed world will begin to suffer long before oil and gas actually run
out. The American way of life – which is now virtually synonymous with
suburbia – can run only on reliable supplies of dependably cheap oil and gas.
Even mild to moderate deviations in either price of supply will crush our
economy and make the logistics of daily life impossible.'
  James Howard Kunstler

'I am the pure product of an advanced, industrialised, post-imperialist country in
decline.'
  Angela Carter

In the nature of things schooling must deal with the future, for schools are, or
should be, preparing young people for what lies ahead. Since predictions are hard,
especially about the future (as Niels Bohr may have said) the best preparation
young people can have is a nimble ability to assess the implications of events as
they happen. But, that said, it helps to have some sense of the future we are moving
toward.

To generalise, there are two ways of viewing that future. One predicts some sort
of continuity: that we shall – doubtless in unexpected ways – build on what we
have now. The contrary view is apocalyptic, predicting (at the least) one of three
types of discontinuity.

The first apocalyptic discontinuity is nuclear war. Since the collapse of state
communism we have had the comforting sense that the nuclear threat has
disappeared. It has not. It has changed, but there are still hundreds of nuclear
weapons in the world, some poorly maintained and guarded. Nuclear technology
has been sold on by rogue scientists and rogue states, of which Pakistan is the best

known. The known nuclear powers (the US, UK, Russia France, Israel, China, India and Pakistan) are developing their armouries while, at least in the case of the US and UK, trying to prevent other countries from doing so. There is, then, a reasonable probability of a smaller or larger nuclear conflict.

The second possible discontinuity is extreme climate change – taking us past the tipping point of global warming. That, we are told, is 'an increase of two degrees centigrade above the average world temperature prevailing in 1750 before the industrial revolution, when human activities –mainly the production of waste gases such as carbon dioxide, which retain the sun's heat in the atmosphere – first started to affect the climate.'[1] Given that temperature rise 'the world would be irretrievably committed to disastrous changes [which] could include widespread agricultural failure, water shortages and major droughts, increased disease, sea-level rise and the death of forests – with the added possibility of abrupt catastrophic events such as runaway, global warming, the melting of the Greenland ice sheet, or the switching-off of the Gulf Stream.'[2]

The third predicted discontinuity is the end of cheap oil. Relative optimists believe that when cheap oil is exhausted (as it will be some time this half-century) we shall have discovered energy sources to replace it. To the pessimists such hopes are in the category of what Feynman used to call cargo-cult science: the belief that good things will no doubt arrive before disaster overtakes us. For the prophets of doom, the gods' cargo is a mirage. 'Based on everything we know right now, no combination of so-called alternative fuels or energy procedures will allow us to maintain daily life … in the way we have been accustomed to running it under the regime of oil. No combination of alternative fuels will even permit us to operate a substantial fraction of the systems we currently run – in everything from food production and manufacturing to electric power generation, to skyscraper cities, to the ordinary business of running a household by making multiple car trips per day.'[3] There are global implications. 'Before fossil fuels – namely coal, oil and natural gas – came into general use, fewer than one billion human beings inhabited the earth. Today, after roughly two centuries of fossil fuels, and with extraction now at an all-time high, the planet supports six and a half billion people. Subtract the fossil fuels and the human race has an obvious problem. The fossil-fuel bonanza was a one-time deal, and the interval we have enjoyed it in has been an anomalous period of human history…We are now unable to imagine a life [without oil] – or think within a different socioeconomic model – and therefore we are unprepared for what is coming.'[4]

We need also to consider what we might call continuous futures, since we cannot know whether a discontinuity will occur, and must hope it will not. Continuous futures build on half a century which has been, in global terms, a time of relative stability – no global wars and no more than a hundred and forty local ones; the warming of the cold war; a few pandemics, and more famines; the rich western countries of the mid-twentieth century still near the top of the international tree fifty years later; and their schools continuing as they were, with little significant change. It is over half a century since Britain's Education Act of 1944, which set the parameters of the British school system for this relatively stable interlude. For some educators this quasi-calm validates their model of schooling as social reproduction: as an educational system which, by and large, reproduces what went before, a conservative society in a more or less stable world.

There is of course another view, noted above: that this has been an historically anomalous moment, a prelude to a time of instability, rapid and perhaps damaging change: and that 'the general equilibrium models, which still dominate mainstream economic theory, are quite incapable of explaining [contemporary] technological revolutions and social changes'.[5] These contemporary indicators include the rapid obsolescence of new technologies; new patterns of ownership and control among mass media; the internationalisation of money markets; the floating of most of the world's currencies; shifting regional alliances (the widening European Community, Nafta, Mercosur, Asean and others); altering demographic patterns (aging and longer-lived populations in most developed economies, younger and longer-lived populations in most LDCs); large-scale migration; climatic transformation; and the global, but uneven, spread of computer-based data networks, with an associated rise of an interconnected 'world economy' (though this is clearly a partial and selective globalisation which mainly benefits a few powerful nation-states, and not the world at large).

Alterations in the wider global landscape have been summarised by Manuel Castells in a typically comprehensive overview: 'Toward the end of the second millennium of the Christian Era several events of historical significance have transformed the social landscape of human life. A technological revolution, centred around information technologies, is reshaping, at accelerated pace, the material basis of society. Economies throughout the world have become globally interdependent, introducing a new form of relationship between economy, state, and society, in a system of variable geometry. The collapse of Soviet statism, and the subsequent demise of the international communist movement, has undermined for the time being the historical challenge to capitalism, rescued the political left (and Marxian theory) from the fatal attraction of Marxism-Leninism, brought the Cold War to an end, reduced the risk of nuclear holocaust, and fundamentally altered global geopolitics. Capitalism itself has undergone a process of profound restructuring, characterized by greater flexibility in management; decentralization and networking of firms both internally and in their relationships to other firms; considerable empowering of capital vis-à-vis labour, with the concomitant decline of influence of the labour movement; increasing individualization and diversification of working relationships; massive incorporation of women into the paid labour force, usually under discriminatory conditions; intervention of the state to widen markets selectively, and to undo the welfare state, with different intensity and orientations depending upon the nature of political and institutions in each society; stepped-up global economic competition, in a context of increasing geographic and cultural differentiation of settings for capital accumulation and management. As a consequence of this general overhauling of the capitalist system, still under way, we have witnessed the global integration of financial markets, the rise of the Asian Pacific as the new dominant, manufacturing centre, the arduous [and still partial] economic unification of Europe, the emergence of a North American regional economy, the diversification, then disintegration, of the former Third World, the gradual transformation of Russia and the ex-Soviet areas of influence in market economies, the incorporation of valuable segments of economies throughout the world into an interdependent system working unit in real time'.[6]

Then there are population issues. In most countries (except those at the heart of the AIDS pandemic) men and women are living longer. The post-genomic revolution in medicine means that we will live longer still – certainly in some parts of the world and eventually in most of it. That affects world population which (though not growing at the alarming rate predicted some decades ago) has increased by about half in the last twenty-five years, and will be significantly larger in years to come. The planet can probably accommodate and feed nine billion people (if that proves to be where the growth curve flattens) but not if we live as we are living now. In some parts of the world populations are growing fast; in others they are not. Growing populations mean that large numbers of young people will need health care, schooling and employment. Where populations are not growing significantly (as in many European countries) there is a contrary problem: a cohort of aging people with dwindling numbers in the workforce, and hence dwindling means of support. An unpredictable factor is large-scale migration, which will happen despite all the attempts of richer countries to close their borders to the poor; but which will vary from country to country (for example, the US has much higher rates of immigration – and may thus be more dynamic – than most Western European countries.)

The world-transforming aftershock of the end to Soviet-style command economies brought with it the end of the twentieth century's 'long war', leaving the United States as not just the only superpower, but one understandably, and sometimes capriciously, determined to order the rest of the world for its own security and benefit.[7] We are still feeling the effects of the rapid collapse of what was recently 'the eastern bloc'; though we are not feeling it with the pain felt by those of its inhabitants who have recently been assigned to the lower ranks of capitalism. Since the bloc's collapse, the international hegemony of democracies and quasi-democracies has enabled them to impose what is known as 'global free trade'. (As noted, we now have a trading system largely made by Americans for Americans, just as its nineteenth-century precursor was, quite understandably, designed by Britain's ruling classes for their own benefit.)

The United States has been prepared to use a range of means – up to and including armed force – to ensure that its markets are unconstrained. But this is only one current form of violence. The Cold War threat of nuclear conflict has been replaced by smaller-scale international clashes, by internal uprisings, and by attacks on the dominant power, while western ideologies are challenged by other creeds, radical Islam among them.

But the shifts which, in the coming decade, are likely to have the most immediate effect on us – and on our schools – are the contest for raw materials and energy, clashes of religion and ideology, the industrialisation of Asia, the information revolution and the post-industrial knowledge-based economies of which the information revolution is a cornerstone.

Resource allocation affects many areas of life. As some natural resources – notably oil and water – become scarcer and more expensive, nations will increasingly devote their energies to securing them. For all of us the choice will be between using less, paying more – which inhibits economic growth – or taking raw materials by force. That last policy ('kick their ass and take their gas' as the bumper stickers have it) is also expensive, even for the world's richest countries, and may not in the end be cost-effective. We are, too, in the early stages of a shift in resource distribution. Richer nations have always seen poorer countries as an area to be exploited for raw materials. But this relationship is changing as Asian economies industrialise. Rather than being a market for the West's industrial production, they themselves are becoming major industrial producers. Rather than being a source of raw materials, they now compete for them. Whatever else we do, we shall need to find alternatives to oil, and ways of making other basic resources go further. That, in turn, implies a shift of emphasis in scientific and economic research and a new type of sustainable and increasingly weightless economy.

One of the drivers of such an economy will be scientific discoveries, building on those revolutionary developments of the twentieth century which included 'unlocking the secrets of the atom, unravelling the molecule of life, and creating the electronic computer. With these three fundamental discoveries, triggered by the quantum revolution, the DNA revolution, and the computer revolution, the basic laws of matter, life and computation were, in the main, finally solved... That epic phase of science is now drawing to a close; one era is ending and another beginning.'[8]

Absent the apocalypse, life and work in the next decades will be shaped by the discoveries of the scientific era now beginning. Some breakthroughs we can already foresee; others we can't yet guess at. In Schwartz's terms, 'some will emerge from research that is already underway'; some 'from the frontiers of today's science' and some 'will be paradigm-changing breakthroughs, after which science and technology are never the same'.[9] One of these 'paradigm-changing breakthroughs' is already occurring with the spread of digital networks: the internet and others. In coming years, it now seems, the internet will be 'the fabric of our lives. If information technology is the present-day equivalent of electricity in the industrial era, in our age the internet could be likened to both the electrical grid and the electric engine because of its ability to distribute the power of information throughout the entire realm of human activity.'[10]

Computers are only a part of a network society, but they are a significant part. We do not yet know the limits of their power, or its consequences. Clearly they will do the sorts of things they now do much better and very much faster. But will there be a tipping point when a geometrical increase in computing power leads to a very different type of machine – one which would pass the Turing test; a machine which we could call intelligent, and wonder whether it would think the same of us? Technological evangelists like Kurzweil believe so: before the century is over, he says, 'human beings will no longer be the most intelligent or capable type of entity on the planet'.[11]

Others argue that the revolutionary phase of information technology is now past, and that the next discontinuity will come in the arena of the life sciences; that 'biotechnology will the next great wave' which will 'ultimately spread through every economic sector, just as computers did before it'.[12] In some parts of the world both information technologies and biotechnologies are already changing what it means to be human. 'Hybrids of living tissue and metal, we increasingly incorporate machinery, synthetic chemicals, inorganic materials, and electronic information into our bodies and environment, and an endless stream of electronically mediated sounds and images into our sensibilities. We have intense personal relationships with electronic and digital devices. We share our world with entities that may be intelligent yet are unconscious, not exactly alive yet not actually dead, quasi-organic and quasi-inorganic. We live with robots, cyborgs, clones, genetically modified animals and plants, and proliferating mutations.'[13]

Such human and non-human transformations will doubtless have extensive consequences: how extensive we can't yet tell. As we see in the following chapter, some natural and social scientists believe there is unlimited scope for new scientific discoveries, and that these may lead to sustainable and equitable economic growth across the world. On that large claim, the jury is out.

Taken together, these changes, present and foretold, lead us into an unfamiliar landscape. There is no doubt that we shall work in different ways as the drivers of our economy change (see chapter 14) and we may view the world very differently. 'There is a growing agreement that many developed countries are undergoing a major transformation of world view, to rival what occurred when the industrial economy replaced the agrarian, rural, pre-industrial economy. Accompanying that shift is a major change to the explanatory pattern. It has been described as the transition to the post-industrial economy, or to the post-modern state, to the communication age, to the global society'.[14] We do not have a global society in any real sense, but 'this new world view, and its allied explanations, are likely to be widespread across the planet [in] the early years of the new century'.[15]

Writing of these changes, Young remarks that, in education, 'how they are responded to, and their implications for educational policy, will depend on decisions made by governments and others which will reflect (a) the position of a country in the world economic order; (b) the national tradition of the country in question; and (c) the policy choices of specific governments'.[16]

The conservative position is that there may have been intellectual and epistemological shifts in our society, but that these have not been fundamental, and do not warrant radical revision of that long-standing body of school knowledge and subject structure which, together, are central to scholastic practice. This is, in itself, a fundamental misconception. Though they may later be falsified or superseded, the theories of general relativity, of quantum mechanics, of sub-atomic physics and of strings have radically changed our view of the physical universe. Space exploration, manned or otherwise, has changed our view of our place in the cosmos. Sub-atomic physics and nanotechnologies are changing the way we consider matter. Psychoanalysts, artists and neuroscientists have changed our view of ourselves. Electronic scanning and gene analysis are changing our picture of the body and the brain. Digital imaging has changed the way we conceptualise, and the way we communicate. Computer-driven networks are changing the organisational forms of industry and society.

These are not changes which can be accommodated by adding new headings to the school curriculum. We are experiencing an intellectual paradigm shift: a change in what we know, and how we know it. In some parts of the world this is leading to changes in the way we live, and the way we work. We are moving from a secure, positivistic, often mechanistic, view of the universe to one which is less secure and more complex: less predictable, more relativist and probabilistic. If we want to equip young people to cope well with this world, schools will need to make an equally radical epistemological shift. Most have not done that. Nor will they, if they continue to train pupils for a vanishing economy and culture; a now anachronistic zeitgeist.

Teaching young people as it does, the school system's task can be seen as a preparation for a future that will not replicate the past. Such preparation is more urgent if our future will indeed be less stable than it has been over the past fifty years. For this book, the question is, how will the inevitable surprises[17] ahead affect schools, students and schooling? How should we prepare the next generation for an economy and society different in kind from that of today?

BEYOND 'THE INTERNATIONAL CONSENSUS'

Schools are not doing well in finding answers. Instead they tend to rely on an unspoken transnational consensus shaped by the governments and agencies which dominate the current process of globalisation – notably the United States, the EU, China and transnational organisations like the World Bank, WIPO, WTO and OECD. Those in the West have developed what is taken to be a universally applicable model of education and training, which nominally leads national educational policies toward 'lifelong learning... international and national accreditation of work skills, multiculturalism, international and national academic standards and tests [and] school choice ... [while] adherence to free market ideologies has resulted in a reliance on the methods of human capital accounting and government intervention to influence student decisions in the education market'.[18] In this widely-promoted model, little attention is paid to what students learn, how they learn, or where they learn. Such imposed models, though often misconceived, have led in some countries to systemic changes in schooling. They are a part of the slow transformation of the developing world's way of schooling.

If we question the international consensus, what else is on offer? The conventional answer would be that schools should shift at least some of their teaching toward what is now happening in the world, and – learning from that – what might happen in years to come. That is unlikely to work, for several reasons. One is that (as we have seen) it is hard for schools, insulated as they are from the world, to teach well when it comes to contemporary issues, much less those in the future. Another is that such teaching, when schools try it, may not work well with young people.[19] In any case, teaching is not what is needed here. What we do need – what we all need – is an ability to investigate what may lie ahead; what may be coming down the road. We can learn to how to use the vast repository of web-accessed data for indicators of the future in any area of interest – work, money, sport, terrorism, health, sex, science – whatever concerns us (and whatever should concern us) at the time.

Such investigations offer an entry to cultures of coming economies: cultures likely to be very different from those that have gone before. If all goes well (and it may not) we shall move into an economy based on 'the culture of innovation, on the culture of risk, on the culture of expectations, and, ultimately, on the culture of hope in the future. Only if this culture survives the nay-sayers of the old economy of the industrial era may the new economy prosper.'[20]

[1] 'Meeting the Climate Challenge: Recommendations of the International Climate Change Taskforce' Center for American Progress 25.1.2005
(http://www.americanprogress.org/site/pp.asp?c=biJRJ8OVF&b=306503)
[2] Ibid
[3] Kunstler 2005
[4] Ibid
[5] Freeman and Louca 2001
[6] Castells 2000
[7] It is not yet clear whether the post-2001 'war on terror' promoted by President Bush and the Pentagon will become – from a US perspective – a satisfactory functional alternative to the twentieth century's long war; or whether it will be, for America, as economically debilitating as that long war was for the Soviet Union.
[8] Kaku 1998
[9] Schwartz 2003
[10] Castells 2000
[11] Kurzweil 1999
[12] Davis 2001
[13] Marcia Tanner, PARC forum, 18.8.2005; openparcforum@parc.com
[14] Beare 2001
[15] Ibid
[16] Young 1998
[17] The term is taken from Peter Schwartz's eponymous book (Schwartz 2003)
[18] Spring 1998
[19] See, for example, 'Young people's attitudes to politics' MORI 2003;
http://www.e-democracy.gov.uk/knowledgepool/default.htm?mode=1&pk_document=59
[20] Castells 2003

CHAPTER 13

WAYS OF SEEING, WAYS OF KNOWING

'Strict determinism failed in biology, not because the arrow of time was not recognised, but because it became obvious that the arrow could change direction.'
    Chris Freeman and Francisco Louca

Schools in this century must deal with the legacy of the last, which altered the ways we see and know the world. The ways in which we see the world were changed by the painters, photographers and film makers of the twentieth century. Even if we never knowingly register a work by Pissarro, Rousseau, Braque, Picasso, Mondrian, Pollock, Nadar, Man Ray, Miller, Eisenstein, Tarkovsky, Vigo or Arbus, their influence comes down to us through innumerable (often debased) images in print and on screen. We no longer believe the camera cannot lie. We know that digital images can be – and are – changed in any imaginable way. We no longer believe that what you see is what you get.

Behind the surfaces lie deeper changes. Our vision of matter itself is shifting. 'In the pre-Einstein era, T H Huxley could define science as "nothing but trained and organised common sense". But quantum mechanics and relativity shattered our commonsense notions about how the world works. The theories ask us to believe that an electron can exist in more than one place at the same time, and that space and time are not rigid but rubbery. Impossible. Yet these sense-defying propositions have withstood a century of tests'.[1] In twentieth-century conceptions of reality, intuition is confounded. As Feynman notes, 'the theory of relativity shows us that the relationship of positions and times as measured in one coordinate system and another are not what we would have expected on the basis of our intuitive ideas'.[2] More, the ways of knowing or testing these counter-intuitive theories are also far from simple observation. 'For over two hundred years the equations of motion enunciated by Newton were believed to describe nature correctly, [until] the first time that an error in these laws was discovered ... both the error and its correction were discovered by Einstein in 1905.'[3] Neither was discovered by direct observation of natural phenomena. And the theories of matter which followed Einstein's thought experiments are also far removed from classical empiricism. To take one recent example, in 2005, the 7000-tonne Atlas detector – 'the world's biggest microscope' – is being used for the first time to track infinitesimal subatomic particles in a collider. Atlas was described by one of its creators as 'sort of counter-intuitive; we need to go to higher-energy machines to see the physics that is just around the corner from what we know already.'[4]

More fundamentally, we now see even the atomic structure of matter as mutable. In a prescient paper published in 1960,[5] Feynman wrote of 'the final question as to

whether, ultimately – in the great future – we can arrange atoms the way we want;
the very atoms, all the way down! What would happen if we could arrange the
atoms one by one the way we want them (within reason, of course; you can't put
them so that they are chemically unstable, for example). Up to now, we have been
content to dig in the ground to find minerals. We heat them and we do things on a
large scale with them, and we hope to get a pure substance with just so much
impurity, and so on. But we must always accept some atomic arrangement that
nature gives us. We haven't got anything, say, with a "checkerboard" arrangement,
with the impurity atoms exactly arranged 1,000 angstroms apart, or in some other
particular pattern. What could we do with layered structures with just the right
layers? What would the properties of materials be if we could really arrange the
atoms the way we want them? They would be very interesting to investigate
theoretically. I can't see exactly what would happen, but I can hardly doubt that
when we have some control of the arrangement of things on a small scale we will
get an enormously greater range of possible properties that substances can have,
and of different things that we can do.' Four decades later, within what we now call
nanotechnology, we are starting to 'arrange atoms the way we want' and are
beginning to find 'an enormously greater range of possible properties that
substances can have, and of different things that we can do'. As creators of hitherto
unknown atomic structures, we shall not again see the material world in quite the
same light. It is more fluid and, in the light of quantum theories, more surprising
than we once thought. As Niels Bohr is said to have remarked, 'anyone who is not
shocked by quantum theory does not understand it'.

Still in the material world, there is our changing climate (see also chapter 12).
We used to think climate was beyond human intervention: as Mark Twain once
said, 'everyone complains about the weather, and no one does anything about it'.
But now we are doing something about it. And, with the Exxon Corporation and
Vice President Cheney dissenting, the consensus is that we are doing damage. We
may be making irreversible changes. We need now to see climate as, in part, a
human construct. Avoiding a climatic tipping point means a change of view on the
part of young people – as well as adults, corporations, governments and
international organisations. The task of bequeathing a liveable world to the
generations ahead involves us all. And we need to understand why our involvement
is necessary. Here schools have a part to play. Most are unclear what that part
might be. It is time they became clear, and accepted that this is a 'political' area
which they cannot, and should not, avoid.

Shifts in our view of the inanimate world are matched by a change in our view of
living creatures, ourselves included. We can create new variants, and new types, of
plants and animals in the laboratory; we can clone animals and will doubtless soon
clone humans. We once thought (and many still think) that men and women were
made in God's image – though of course different people have different gods to be
the image of. But the moral for all believers was that we were not our own creators:
whatever intelligent designer created us, it was not a process we could interfere
with. Now some people, in some parts of the world, do regularly interfere with the
process of creating and shaping humans. It is, understandably, a controversial

project. 'Many of the current debates over biotechnology, on issues like cloning, stem-cell research, and germ-line engineering, are polarised between the scientific community and those with religious commitments'.[6] To view humans as humanly engineered is a profound shift in our way of seeing. But human instincts – for survival, for health, for longevity, for success – mean that such biotechnological developments will accelerate rather than decrease, and the opposition will doubtless be more bitter. It may be that post-genomic biotechnology in future 'will mix great potential benefits with threats that are either physical and overt or spiritual and subtle' and that, therefore, 'we should use the power of the state to regulate it'.[7] Whether or not that will finally be possible, and whether all states would agree, these are issues that schools should deal with – both the world-transformative potential of the new biology, its ethical implications and its social consequences. Not surprisingly, few schools do this adequately; fewer do it well.

Many of these altered ways of knowing (including the examples above from physics and biology) depend on recent increases in computing power. 'One hope for sustained scientific progress may be the development of computer systems with new levels of miniaturisation, speed and complexity. Pure science projects that promote the development of these new technologies will play a starring role in the future'.[8] In this context, writing of bioscience, Baltimore suggests that, 'one consequence of trying to decipher the three billion units of information in DNA is that we soon reach the limits of human comprehension. Only computers can store such data, and only computers can find the chosen piece of meaningful structure in a sea of DNA.'[9]

Around scientific computing are grouped other new technologies. 'The scientific budgets of most countries have already had to come to terms with scientific activities that were once inexpensive ventures requiring little more than a few test tubes, books, chemicals, home-blown glassware, and low-tech equipment, but now need large computer systems, spectrometers, electron scanning microscopes, small accelerators, and other very expensive pieces of hardware.'[10]

Dealing with natural or social sciences which have, in this way, become information sciences is clearly a problem for schools. Most cannot afford sophisticated instrumentation. They lack computing power or, if they can access high-speed computers – perhaps through grids – they lack the skill to use that facility for scientific experimentation.

Computers also influence our view of ourselves. Cartesian man was a clockwork creature; for some Victorians the universe was mechanical, understood by rational thought and experiment; in the early twentieth century, man was an industrial automaton; for many thinkers of the late twentieth-century and early twenty-first, we are human embodiments of artificial intelligence – though often less capable than our emergent machines. Since the first viable computers, some of those who work with them have wondered about their future capacity. 'I propose to consider the question,' Turing wrote, '"Can machines think?" This should begin with definitions of the meaning of the terms "machine" and "think".' The definitions might be framed so as to reflect so far as possible the normal use of the words, but this attitude is dangerous. If the meaning of the words "machine" and "think" are to be found by examining how they are commonly used it is difficult to escape the conclusion that the meaning and the answer to the question, "Can machines think?" is to be sought in a statistical survey such as a Gallup poll. But this is absurd.'[11] Half a century later, Ray Kurzweil, artificial-intelligence evangelist, is less tentative. He has advice for God. Mammalian neurons, he notes, 'are marvellous creations, but we wouldn't build them the same way... neurons are extremely slow; electronic circuits are at least a million times faster. Once a computer achieves a human level of ability in understanding abstract concepts, recognising patterns, and other attributes of human intelligence, it will be able to apply this ability to a knowledge-base of all human-acquired – and machine-acquired – knowledge.'[12] Many of those whose views are less apocalyptic still, consciously or unconsciously, cast humans as wetware; as digital devices with a pulse rate. 'Although writing remains our primary information technology, today when we think about the impact of technology on our habits of mind, we think primarily of the computer.'[13]

Instrumentally, this confusion is easy to understand. Over the past decades new technologies – often computer-enhanced – have edged hesitantly toward humanoid status. We are beginning to find people who attend to cybernetic pets, who depend on helpful robots, chatterbots, agents, search engines or digital tutors. Of course many of these devices now combine the worst qualities of humans and machines; but that, optimists hope, will change. Computing has indeed enlarged the limits of what is humanly possible. We see pictures sent from Mars, and analyse the surface of the planet. We look back to the beginnings of the universe. We examine bodies far too small to be seen with optical magnification. We do computations which once would have taken impossible spans of time. In seconds we can access data which might have taken months, or years, to find. We watch the workings of our brains. We can, in a multitude of ways, extend the reach of human intelligence. Each year, we extend it further – ultimately to points we cannot foretell.

The world-transformative disciplines of the early twenty-first century are coming together. Kaku argues that scientific progress in the future will be propelled 'by the intense interplay between quantum physics, molecular biology and computers ... this interplay between the three scientific revolutions is one of the most important factors driving the science of the future'.[14] Unfortunately that hermeneutic interplay has not made it easier for schools to deal with the individual disciplines, their convergence, or their reshaping of knowledge. We have changed both our ways of seeing the material world – it is less solid, and more mysterious, than we once believed – but also our ways of knowing it. The experimental evidence for our hypotheses is increasingly indirect. But that is true 'of almost all recent discoveries in physics. As physics evolved in the twentieth century, it moved away from things that can be directly observed to things that can be "seen" only through measurements coupled with a train of theory. For example quarks – components of the proton and neutron that underlie the secondary school picture of the atom – never appear in isolation. We find them by following the trail of evidence they leave as they influence other particles. It is the same with the intriguing kinds of stuff known as dark energy and dark matter... We know that dark matter and dark energy exist because they have effects on surrounding matter.'[15]

There are other knowledge-shifts which have happened more recently: some in electronics, some in computing, some in digital networking, some in biotechnology, some in nanotechnology. (For convenience these are here grouped as 'new technologies'.) In a relatively short space of time these technologies are changing the ways in which some view the world, the ways in which they apprehend it, and the ways they think about it. This is not unexpected. We have always seen aspects of the world, and aspects of humanity, in the light of our dominant technologies. 'The invention of written language brought about a radical shift in how we process, organise, store and transmit representations of the world,'[16] but, as Neil Postman remarked, this was not an unmixed blessing. 'The advantages and disadvantages of new technologies are never distributed evenly among the population. This means that every new technology benefits some and harms others. There are even some who are not affected at all. Consider again the case of the printing press in the 16th century, of which Martin Luther said it was "God's highest and extremest act of grace, whereby the business of the gospel is driven forward".' By placing the word of God on every Christian's kitchen table, the mass-produced book undermined the authority of the church hierarchy, and hastened the breakup of the Holy Roman See. The Protestants of that time cheered this development. The Catholics were enraged and distraught.'[17]

A NEW CONCEPTUAL MAP?

For schools the implications of these shifts in the organisation of knowledge are significant, and largely unexplored. 'For only two centuries, knowledge has assumed a disciplinary form; for less than one it has been produced in academic institutions by professionally trained knowers.'[18] Yet we have come to see these circumstances as so natural that we tend to forget their historical novelty and fail to imagine how else we might produce and organise knowledge. 'Our world now seems so naturally divided into, say, biology, sociology and musicology that when we try to imagine alternatives to these disciplines, we think merely of combining them: biochemistry, sociolinguistics, ethnomusicology.'[19]

Such assumptions underlie school curricula. We find it hard to imagine curricula which are not broken down into the 'school subjects' – English, maths, biology, and so on – to which we have become accustomed as a prism through which pupils view the world. We find it equally hard to imagine teaching and learning which deals seriously with 'new knowledge' – much of which is not very new, since its roots are in the early twentieth century. We may intellectually accept that Newton's mechanical model of the universe has been challenged by the notions that time and space are one; that light waves curve; that the gravitational force of black holes creates a seemingly impenetrable event horizon; that particles can be in more than one place, and in more than one state, at the same time; that qubits can be entangled in ways we cannot yet explain; that Euclidean geometry and other traditional mathematical systems are not absolute, but are among a variety of possible systems; and that objective observation of many phenomena may not be possible. But this does not mean that these relatively new ways of knowing are adequately taught in schools. It is easier to stick with time-honoured, and more intuitive, ways of seeing the world – even though they may discourage the new thinking on which our human future depends.

When what we see is seen anew, we who see are also changed. We are no longer the autonomous intellects we might once have believed. Our changing vision of the material world is matched by an altered view of humanity and by the realisation that there are no objective views. We are beings shaped by our instincts – sexuality predominant among them – and, to a still uncertain extent, by our evolutionary legacy. We are moulded and limited by the preconceptions of our social class (an insight which, as we have seen, has not yet prevented educational administrators of one social class working at the expense of others).

The ways we know the world have changed; and thus the ways we interact with the world. At home and at school, most of us deal daily with low-level computers (and, as business and government interfaces, with higher-level machines); they are part of our private life and, often, of our education. At home and at school, students 'are absorbing more than the content of what appears on their screens. They are learning new ways to think about what it means to know and to understand'[20] – and these 'new ways to think' may be very different from those of their teachers.

One of these new ways to think – now imperfectly understood – is a reconceptualisation of ontology. 'The question ontology asks is: what kinds of things exist or can exist in the world, and what manner of relations can those things have to each other? Ontology is less concerned with what is than with what is possible ... in a particular domain, what kinds of things can we say exist in that domain, and how can we say those things relate to each other?'[21] Traditionally we think in categories, and schools (being traditional places) are organised by categories: categories of year groups, gender, academic and non-academic, special needs, classrooms, subjects, and so on. In recent years categorisation of people – in schools and elsewhere – has been subject to some critical examination, but there have been few comparably thoughtful critiques of subject categorisation. And yet, at the simplest level, the web radically changes our ideas of categorisation. When we search for information we no longer look on some virtual library shelf. We ask for the information and assess the results of our request: results which may come from very many different virtual shelves, some with labels that seem to have nothing to do with our original request. 'One reason Google was adopted so quickly when it came along is that Google understood there is no shelf, and that there is no file system. Google can decide what goes with what after hearing from the user, rather than trying to predict in advance what it is you need to know. Let's say I need every Web page with the word "obstreperous" and "Minnesota" in it. You can't ask a cataloguer in advance to say "Well, that's going to be a useful category, we should encode that in advance." Instead, what the cataloguer is going to say is, "Obstreperous plus Minnesota! Forget it, we're not going to optimize for one-offs like that." Google, on the other hand, says, "Who cares? We're not going to tell the user what to do, because the link structure is more complex than we can read, except in response to a user query".'[22] This matters because schools are run on categories, often used unconsciously, or at least without reflection. England's national curriculum is, par excellence, an attempt to force everything a young person needs to know into a set of officially authorised boxes. If our ontology changes – if we look at the world through a different set of categories, or a different type of categorisation – then what schools do must also change significantly.

A related change is in popularly-created, tagged, web-based categories – folksonomies – which users clearly find a valuable addition (or alternative) to traditional taxonomies. If it were otherwise, folksonomies would not exist.

Networking changes many other aspects of our lives. At work, we do much of our business digitally. Whether travelling or at rest, we assume computers are working for us in various ways; not least in life-supporting systems. At least in more affluent countries, we know that we can take a phone where we go; that, wherever we are, we can send and receive calls, photos, sound files, video files, email and text messages. We assume ubiquitous access to vast stores of information. Much of what we call memory is now stored in digital form. We are surrounded by still and moving images and newly-updated news. Our lives are coded in data banks, and mined by those who want to know about us.

These digital developments also change the way we think about the world. They change our ways of apprehending the world. Knowing is individual, but how we come to know is shaped by the intellectual climate of the time; and that, in the early years of the twenty-first century, is radically shaped by these new technologies. Data networks let us recast our projected selves – 'possibilities which are particularly important for adolescents because they offer what Erik Erikson described as a moratorium, a time out or safe space for that personal experimentation that is so crucial for adolescent development'[23]... while 'for those who are lonely, yet afraid of intimacy, information technology has made it possible to have the illusion of companionship without the demands of friendship'.[24]

At the level of information, we have access to more data – infinitely more – than any other generation. This is not an unalloyed benefit. Though there is more accessible information, there are also new techniques for those who wish to know about us; who wish to control what we think and what we do. Our privacy is diminished. Whereas it was once a serious business when governments tapped our phones and read our mail, we now take it for granted that the state agencies we pay for, yet know nothing about, will pry into every electronic aspect of our lives. It happens all the time, unnoticed.

At another level we live, increasingly, in 'a culture of presentation, a corporate culture in which appearance is often more important than reality'.[25] In contemporary political discourse – on television, radio, and on the net – 'use of rhetorical devices at the expense of cogent argument regularly goes without notice'. We know about public life in new ways, with new consequences. 'The radicals who have changed the nature of politics in America are entrepreneurs in dark suits and grey ties who manage the large television industry in America. They did not mean to turn political discourse into a form of entertainment. They did not mean to make it impossible for an overweight person to run for high political office. They did not mean to reduce political campaigning to a 30-second TV commercial. All they were trying to do was to make television into a vast and unsleeping money machine. That they destroyed substantive political discourse in the process does not concern them.'[26]

The digital universe has its limits. Despite the claims of technological evangelists, new ways of knowing and interacting are not ubiquitous. Parts of the world are excluded from the new episteme. In our culture too, there are epistemic islands, insulated from ambient change. School systems are such islands. Locked in the age of print, only superficially affected by their expensive experiments with industrial computing, schools are cut off from the digital culture around them. For some commentators, this is entirely to the good. Postman repeatedly and vociferously argued that new technologies will destroy all that is best in civilisation. Following Aldous Huxley, he worried particularly about the media we like best; those which entertain us, and turn us away from the puritanism of print (and, perhaps, away from schooling). 'What Huxley feared was that there would be no reason to ban a book, for there would be no one who wanted to read one. Orwell feared those who would deprive us of information. Huxley feared those who would give us so much that we would be reduced to passivity and egoism. Orwell feared that the truth would be concealed from us. Huxley feared the truth would be drowned in a sea of irrelevance. Orwell feared we would become a captive culture. Huxley feared we would become a trivial culture, preoccupied with some equivalent of the feelies, orgy porgy, and centrifugal bumblepuppy. As Huxley remarked in Brave New World Revisited, the civil libertarians and rationalists who are ever on the alert to oppose tyranny "failed to take into account man's almost infinite appetite for distractions". In 1984, Huxley added, people are controlled by inflicting pain. In Brave New World, they are controlled by inflicting pleasure. In short, Orwell feared that what we hate will ruin us. Huxley feared that what we love will ruin us.'[27]

Postman may have been right when he predicted that new technologies would devalue some of what was best in the culture of literacy. But his solution – that we must somehow find a way back to the alphabetic garden – is an unattainable wish. As he knew, and we know, technologies are genies which cannot be forced back into bottles. Expelled from that garden, we have no way back. Instead, we need to apply all we have learned to be politically and morally valuable to an age of new technologies, new economies, and new literacies. 'In the decade ahead we need to rebuild the culture around information technology. In that new sociotechnical culture, assumptions about mastery would be less absolute. The new culture would make it easier, not more difficult, to consider life in shades of grey; to see moral dilemmas in terms other than a battle between good and evil. For never has our world been more complex, hybridised, and global. Never have we needed to have so many contradictory thoughts and feelings at the same time. Our tools must help us to accomplish that, not fight against us' for 'if we take the computer as a carrier of a way of knowing, a way of seeing the world and our place in it, we are all computer people now.'[28]

[1] Horgan, J 'Come on, use your common sense' *The Guardian* 18.8.2005
[2] Feynman 1997
[3] Ibid
[4] www.guardian.co.uk/science 26.8.05
[5] Feynman 1960
[6] Fukuyama 2003
[7] Ibid
[8] Barrow 1999
[9] Baltimore, D in Denning (ed) 2001
[10] Barrow 1999
[11] Turing 1950
[12] Kurzweil 1999
[13] Turkle 2004
[14] Kaku 1998
[15] Randall, L 2005
[16] Turkle 2004
[17] Postman 1998
[18] Young 1998
[19] Ibid
[20] Turkle 2004
[21] Shirky 2005
[22] Ibid
[23] Ibid
[24] Ibid
[25] Postman 1998
[26] Ibid
[27] Ibid
[28] Turkle 2004

CHAPTER 14

HOW WILL WE WORK?

'For a nation, the choices that determine whether income doubles with every generation, or instead with every other generation, dwarf all other policy concerns'.
  Paul Romer

'The shift to a knowledge-based economy demands that traditional relationships between education, learning and work are fundamentally reappraised. The long-running debate over whether, and to what extent, education should be a preparation for work, as well as life, is being overtaken by events.'
  Alan Burton-Jones

I got a job working construction
For the Johnstown Company
But lately there ain't been much work
On account of the economy.
  Bruce Springsteen

If a main function of schooling is to support our national economy, we need to look ahead to the kind of economy we shall have when those now young are adult. There is added urgency since, looking back, we see that schooling has rarely been an optimal preparation for life beyond school.

As we have seen, there are many future scenarios. They now range between two poles, one more optimistic than the other. The darker scenarios include nuclear war, irreversible climate change and a collapse of civilisation with the ending of our time of cheap oil (see chapter 12). The more optimistic future, considered below, holds that there is no limit to human inventiveness, or to the things that can be invented. We can invent our way out of any difficulty if we – and other nations – free ourselves from the weight of our past.

In Britain's case, our industrial story has a beginning, a middle and an end, as good stories should. The UK's long descent from the world's leading industrial power to one of the also-rans was due in part to what Correlli Barnett calls the country's 'education for industrial decline'. In the last years of the twentieth century that slow impoverishment was reversed by Britain's new role as a relatively low-wage and low-skill and mainly service economy. Unions were weakened in the 1980s and 1990s, making it easier to hire and fire; benefits were reconfigured to push the poor into work at lower real wages than they might have expected a decade earlier. In tandem, from the mid-1990s, easier borrowing, low inflation and relatively low interest rates encouraged economic expansion,

147

consumer spending and personal indebtedness.[1] The result was a British economy, at the beginning of the twenty-first century, with higher employment and marginally higher growth than some of the country's European competitors, giving our politicians a soapbox from which to lecture the rest of the European Union.

Even if we ignore the dark scenarios of climate change and oil depletion, our economic hubris may be premature. The *Economist* has described services as anything sold in trade that can't be dropped on your foot. But many of the services which can't be dropped on your foot can be outsourced across digital networks, to places where they can be completed more cheaply than here. Though Britain has, since the mid-eighties, benefited from being a relatively low-wage economy with low job security, globalisation has brought – and will increasingly bring – competition from many countries where wages are even lower and job security is largely absent. China and India are most often cited in this context, but there are low-wage countries much closer: among them Albania, Moldova, Ukraine, Bulgaria, Lithuania, the Czech Republic, Belarus, Latvia, Estonia, Hungary, Poland, Romania, Slovakia and Slovenia.

Further, a service economy is still a large consumer of energy and other natural resources. Britain, as elsewhere, is affected by the increasing cost and declining availability of raw materials (gas, oil, iron ore and so on). If economic growth relies on steadily increasing inputs of these materials it is likely to be unsustainable, as primary resources become less plentiful, less accessible and more expensive and as the G8 countries compete for them with newly industrialising countries, notably in Asia.

Beside the cost of raw materials there are the less visible costs of current economies. Economists and environmentalists agree that both industrial and service economies generate unwished-for side effects (notably pollution, environmental degradation and accelerated climate change) and these negative externalities may increase faster than the production of goods. Here too, there are limits to growth.

Ricardo and Keynes – dominating figures in economic thought in successive centuries – both believed that wealth creation must decline; and that this decline, combined with population growth, would impoverish us all. But, as sometimes happens, the world – or most of the world – is not (or not yet) behaving as theory said it should. Growth has continued longer, and more steadily, than economic pessimists believed possible, even in countries where industrial production is declining. And, though many of us live in poverty, the world supports more people than Malthus, or Ehrlich, thought possible. The question for Britain in the twenty-first century is how to manage the future: absent an apocalyptic discontinuity, how do we combine sustainable economic growth with social justice? The question for this book is how education might help do that.

In the first years of the twenty-first century there is growing (but by no means universal) consensus that Britain is moving toward a knowledge-based economy. At first take, this is an odd notion. It is hard to think of any product or service which does not already have some knowledge component. Some thinking must have gone into whatever it is, as well as materials and human labour. But knowledge economies differ from what went before in the proportion of knowledge to materials and labour in any given enterprise. In 'new growth theories' we can say that knowledge is used to reduce the proportion of materials and labour, and to find innovative and sustainable ways of using both.

One set of growth theories is exemplified by the work of Paul Romer, 'according to which aggregate productivity is a function of the degree of product variety. Innovation causes productivity growth in the product-variety paradigm by creating new, but not necessarily improved, varieties of products. This paradigm grew out of the new theory of international trade, and emphasized the technology spillovers according to which the productivity of resources devoted to developing new product varieties was greater the greater the variety of products that have already been developed'.[2]

Romer argues that this way of thinking overturns the long tradition of decreasing or diminishing returns, the cornerstone of traditional economic models. If we are thinking of economies dependent on capital, land and labour, a model of diminishing returns makes sense. But, Romer argues, what classical economists overlooked is that economic growth does not depend simply on producing 'more of the same' things, from expendable resources. 'Economic growth occurs whenever people take resources and rearrange them in ways that are more valuable. A useful metaphor for production in an economy comes from the kitchen. To create valuable final products, we mix inexpensive ingredients together according to a recipe. The cooking one can do is limited by the supply of ingredients, and most cooking in the economy produces undesirable side effects. If economic growth could be achieved only by doing more and more of the same kind of cooking, we would eventually run out of raw materials and suffer from unacceptable levels of pollution and nuisance. Human history teaches us, however, that economic growth springs from better recipes, not just from more cooking. New recipes generally produce fewer unpleasant side effects and generate more economic value per unit of raw material.'[3] Ideas, it seems – certain sorts of ideas in certain institutional contexts – are a principal engine of economic growth. Growth can be driven by inventing or discovering new things (some of which may be non-material) or by making things, which people continue to want, in new ways. The dynamic of such growth (and of the new economics which tries to explain it) is new knowledge. Creating and using knowledge was of course involved, but was not seen as central, in industrial economies. It is now. The ways in which knowledge will be created, and the ways it will be applied, distinguish the post-industrial age from the industrial.

In an economic context, knowledge is characterised in particular ways. 'Because ideas can be infinitely shared and reused, we can accumulate them without limit.'[4] Ideas are neither finite nor expendable. 'Knowledge has different properties from other economic goods... the ability to grow the economy by increasing knowledge, rather than labour or capital, creates opportunities for nearly boundless growth.'[5]

Of course this does not mean that we will have boundless growth. We have noted (chapter 12) scenarios which predict the opposite: global chaos and misery. History records our talent for finding and applying destructive knowledge to counter the productive – nuclear weapons being, as Einstein predicted, a prime example. We have a perverse gift for causing misery, to ourselves and to others. But this chapter focuses on the positive: on productivity and growth. And as Romer says, if we have compound growth in productivity, it will make more difference than most of us realise. 'People are reasonably good at forming estimates based on addition, but for operations such as compounding that depend on repeated multiplication, we systematically underestimate how fast things grow.'[6]

The knowledge we are discussing may be anything but esoteric. 'Knowledge includes everything we know about the world, from the basic laws of physics, to the blueprint for a microprocessor, to how to sew a shirt or paint a portrait.'[7] In economic jargon, knowledge is a 'non-rival good', but is 'excludable'. It is 'non-rival' because more than one person at one time – indeed thousands of people – can use any single bit of unprotected knowledge; which is clearly not true of other goods, like spades or lathes. Protected ('excluded') knowledge is that which comes under patent, or copyright or similar regulations; or which is known to only a few people, or to one person. Knowledge can be, and often is, embedded in physical products: the products themselves are rival goods – most can be used by only one person at a time. The knowledge underlying them (unless legally or otherwise protected) can be used by anyone.

'The source of economic progress is ideas. We have basically the same stock of physical resources we have always had. Our higher standard of living stems from our improved ability to rearrange these physical objects into forms that provide greater value ... Unlike the critics of the patent office at the turn of the twentieth century, who believed it could be closed because nearly everything useful had already been invented, it is extremely likely that we will never come close to discovering all or even a very significant fraction of all of the possible useful products, inventions and processes we might create from the physical objects available to us.'[8]

One of Romer's illustrations of invention's possibility comes from chemical synthesis: the combining of different chemical elements in different ways, under different conditions, in order to see if some new and useful product might be produced. 'The periodic table contains about a hundred different types of atoms, so the number of combinations made up of four different elements is 100 x 99 x 98 x 97 or about 94 million. A list of numbers like 1, 2, 3, 7 can represent the proportions for using the four elements in a recipe. To keep things simple, assume that the numbers in the list must lie between 1 and 10, that no fractions are allowed, and that the smallest number must always be 1. Then there are about 3,500 different sets of proportions for each choice of four elements, and 3,500 x 94 million (or 330 billion) different recipes in total. If laboratories around the world evaluated 1,000 recipes each day, it would take nearly a million years to go through them all. (In fact, this calculation vastly underestimates the amount of exploration that remains to be done because mixtures can be made of more than four elements, fractional proportions can be selected, and a wide variety of pressures and temperatures can be used during mixing).'[9] If we continue to produce new and useful ideas, and if this knowledge is used productively and sustainably (which is by no means always true), then we can produce more and better goods and services, using smaller amounts of physical resources and more renewable resources, with less degradation of the environment.

Quality of innovation remains a problem with the theories of Romer and his associates. Romer seems to feel that growth stems simply from quantity of innovation. That may be true, but if some or all of the innovations are damaging to people or the environment (as, for example, many nuclear power stations proved to be) then the costs of growth may be unsustainable. For this reason Aghion and Howitt prefer a neo-Schumpeterian model of growth which, like Romer's, relies on continuing innovation, but which 'focuses on quality-improving innovations that render old products obsolete, and hence involves the force that Schumpeter called "creative destruction".'[10]

Despite the relatively optimistic outlooks of both Romer's 'product variety' and Aghion's neo-Schumpeterian models, there are difficulties with an innovation process which relies (as it must) on continuous knowledge production. Since other people can use any piece of knowledge you have discovered, why invest in its discovery? Clearly, the way to profit from 'your' knowledge is to make it excludable – that is to protect it by patent, copyright or other means. If you can do that for any length of time (as, for instance, Larry Page and Sergey Brin have done) you might get rich. 'Because knowledge has increasing returns (continuously declining marginal costs), having the largest market share produces the highest profits. As the leading producer faces permanently declining costs – the next unit of output can be produced even more cheaply than the last – whoever has the leading position in the market can maintain and extend it.'[11] The classic recent example is Microsoft, which invests huge amounts in producing carefully protected (though not always original) knowledge, and in harassing those unwilling to pay for its use.

Once produced, it costs companies almost nothing to replicate and sell their protected knowledge, on disc, or on the web. Up to the time of writing, Microsoft has done well from this quasi-monopolistic control of an area of knowledge. One of the dilemmas of knowledge production, then, is how to reward investment in research and development, without creating knowledge monopolies which stifle innovation.

HISTORY, GEOGRAPHY, CULTURE AND POLITICS

Though theoretically unconstrained, knowledge production is not, in practice, independent of history, geography, culture or politics. Cortright notes that where economies end up 'is a product of the development path that they follow. Small chance events occurring at the right time can have persistent long-term effects.'[12] Or, conversely, social events can have long-term negative effects. Six hundred years ago, China was the world's most technologically advanced civilisation. It then experienced cultural and political changes that stifled further innovation and, in succeeding centuries, took the country technologically backwards. Britain's period of technological dominance lasted less than a century; but the country has, in many areas (certainly in schools) since been shackled to the mindset of that time.

If economic success is linked to intellectual freedom and to Schumpeter's 'creative destruction', then Britain is better placed than many countries. But – given our class structure, our insularity, our anachronistic education system, our equation of morality with custom, and our periodic fits of officially sanctioned intolerance – we lack an ideally fertile soil in which to grow a new, knowledge-based economy. If, as Romer suggests, 'the most important job for economic policy is to create an institutional environment that supports technological change'[13] then, in education and elsewhere, Britain has some way to go.

Institutions – education systems among them – determine the growth and productivity of knowledge economies. And the pressures on productivity are growing. The drive for increased productivity in post-fordist globalised capitalism focuses the attention of decision-makers on the connection between education and economics.[14] Classical economists, and business lobbies, argue that the government's main economic function is to hold the ring for the unfettered operation of markets. This notion, though comforting for those who hold it, is mistaken. 'Beliefs about the value of new knowledge, risk-taking, and trust in social institutions influence the rate and type of economic growth in a society. The structure of incentives in society is shaped by institutions, which means that ultimately the effectiveness of markets is dependent on collective, political processes. Markets alone cannot produce the set of conditions needed for the efficient functioning of a market economy.'[15] Of course it is true that governments can do a great deal that is economically damaging. But they can, if so minded, make institutional changes which foster economic growth. One of those is to develop adaptive school systems which encourage innovation and originality.

School systems do need to be adaptive. It is not enough for schools to encourage innovation this month, or next, or while innovation is fashionable. The process of adaptation must continue over time. It has to do with 'the willingness of a society to acquire knowledge and learning, to induce innovation, to undertake risk and creative activity of all sorts... We are far from knowing all the aspects of what makes for adaptive efficiency, but clearly the overall institutional structure plays a key role, to the degree that the society and the economy will encourage the trials, experiments and innovations that we can characterise as adaptively efficient. The incentives embedded in the institutional framework direct the process of learning-by-doing and the development of tacit knowledge that will lead individuals in decision-making processes to evolve systems that are different from the ones that they had to begin with.'[16]

Traditionally we have a picture of the lone inventor as innovator: an Edison, a Ford, an Einstein. This may be the case; but often is not. Invention and innovation are more typically social processes: they arise from communities of people working on similar problems. These communities may work face-to-face or, with excellent communication links, may work at a distance from each other.[17] Either way, we see that school systems, which still treat schools as isolated islands – and pupils as isolated intellects within them – are at a disadvantage. We think of school pupils (and school teachers) as individual workers, in a world where creation and innovation are socially located, and commonly collaborative. Changing these scholastic arrangements – and their underlying mindset – needs to be done; but it will not be easy (see chapter 21).

As digital networks get better, faster, wider and more user-friendly, pupils and teachers will work increasingly in knowledge-creation groups with others at a distance. Such communication – however good the network – favours codifiable knowledge. 'Codifiable' here means knowledge which can be expressed reasonably clearly and succinctly. But much useful knowledge is not of that kind. It is tacit: it concerns things we know, but which may not reach the level of language. There is a story about Elizabeth David, the cookery writer, who was collecting recipes in France. At a rural restaurant famous for its omelettes, Ms David asked the patronne how they were made. 'Well, madame,' said the patronne, 'First I break some eggs, then I put them in a pan with butter, then I whisk them all together.' Whatever made those omelettes special was to remain in the tacit realm. The writer, seeking codifiable knowledge, left without a recipe worth publishing.

The internet has been optimistically heralded as 'the death of distance'. But reports of its death are exaggerated. Distance is alive. Geography still matters. We see this in innovation clusters like California's Silicon Valley or Boston's Route 128.[18] The same is true, more generally, of many cities. 'At the crossroads of trade, cities promote the mixing of a wide range of people, ideas and products, generating new work, and triggering productivity and growth.'[19] Creative men and women work in cities to be near other creative men and women. They debate; they exchange ideas. Clearly there are knowledge spillovers which come only from proximity; spillovers which are in part tacit, and are not yet digitally transmissible. In education, just because tacit knowledge does not travel well, schools will have to break down their isolation and develop their own internal capacity for knowledge-creation. Learners need to find they can learn at a level beyond language.

Linked to these factors is the notion of critical creative mass. A group of creative people may add up to more than the sum of its parts: the group may produce more new knowledge than its members individually could have done. Why? One answer, Romer writes, 'is that the more people you're around, the better off you're going to be ... If somebody discovers an idea, everybody gets to use it, so the more people you have who are potentially looking for ideas, the better off we're all going to be.'[20] Several conclusions follow. For school systems in knowledge economies, the most significant is that we are foolish to offer a good education to only part of our population. If a larger group of educated people means that you are likely to increase disproportionately the generation of new knowledge, then, on grounds of economics as well as equity, we should extend real educational opportunity. (What this should not mean – though now it often does – is that extended formal education is matched by a corresponding decrease in quality.)

In summary, and following Cortright, we could suggest that strategies for fostering knowledge economies might include:

- creation of new knowledge in business settings, as well as educational and research institutions;
- diversity of approach, since it is difficult, often impossible, to know what will work in the medium or longer term;
- encouraging local concentrations of knowledge and expertise;
- assessing the usefulness of ideas, whatever their source for 'innovation by front-line workers is as important to the knowledge economy as undertaking scientific research'.[21]

In this context, Romer emphasises that economic development is not a zero-sum game: the fact that one group wins does not mean that other groups must lose. 'Knowledge-based growth can stimulate a self-reinforcing cycle, in which faster growth triggers additional knowledge creation, and more growth.'[22]

For school systems, preparing for a knowledge economy means, first, a change of emphasis – from 'schools as information-transmission places' to 'schools as knowledge-building places', and as places for acquiring, and valuing non-codifiable knowledge: the knowledge that students bring with them to school (see chapter 21). Secondly, it means combining diversity of approach with genuine equality of opportunity – since we cannot know which approaches will best fit young people for a new economy; and nor can we know who will contribute the new knowledge on which that economy depends, or precisely how they will contribute.

The industrial age assumed that significant contributions to knowledge would come from its elite; from 'high-flyers'. It was they who would make the scientific and technological discoveries which advanced industry, and improved productivity. We still need such brilliance, but new economies have a more catholic conception of productive knowledge creation: it can happen anywhere, at any time.

Writing of the digital revolution in US business, Brynjolfsson notes that much of the current American productivity growth comes not from the high-flyers, but from 'the creative, diligent, and painstaking work done by those who have been rethinking supply chains, customer service, incentive systems, product lines, and the thousand-and-one other processes and practices affected by computers. Investments of intangible capital constitute the real source of today's productivity growth.'[23]

In knowledge economies, 'firms will increasingly take advantage of each person's innate curiosity and willingness to experiment... every worker in an organisation, from top to bottom, can become a "knowledge" worker, if given the opportunity to do so.'[24] Conversely, innovative workers cannot do their best in a traditionally rigid business environment. There are 'positive feedback loops between information technology, organisational flexibility, and highly skilled labour, at the level of the firm'. The networked business 'is based on a flat hierarchy, a teamwork system, and open, easy interaction between workers and managers, across departments, and between levels of the firm'.[25]

In short, economic progress is achieved not just by landmark discoveries, or by solitary genius. Rather, it is built incrementally both from individual discoveries and from thousands, or millions, of small advances, often made long after the initial landmark finding; and often made by people who are not scientists, or researchers, or managers. 'Many productivity improvements come from the application of fairly simple ideas in bold or novel ways.'[26] In business, this search for improvement means paying attention to everyone's ideas – not just those of management. In schools, it means paying attention to pupils' ideas, not just to those of their elders.

Preparing for a knowledge economy means that schools must find a way of keeping pupils safe – which usually means relatively confined – while forming mutually productive, real or virtual, links with local concentrations of specialised knowledge and expertise. 'Businesses and places that provide good environments for understanding problems and creating knowledge are just as important to the new economy as are those conducting scientific research'[27] (see chapter 21).

Finally, school systems need to reorganise not only to encourage innovation, but also to reassure parents – in particular, affluent parents – that opening opportunities for pupils labelled 'less academic' will not threaten the prospects of 'academic' and (almost invariably) middle-class young people. Knowledge economies, in more optimistic scenarios, are not zero-sum games; nor can they rely for new knowledge on elite social groups. Growth in one economic sector – or improving the lot of one group – need not be at the cost of another. We must make sure the same applies in school systems. Currently, that is not the case; or at least, to many parents it seems not to be the case.

---

[1] Market analyst Datamonitor said the total outstanding debt on the cards reached £53.5 billion at the end of [2003], while the total number of cards in circulation has risen by 58% since the end of 1999 to nearly 65.5 million. Manchester News 15.4.2004
[2] Aghion, P and Howitt. P, 'Appropriate growth policy: a unifying framework': the 2005 Joseph Schumpeter Lecture, delivered to the 20th Annual Congress of the European Economic Association, Amsterdam, August 25, 2005.
http://post.economics.harvard.edu/faculty/aghion/papers/Appropriate_Growth.pdf
[3] Romer 1999
[4] Cortright 2001
[5] Ibid
[6] Romer 1994
[7] Cortright 2001
[8] Romer 1994
[9] Ibid
[10] Aghion and Howitt 2005
[11] Cortright 2001
[12] Ibid
[13] Romer 1994
[14] Hickox and Moore 1991

[15] Cortright 2001

[16] North 1990

[17] This will be increasingly possible, of course, as networked societies mature.

[18] There are other benefits within agglomerations of similar industries: reciprocal sub-contracting, or commonality of suppliers, for instance.

[19] Cortright 2001

[20] Romer 2000

[21] Cortright 2001

[22] quoted in Cortright 2001

[23] Brynjolfsson 2004

[24] Romer 1993

[25] Castells 2003

[26] Cortright 2001

[27] Ibid

CREATIVITY, INNOVATION, ENTERPRISE

'The granting [of] patents 'inflames cupidity', excites fraud, stimulates men to run after schemes that may enable them to levy a tax on the public, begets disputes and quarrels betwixt inventors, provokes endless lawsuits...The principle of the law from which such consequences flow cannot be just'
   The Economist, 1851

'We tend to think you can be taught to do things, and when you have been taught the right way or you observe the right way or you have read the right way, that is what we should do. And the wonderful thing in business is that that doesn't work. The rules tomorrow are very different to the rules today. And just encouraging people to think differently and just to try and take a few risks, think dangerously and to do something that hasn't been done before and to do something that sounds mad.'
   Sir James Dyson

'Employers are continually asking for employees to be able to create ideas, to be innovative and work as teams. Despite this, activities that encourage critical thinking are a rarity in our schools. Creative programmes that foster innovation are seen as risky, and yet are essential for the future of our nation.'
   Richard Wallis, head teacher

As 'innovation comes closer to being the sole means to prosper and survive in highly competitive and globalised economies'[1] politicians push schools toward the teaching of innovation, creativity (which is held to be a driver of innovation) and 'enterprise' – seen as the commercial application of both. As Florida says, somewhat optimistically, 'we have evolved economic and social systems that tap human creativity and make use of it as never before. This in turn creates an unparalleled opportunity to raise our living standards, build a more humane and sustainable economy, and make our lives more complete'.[2] If only.

As we understand it, projects may be creative, but not innovative. A student may, for example, do a creative and perfect copy of Matisse's 'Harmony in Yellow', but the painting will not be innovative, or particularly valuable to others, since the innovation occurred when Matisse did the original. (This disjunction is of course a constant source of frustration to accomplished forgers who wish to be recognised as artists in their own right.)

There are more commercially oriented distinctions: 'creativity only becomes innovation when ideas become useful. In the business world, that means when a new product or service is launched, or starts to make money. Creativity is a behaviour; innovation is a process.'[3]

Any commercial enterprise will involve some level of innovation – implementations of invention – thought to be useful to others beside the innovator. In most cases the market decides whether or not this is the case, or whether the innovation is useful enough to be profitable.

In Britain in the twenty-first century there is, in governmental circles, a new emphasis on creativity and innovation. According to the Prime Minister, in 2004, 'the creativity and inventiveness of our people is our country's greatest asset and has always underpinned the UK's economic success... innovation, the exploitation of new ideas, is absolutely essential to safeguard and deliver high-quality jobs, successful businesses, better products and services for our consumers, and new, more environmentally friendly processes.'[4] The challenge, Mr Blair continues, 'is to create the conditions where all our firms put innovation at the centre of their strategies for the future'.[5] In this context, Aghion and Howitt argue that 'higher education investment should have a bigger effect on a country's ability to make leading-edge innovations, whereas primary and secondary education are more likely to make a difference in terms of the country's ability to implement existing (frontier) technologies.'[6] For Britain, this is not an either-or proposition: the country needs to be (at least in some areas) at technological frontiers; but it also needs to imitate and implement existing technologies.

In relation to UK education, the themes of creativity, innovation and enterprise were developed by Howard Davies, a former head of Britain's Financial Services Authority. In what has become known as 'the Davies Report',[7] the authors quote an OED definition of an enterprising person:

'An enterprising individual has a positive, flexible and adaptive disposition to change, seeing it as normal and as an opportunity rather than a problem. To see change in this way, an enterprising individual has a security born of self-confidence, and is at ease when dealing with insecurity, risks and the unknown. An enterprising individual has the capacity to initiate creative ideas and develop them into action in a determined manner. An enterprising individual is able, even anxious to take responsibility, is an effective communicator, negotiator, influencer, planner and organiser. An enterprising individual is active, confident and purposeful — not uncertain and dependent.'

For British schools this politically driven push toward the development of enterprising persons is problematic, for it goes against the grain of the didactic method which – either by inclination or order – most schools still practice. Schools are not usually places which encourage a 'flexible and adaptive disposition to change'; nor do they purposefully develop students who are 'at ease when dealing with insecurity, risks and the unknown'. Commonly the opposite is true: as every schoolboy knows, favoured pupils are those who follow rules, take no risks, and efficiently memorise received knowledge.

'Teaching innovation' is an inherently contradictory project, since the essence of innovation is new and unexpected practice which cannot be taught, at least not in any conventional sense. Christensen illustrates this when he points out that in recent times some of the world's best-managed companies (Sears, DEC, Wang, Xerox, American Steel, among others) have been crippled or bankrupted by failing to see the significance of innovations; and that 'the decisions which led to failure were made when the [corporations] in question were widely regarded as among the best companies in the world'.[8] Had these companies been able to 'teach innovation' to their employees they would now be better off than they are. Or, in some cases, they would still exist.

The case of Xerox PARC is perhaps the best known and best documented of the late twentieth century's startling failures to handle innovation. PARC – the Palo Alto Research Center – was an offshoot deliberately set up, away from the main Xerox establishment, in order to liberate innovation. In that, it was successful. PARC developed crucial components (among them the graphical user interface) of what would become the personal computer. Unfortunately for Xerox, the parent company failed to recognise the value of these innovations, and did not commercialise them. The knowledge unappreciated within Xerox 'leaked rapidly out and down the road to Apple, and from there to Microsoft and a thousand other software developers'.[9]

If it is difficult for the world's best-managed firms to deal with innovation, it is even harder for schools. Schools have a long history of discouraging creativity and innovation: as we have seen, creativity is often a handicap in a well-ordered school. Changing that pattern is rather like turning a water mill into microprocessor plant. It can be done, but not just by adding one or two new ingredients. What is needed is a change of culture and expectation: a move away from the belief that schools should deal only with the traditional and predictable. Schools' processes, like those of slow-moving firms, 'are set up so that employees perform tasks in a consistent way, time after time. They are meant not to change, or, if they must change, to change through tightly controlled procedures'.[10]

Currently, if there is innovation in schools (as in curricular or assessment changes) it will probably come from properly authorised adults, usually in a layer of bureaucracy above schools and teachers. Under England's 2002 Education Act if teachers themselves wish to innovate they need permission from above.[11] Imposed innovation is likely to discourage creativity; innovation from below is itself discouraged.

So where should we now look for creativity in schools? We expect to find it in art rooms (where there is, at times, extraordinary and wonderful student work) and perhaps in English classes though, in England, government and quangos now discourage both creativity and the closely linked quality of enjoyment. Analysis is preferred. The writer Philip Pullman notes that, on reading 'through the sections on reading in Key Stages 1 to 3 of the National Literacy Strategy [for England and Wales],…I was very struck by something about the verbs. I wrote them all down. They included "reinforce", "predict", "check", "discuss", "identify", "categorise", "evaluate", "distinguish", "summarise", "infer", "analyse", "locate"...and so on: seventy-one different verbs, by my count, for the activities that come under the heading of "reading". And the word "enjoy" didn't appear once... I am concerned that in a constant search for things to test, we're forgetting the true purpose, the true nature, of reading and writing; and in forcing these things to happen in a way that divorces them from pleasure, we are creating a generation of children who might be able to make the right noises when they see print, but who hate reading and feel nothing but hostility for literature.'[12]

Outside art and English classes things are simpler: learners' creativity is minimal, and is expected to be minimal. If the main business in classrooms is information transmission, creativity clearly has no place. We need not be creative to absorb and reproduce data. Even students' planned activities require little or no creativity, for they too are commonly oriented to memorising a set quantum of information or of algorithms. From within the didactic paradigm, most schools see creativity as irrelevant to higher-status subjects like mathematics, or the natural and social sciences.

Many educators have contested that view. One of the most cogent, in recent times, is Marlene Scardamalia who is concerned with students' knowledge-building, rather than knowledge-banking. Scardamalia writes that, 'in the "knowledge age," the health and wealth of societies depends increasingly on their capacity to innovate. People in general, not just a specialized elite, need to work creatively with knowledge... This presents a formidable new challenge: how to develop citizens who not only possess up-to-date knowledge but are able to participate in the creation of new knowledge as a normal part of their lives.'[13] Knowledge-building in schools, she continues, is a creative act: 'the job of an elementary school class that takes a knowledge building approach is to construct an understanding of the world as they know it.'[14] School students 'can begin functioning as real scientists as soon as they are able to engage in a form of social practice that is authentically scientific – that is concerned with the solution of recognizably scientific problems in recognizably scientific ways. Analogous arguments can be made about authentic functioning in history, literature, and other disciplines that students may venture into in their knowledge building efforts.'[15]

There is a problem here. We have seen that, as schools now are, it is difficult for teachers to work creatively with students as builders of knowledge – knowledge which will be new to them and, very occasionally, new to the world. Indeed it is difficult in schools to combine traditional teaching with any sort of creativity, since the two modes are likely to be in opposition. Further it is generally agreed that, though creativity cannot be taught in any strict sense of the word it can be fostered by arranging for students to work with genuinely creative people (as British art schools sometimes do, and did more often in the less-regimented past) or by letting groups of learners use creative tools – game-creation engines for example, or open internet access, tools for machinima, sensor arrays, cameras, web-publishing and blogging facilities, music mixers, animation programs, fabricators, script processors, or collaborative digital workspaces – with basic guidelines for their use. Of course this means entering a world which is new, unexplored and often daunting to teachers. Indeed it may be that, if we wish to foster creativity, schools, as they are now, are not the place to do it: at least while they still see their main task as teaching facts and low-level skills. As a young English entrepreneur said, looking back at his schooling, 'I think a huge shift would be when children actually stopped to reflect and learn about learning. Then learning is something very different. It isn't something that grown ups throw at you – something you've got to do. Instead it becomes a key to curiosity and vitality and with it you can do anything.'[16]

Despite the difficulties, it seems reasonable to British politicians in the early years of the twenty-first century that schools should be told to offer 'enterprise education', with emphasis on fostering creative, innovative and entrepreneurial qualities, and readiness to enter the world of enterprise. The ultimate objective, according to the 2002 Davies Report[17] 'is a more dynamic economy, with a more rapid rate of job and business creation. That in turn requires a more enterprising workforce, with the skills and attitudes necessary to manage more flexible careers and to understand and manage risk.' Reviewing school provision, the Report found that 'whilst young people recognise the challenges and rewards involved in starting and running a business, many are unsure of their own ability to meet the challenges successfully. They lack the skills and confidence to turn positive attitudes into action during their future careers … while some schools have implemented imaginative programmes, usually with business support, those experiences are available to relatively few students nationally – fewer than thirty per cent of young people take part at any point in their school careers. It is also clear that few schoolchildren are exposed to basic concepts about finance and the economy, which form part of the essential toolkit of the effective entrepreneur.'[18] One of the few research studies of entrepreneurs' practice is in general agreement: 'currently education in the UK is not equipping young people with the competencies needed for either enterprise or for working life'.[19]

Since 2002, and partly based on the recommendations of the Davies Report, the Department for Education and Skills has been developing an expensive programme of enterprise education in schools. (This followed a bureaucratic turf war with the Department for Industry which, with some justification, felt that industry and enterprise were part of its remit.)

Enterprise education has had all the problems suffered by other recent school implants. A programme designed to prepare young people for life beyond school – but conceived, evaluated[20] and sustained within the education system – has the character of Plato's crepuscular cave, whose inhabitants, seeing shadows on the cave wall, try to picture the world outside. Clearly teachers are far removed from entrepreneurs: one group choosing security and stability, the other adventure and risk. This is not a reflection on either group; but it does mean that there is a wide gap in understanding between the two. Entrepreneurs, for various reasons (among them impatience), tend to make poor teachers; and teachers, in choosing their profession, have opted for life less entrepreneurial. The Department for Education has tried to remedy this deficit of understanding by appointing enterprise advisers – but they too are rarely business people, and certainly not successful ones.

Another way out of the scholastic cave is the 'school-business link', which has both its uses and its problems. Quality of links varies, as Davies and his team found: 'it is clear that the quality of local partnership brokerage varies enormously, partly due to the absence of any clear quality framework underpinning [this] work'.[21] A later review concluded that 'few schools have coherent programmes of business education' and that there was 'frequent failure to fully exploit business links'.[22] When they are fully exploited, business links are supposed to work both ways: schools and pupils learn about business and enterprise while 'business methods' improve the ways in which schools are run. Anecdotal evidence suggests that the latter rarely happens in the UK. In the US, the home of business and enterprise education, 'despite an estimated 200,000 business partnerships with public schools, fundamental aspects of public education have barely changed in decades. And performance is still weak.'[23]

Pupils visiting businesses certainly learn something they would not have learned in the classroom but, given the constraints of time on both sides, what they learn is almost inevitably superficial. Work experience should offer more than business visits, and often does. But given pupils' lack of relevant skills they are often assigned simple, repetitive tasks in the workplace, which may teach little more than the fact that a good deal of paid work (at least at this level) is neither interesting or challenging.

Given the restriction of business visits and work experience, many schools supplement enterprise education with what the Davies Report calls 'mini-company schemes': a 'business' within a school. These are commonly curbed by the limitations mentioned above: if teachers were good at running companies, they might well be doing that. Not surprisingly, mini-company schemes tend to lack the hard edges of commercial life. When the Department for Education was promoting its enterprise education efforts in 2004 it pointed journalists toward a school whose business scheme was then publicised by the British media. Under the heading 'Schools in England are getting official advice on how to teach students to be more enterprising' the BBC described a school's mini-company scheme, which occupied 180 pupils and involved making fifty origami ducks. The ducks were then to be shipped to France.[24] We are not told what market research established the size of market in France for hand-made origami ducks nor, given the labour-intensity of the operation, whether exporting fifty paper ducks was a profitable business. But it seems to have satisfied those who oversee business education.

In summary then, we now have an expanded programme of enterprise education in schools and, it is generally agreed, that programme will need to foster pupils' inventiveness, creativity and, naturally, qualities of independence and enterprise. But, as we have seen, these are precisely the qualities which most schools do not encourage in their pupils and which England's centrally mandated National Curriculum, and its national assessment system, are designed to discourage. Looking back on his schooling a young English entrepreneur commented that he found school very structured. 'It was very much going in and they would teach you about history, or they would teach you about geography or they would teach you about science. I was coming home and learning all these fascinating things about the other world and how the rest of the world operated and then going back and having it drilled into you that Oliver Cromwell did this and that kind of thing. But I was getting much more of a life experience outside school. And should that be the case? Should you have to go off and find your life experience when you are a teenager growing up or should school somehow integrate you with all that is going on out there? So I found school very constrained in what we were allowed to look at and what we were allowed to develop interest in.'[25]

Further, schools themselves are, as we know, conservative institutions, insulated from developments in the world outside them, with a technology – a modus operandi – slower to change than almost any other. Just as schools are not role models for the democratic practices promoted in citizenship classes, they are commonly the reverse of what we look for in successful enterprise. Why then, we might ask, have politicians chosen schools, of all places, to introduce young people to the fast-changing, technology-driven and inherently unstable world of twenty-first century enterprise?

The answer is: because they can. With central control of the curriculum, the politicians in charge of state schooling can, at will, shoe-horn new subjects – 'citizenship', 'ICT', 'enterprise education' – into an already crowded curriculum. Further, something like enterprise education can be done more cheaply by forcing it into the school timetable than by using other, and perhaps more effective, channels. If we were serious about doing enterprise education well, we would need to make significant changes to our school system. No doubt that will one day happen. But, since it would be an exercise both difficult and expensive, it is unlikely to happen soon.

What we can practically do, and do soon, is make more effective use of new technologies which allow many of us – who would not have been thought creative – to create. And digital technologies could strengthen school-business-enterprise links in other ways.

With agreement on both sides, networked webcams could let pupils at school watch people at work in businesses and enterprises; with an audio link, staff in a company could explain what they are doing, and why they are doing it. This might be followed by brief sessions in which students put their questions to the people they have been observing.

As a second option (and again with agreement) learners could research, plan, film and edit a documentary on some aspect of for-profit or social enterprise. The finished video would be published to the web. Experience shows that documentary-making is a much more focused and productive project than a simple 'workplace visit'.

A third option is the virtual workplace: the setting and processes of a workplace created virtually in schools. Groups of pupils deal virtually with the quotidian procedures and crises of a real business. Such virtual workplaces should be created

163

in collaboration with the businesses they represent, and kept up to date to avoid the anachronistic quality of many textbook case studies.

All these are ways of recognising the hermetic quality of schooling, while fruitfully connecting with reality outside. All too often the school system's answer is to present students with educators' imagined scenarios of innovation and enterprise. Our task now is to find ways for learners to go beyond those, and to deal (virtually or face to face) with the real, unpredictable and rapidly changing commercial world.

---

[1] David and Foray 2002

[2] Florida 2002

[3] 'Welcome to the revolution' Sticky Wisdom, London: 2004

[4] Department of Trade and Industry: Innovation Report: 'Competing in the global economy: the innovation challenge' Department of Trade and Industry 2003 http://www.dti.gov.uk/

[5] Ibid

[6] Aghion and Howitt 2005

[7] Davies, H (2002) Enterprise and economy in education, London: HMSO

[8] Christensen 2003

[9] Seely Brown and Duguid 2000

[10] Christensen 2002

[11] See Part I of the Education Act 2002: Provision for new legal frameworks; Chapter One: Powers to facilitate innovation; but see also chapter 8 of this book for British schools' legislation (proposed in 2005) which deals in part with innovation.

[12] Pullman 2003

[13] Scardamalia & Bereiter 2002

[14] Scardamalia and Bereiter 1999

[15] Ibid

[16] Quoted in Darby 2001

[17] Davies 2002

[18] Ibid

[19] Darby 2001

[20] See, for example, Higham, J and others (2004): 14-19 Pathfinders: an evaluation of the first year, Brief RB504, London: DfES

[21] Davies 2002

[22] Butler, D (2003) in 'Business Education' Ofsted subject reports conference series 2002/03 HMI 1641 e-publication

[23] Kanter, R M (2001) in Harvard Business Review on innovation, Harvard Business School Press

[24] BBC News Online 17.11.2004

[25] Tom Hadfield, quoted in Darby 2001

IV RESHAPING THE SCHOOL SYSTEM: RESISTING CHANGE

CHAPTER 16

TEACHERS

*'Her departure from the profession wasn't without bitterness: she'd done
everything she was supposed to do, and excelled in every way, but after five
years in the classroom in one of the most expensive cities in the country, she was
still making less than $30,000 a year.'*
    Dave Eggers

In what the post-1997 British Labour government describes as its project to
modernise British schools, teachers are often collectively cast – by politicians – as
roadblocks to progress. They resist the introduction of unqualified 'teaching
assistants' (who often turn into unqualified class teachers); they disapprove of
turning over parts of the school system to private companies. (A consultants'
analysis for businesses wishing to move into the education sector concludes that
'this [Labour] government is genuinely committed to the use of the private sector
in the delivery of public services...[though] there are currently few players with
the capacity or track record to participate in this potentially massive market...there
is currently a window of opportunity to buy and build a substantial outsourcing
business with an initial focus on education but with the clear future intention of
moving into other government sectors'.[1])

Teachers' unions claim that the small cluster of twenty-first century 'school
academies', (enthusiastically promoted by Mr Blair and his subordinates) may
improve schooling for some pupils – though even that is not clear at the time of
writing – but, given the significant diversion of funds from 'ordinary schools' to
these more favoured schools, they will at the same time make schooling nationally
more unequal than it is already. With their interest in equity and public service, it is
not surprising that teachers are viewed negatively by those politicians and
administrators who claim to be modernising schools.

Teachers are also wary of the centrally mandated initiatives which now rain
down on schools. Rightly or wrongly, they believe that most of these will be ill-
planned, under-researched, over-administered, short-term, under-financed, and
irrelevant to the central business of schools, if we believe that central business has
to do with learning.

Teachers have, however, little power to block politically inspired change. Their
unions – never politically strong – were visibly weakened in the wider anti-union
campaigns of the 1980s and, more specifically, by politically inspired efforts to
deskill teachers and to erode their already tenuous professional status. In the late
1990s Conservative functionaries were replaced by Labour appointees who, from
1997 to 2000, characterised teachers as simultaneously trendy, reactionary,

incompetent and ignorant: unworthy of a voice in education policy. Teachers are further handicapped by the oft-repeated assertion that education should be above or outside politics: a teacher should not stray beyond the walls of her classroom. A surprising number of teachers still accept this restriction, despite the fact that schooling is one of the most highly politicised areas of society. As a result, teachers have suffered a steady loss of autonomy as British governments extend their control over school curricula (what teachers teach) and teaching method (how they teach). The significant educational and organisational decisions have been taken out of teachers' hands. If teachers ever had professional status, they have it no longer. Collectively teachers now fail the criteria of professionalism: they lack the power to determine who teaches, what they teach, and how they teach.

Currently our school system is an analogue of traditional industry. Changes are imposed from above: an essentially authoritarian procedure. Schools' paymasters, in government departments, decide on a new assessment regime, or a 'literacy and numeracy strategy', or the formulation of 'league tables' – and then impose them on schools. With an authoritarian head teacher, or deputy head, this pattern of imposition may be replicated within the school. It is, as Papert says, a command economy in miniature. 'One of the key arguments used to justify the [soviet] command economy [was] that a tightly programmed, highly planned economic system would necessarily be more efficient than one that operates through myriads of individual uncoordinated decisions.'[2] Such a fully rational economy with no waste would clearly be more efficient 'than the chaos of the capitalist market economy'.[3] This was a defensible position while the gosplanned soviet economy was sheltered from international competition. When perestroika blew away that shelter the command economy quite rapidly collapsed. Fortunately for our still-sheltered school system its central command has not been similarly tested. It is still possible to see teachers as a sometimes reluctant, but ultimately obedient, centrally directed workforce.

In terms of both organisational health and education, this may not be an optimal approach. Any informed discussion of change management will stress that those who have to use new techniques should be involved in choosing and implementing them. These are principles commonly and briskly ignored within school systems unless teachers, like their industrial counterparts, threaten to strike. This they rarely do.

Issues of training for and acclimatisation to change are commonly overlooked. We all need help, and time, to be comfortable with new developments; teachers rarely get enough of either. Digital technologies are a case in point. They will be increasingly important as school systems begin to educate for knowledge economies (see chapters 20 and 21); yet the training teachers are offered in this arena is often the wrong kind, and the wrong amount. It is the wrong kind because education's administrators commonly have a poor understanding of networked society; and the wrong amount because those who budget spend most of the available funding on hardware. Software usually comes second, and training last. As a rule of thumb, corporations budget for training three times the cost of computing kit. Schools do not. In the largest UK exercise of its kind (the so-called

NOF programme of 2000–2002) teachers were expected to turn up, in their own time, to be lectured on computers and computing. Very few people become experts in new technologies – or anything else – through short courses of lectures supported by printed notes. In this case, very few teachers did become expert.

Several obvious but apparently elusive conclusions follow. First, if we want effective change in schools, teachers need to be treated as partners in formulating and implementing those changes – not as workers whose task is to obey orders from above. Secondly, the changes should make teaching easier and more effective, in the sense of helping students to learn. Third, schools need to be in closer touch with the social, economic and technological changes happening around them. Finally, we need research on the effects of systemic change; proper programmes of change management; time for teachers to acclimatise to new techniques; and adequate training in any innovation. These are not quick or inexpensive processes, which might persuade those advocating scholastic novelties to consider them more thoughtfully.

---

[1] Capital Strategies 2000
[2] Papert 1992
[3] Ibid

CHAPTER 17

PARENTS

In Britain we read, in the conservative press, that 'parents think this', or 'parents say that'. Commonly these nameless parents are objecting to some innovation: to the dumbing-down of an examination, to some meritocratic measure, or to the introduction of meretricious school subjects: media studies for instance. But almost certainly, if we looked more closely, we would find that those in such articulate groups are not representative parents. The people who get such publicity are likely to be an articulate minority, determined to get their children into 'good universities', as a gateway to good (that is, well rewarded) careers. In this respect affluent parents' belief that academic schools should be left alone are, generally, justified. The then UK Minister for Higher Education, speaking in 2002, noted that only 15% of entrants to what she called 'top universities' came from families in the lower half of the UK income range. Thus 'more than 85% of those who go to our top universities come from the top three income groups'.[1] But most of the parents publicised by the conservative press are not those who send their children to fee-charging schools. They might, if they had more disposable cash. As things are, these are people who must make do with 'academic' state schools. Understandably, they wish to be sure that these schools are an efficient conduit to one of the universities of their choice.

Using the state school system might appear cheap and easy, but it may not be either. Britain still has the remnants of a system which once (in the mid-1960s) aspired to equality of educational opportunity. Ambitious parents need, therefore, to circumvent any remaining egalitarian mechanisms, using private tutors, cultural capital and postcode manipulation in order 'to outwit policies designed to promote meritocracy'.[2]

'Parental choice' in Britain, as now widely promoted, is pretty much a myth. If you want your children to go to a 'good school' which does not charge exorbitant fees, you may well have to move to a more expensive house, be creative with your address, or else find God. A study in 2003 concluded that buying a house near a good state school in London could add up to £80,000 to the price. A parent who had paid such a 'school surcharge' for a house was quoted as saying, of herself and her husband, 'We were both privately educated, and I would like to send [my daughter] to private schools, but the costs are huge. We worked out that, by sending her to the local infant and junior schools, we could save £40,000 to £50,000 in fees'.[3] The researcher who led this study of London house prices commented that these parents had paid one of the lower education surcharges. In other urban areas, 'if you cannot afford the [private school] fees, you will not be able to afford the house that gets your kids access to the best state school either'.[4] How is it, a journalist asked recently, that 'despite a government spend of £50 billion on education – £850 for every man, woman and child in the country – the presence of a well-regarded school adds £50,000 to the price of a house?'[5]

Failing to get into a good state school, an ambitious agnostic parent may try for a good church school. For reasons too profound to be investigated here, church school pupils are seen as more likely than their state counterparts to be successful in climbing academic ladders. So desperate parents get religion, attend church, and lever their infants into ecclesiastic schools.

This accelerating scramble for school places is unseemly, undignified, and entirely understandable. A former Downing Street aide, Fiona Millar, in 2004 began a personal crusade to get middle-class parents to send their children to their local state comprehensive, thus 'improving education for everyone'.[6] Such altruistic gestures are commendable and, at least in England, unlikely to succeed. We all want the best for our children, and, as one mother said, we send schools the best children we have. If 'best' for some parents means 'getting my child into a good university' this is a zero-sum game: only some will succeed. The most genteel parents push others aside to make sure their own children have first choice.

Of course, some parents are more skilled than others at working the system. 'Until some way is found radically to reorganise the school system so that it is at once less of a lottery and less stratified, parents will carry on scrabbling for school places, honestly and dishonestly. They will continue to regard each other with suspicion and jealousy, and will remain tiresomely obsessed with the question of where their and other people's children have managed to scrape in'.[7]

If parental ambition were just a matter of scuffling for school places, it might not matter too much, except to those who win, and those who lose. But the consequences are wider. Having got their children into a favoured school, these affluent, articulate parents take the next natural step: they make sure that nothing will hinder the further progress of their young. These well-blessed culturally-capitalised children are likely to be highly literate and to have (or be trained to have) skills in retaining and reproducing information, without closely questioning its value. Reasonably enough, their parents work to maintain school as a setting which rewards precisely those qualities. Despite some puppy-like rushes at assessment reform, university entrance exams in Britain still reward those who are bookish, and who can neatly repeat what was earlier transmitted in the classroom. These exams have significant upstream effect: they alter everything that happens in secondary schools. They affect the school careers of those who aim to pass university entrance exams, those who will not take them, and those may take them, but have no hope of high marks.

Affluent parents, and their allies in the British press, take issue with any attempt to make schools less academic; to attune them more closely to the present day, or to life around them. Any move toward relevance might reduce the upwardly mobile child's chances of success, and make competition tougher by encouraging the streetwise children of the poor. This view is well expressed by the commentator

Melanie Phillips, who has made a profitable middle-aged journey from the left of the political spectrum to the right. Commenting on (ultimately discarded) proposals to reduce the distorting influence of 'academic' schooling, Ms Phillips asks, is there 'a decline in academic rigour? Solved – by stamping out academic rigour altogether. Too many exams burdening pupils? Solved – by destroying the very meaning of exams'.[8] With such influential and well publicised advocates of traditional schooling, affluent parents have little to fear.

Hoping that ambitious parents will behave altruistically is like expecting the lion to lie down with lamb. As the saying goes, only one gets up in the morning. In unequal class-stratified societies – that is, in most societies – schools will cease to be competitive cockpits only when they no longer promise access to scarce goods. To start that process, we need to detach schooling from university entrance. Universities will have to find their own ways of selecting entrants, rather than free-riding on school assessment and, in the process, distorting compulsory education.

Poorer parents often have more urgent issues than pushing their children through school: they worry about staying in work, paying the bills and the rent. They are inclined to trust, or hope, that teachers know what they are doing. Ambitious, affluent parents – outside the fee-charging sector – have no such faith. Doing their best for their children, they help to shape state school systems, and make them resistant to change. That is entirely understandable, but it does mean, in England, that we have a school system adapted to some century other than this.

Affluent parents' influence on our schools might seem to breach the system's closure, but it does not. This group of parents is happy to accept the system's own assessments – and self-assessment – since their aim is to have their offspring do well within the education system, as judged by the system's criteria. A school whose pupils do well in university entrance examinations is thought, by both administrators and parents, to be a successful school. At the time of writing, judgment by league tables appears to satisfy everyone, except perhaps the majority of pupils, and, of course, those who are trying to build a new and more innovative national economy.

---

[1] Margaret Hodge, reported in *The Guardian*, 14.1.2002
[2] Mulgan 2005
[3] *London Evening Standard* 4.9.03
[4] Ibid
[5] Bedell 2002
[6] Ms Millar was thereafter accused by the English *Sunday Times* of 'spelling doom' for middle-class parents
[7] Bedell 2002
[8] Melanie Phillips, 'The immolation of British education' *Daily Mail* 18.10.2004

BUSINESS

'The consequences of technological change are always vast, often unpredictable and largely irreversible. That is also why we must be suspicious of capitalists. Capitalists are by definition not only personal risk takers but, more to the point, cultural risk takers. The most creative and daring of them hope to exploit new technologies to the fullest, and do not much care what traditions are overthrown in the process or whether or not a culture is prepared to function without such traditions. Capitalists are, in a word, radicals. In America, our most significant radicals have always been capitalists – men like Bell, Edison, Ford, Carnegie, Sarnoff, Goldwyn. These men obliterated the 19th century, and created the 20th, which is why it is a mystery to me that capitalists are thought to be conservative. Perhaps it is because they are inclined to wear dark suits and grey ties.'
Neil Postman

If business people are indeed radicals, it is hard to see why they continue to favour a style of schooling which, some time last century, had outlived its economic value. Business, we might think, is one pressure group which would want to move with the times, or even be a little ahead of the curve. As Pearn says 'the pressure of change in the external environments of organisations, whether manufacturing or service providers, whether public, private or voluntary, is such that they need to learn more consciously, more systematically, and more quickly than they did in the past... they must learn not only in order to survive but also to thrive in a world of ever increasing change and ever shortening predictability horizons, whether these are social, technological, political, local or global.'[1] In short, if they are to cope with change in the twenty-first century, businesses need to become learning organisations. And if schools are to meet the needs of business, schools too need to become learning organisations, staffed by people who wish to learn, and who have learned to learn. We might expect business to argue for this.

Is that argument happening? It is not. In the first years of the twenty-first century, most business leaders still echo the conventional wisdoms around schooling. Business managers call for more educational targets (but not for better definition of those targets); for maintaining standards (without defining those standards, or evaluating their usefulness in the world outside education); and for more testing (without questioning what is tested). According to the Confederation for British Industry, schools' task is to teach pupils reading, writing and figuring. 'The CBI said its 2004 survey figures found 83% of businesses thought the education system's first priority should be improving literacy and numeracy levels.'[2] In other words, schools should do no more than they have been doing – or trying to do – for the past two centuries. Doubtless we should all be literate and numerate. But seeing that as the sum of mass schooling's achievement is remarkably short-sighted.

A modest educational prescription may fit with corporate and ministerial inclinations, but seems unlikely to produce the workforce businesses will need in the new economies of coming decades. Why then does the business lobby behave as it does?

Since there is little critical contemporary research on corporate attitudes to education, we can only guess why British business acts against what seem to be its own best interests. A first guess might be that many who speak for businesses do not well understand the social, technological and economic changes going on around them. Alternatively, business people may understand these changes, but believe that they do not apply to their own business model. As Christensen says, 'companies stumble for many reasons... among them bureaucracy, arrogance, tired executive blood, poor planning, short-term investment horizons, inadequate skills and resources, and just plain bad luck.'[3] But, he continues, well-managed companies also misread events: 'companies that have their competitive antennae up, listen astutely to customers, invest aggressively in new technologies... still lose market dominance'.[4]

A third explanation for business complacency is that a generally low level of education and training 'broadly speaking, represents what employers deem their workforce needs to know' and is thus a rational business decision, given the developmental level of most companies. In other words, the barriers to educational change are, in part, those of contemporary British business structure. Among these corporate barriers to educational change, Keep lists 'factors such as stock market and investor pressure to realise short-term shareholder value and maximise profits; product market strategies that are built around the delivery of a narrow range of relatively standardised goods and services, and around price leadership; and the continuing existence of large swathes of employment where low trust, low involvement styles of people management co-exist with Taylorised forms of work organisation and job design where there is little room for genuine discretion, reflection, innovation or learning for those on the shopfloor/front-line.'[5] As always, there are exceptions. Some businesses manage change well. More do not. In this respect US firms tend to do better than their European counterparts, which is one reason why US productivity is higher than in the Eurozone. 'The [US productivity] growth rate jumped to more than 2.5 percent in 1995 and has averaged more than 4 percent since 2001. The difference is dramatic. It takes 50 years for living standards to double if productivity grows at 1.4 percent per year, but only 18 years to double at 4 percent growth...To sustain the productivity surge, today's managers must develop incentives that encourage their workers – as well as themselves – to be more creative, self-starting, educated, and willing to experiment. Jobs that call for simply following recipes will become scarcer, and demand for an innovation-driven workforce will continue to grow.'[6] Though the US has a large educational underclass, and many deplorable schools, it is better than Europe at developing these 'creative and educated' workers – in part because of a different attitude to new technologies, and a different level of openness in learning about them. Most of that learning is done outside school; but schools which are themselves learning organisations are the best preparation we can offer the changing world of business in an information or a knowledge economy. In Britain, a business demand for schools (and for businesses themselves) to become learning organisations is likely to follow a shift from competing as a relatively low-cost economy to competing on unique value and innovation.

In a report commissioned by the Department for Trade and Industry, Porter describes this time as the UK's difficult 'transition to a new phase of economic development' in which 'government, companies, and other institutions need to rethink their policy priorities'. A public consensus on the direction of the transition and on the next stage of the country's competitiveness, Porter continues, 'would help to manage the uncertainties of this process. The absence of such a consensus at a time when the old policy approach is running its course explains much of the puzzlement and even pessimism in the current UK debate. We find that the competitiveness agenda facing UK leaders in government and business reflects the challenges of moving from a location competing on relatively low costs of doing business to a location competing on unique value and innovation. This transition requires investments in different elements of the business environment, upgrading of company strategies, and the creation or strengthening of new types of institutions'.[7] But, Keep adds, 'many firms are very happy with the old way' in part because 'the UK has a relatively low-wage economy, with a large number of poorly paid workers. Many people can only afford to buy goods and services on the basis of price rather than quality, customisation or specification. Satisfying this market produces competitive strategies based on price and standardised products, and firms full of low-paid and low-skilled employees... Most British companies have focused on this domestic market. Research indicates that 39% of them see their competitive focus as local, 21% as regional, 29% as national, and only 10% as international. Most of them rely on UK consumers, many of whom have limited purchasing power. Moreover, globalisation may have very limited impact on domestic markets, especially for many interactive services, eg hotels, retailing and childcare'.[8] Therefore, it seems that, for many firms 'the training currently being provided, broadly speaking, represents what employers deem their workforce needs to know. In other words, companies 'are acting rationally with regard to the markets they face and this strategy is delivering reasonable profits and business success... Unfortunately, for society as a whole, the results may be far from good enough.'[9]

Currently, many British companies see routes to expanded markets which they take to be easier than new systems of production, management and skilling. 'Despite a policy rhetoric that continues to proclaim that skills are the only source of sustainable competitive advantage for organisations in the developed world, the reality is that firms have available to them a variety of other perfectly viable routes to success... For example, as the merger and acquisition wave in banking, insurance, oil, pharmaceuticals, car manufacturing, the media, advertising and the food and drink industries attests, buying out competitors and reaping economy of scale advantages in a global economy represents a much favoured route to success.'[10]

There is also an issue of inertia. In their day-to-day dealings some companies and corporations may be departing from traditional industrial practice; but, as Schumpeter said, mindset and language may linger in a vanishing industrial era. It would follow that inadequate education for a future workforce may not be seen as a drawback; on the contrary, it may seem an insurance against restlessness in those menial jobs which are still prevalent in Britain's relatively low-pay and low-skill economy. In these circumstances, an ideal workforce might be – as it has been for a century and a half – one that is no more than partially trained; consisting of workers who are basically literate and numerate, and willing to obey managerial direction; workers who do not expect to take initiative. If those are desiderata for a large part of the business community, then British schools are probably doing as well as we could hope.

This notion of business marching backwards to the future is supported by the expansion, throughout the 1990s, of what we might call random computerisation. Though this computerisation is ostensibly part of what commentators call the information revolution, it is a revolution that many business people seem not to understand well. Since the 1980s businesses in many countries have spent immense amounts on information technologies. Yet, in terms of profit and productivity, there seems to have been a disproportionately low return on investment. In a much-quoted remark, the economist Robert Solow observed that 'You can see the computer age everywhere but in the productivity statistics'. Why is this? Or, why was this?

In the UK, it is not difficult to find explanations. First, many business people have only a loose understanding of the limitations and the potential of computers and data networks, and do not use digital systems as well as they might. Since computer generations are short, businesses may be at least one digital generation behind the curve. If we think back, the first generations of computers were awkward and limited beasts. They were hard to use; it was assumed that only specialists could use them. They would not do most of the things we felt they should be able to help us with. Computers did not adapt to us: they sat there stolidly, waiting for us to adapt to them. And, mostly, they were stand-alone machines. As with electricity networks in another generation, it took a while to see the force of Sun's slogan, 'the network is the computer'. It took longer to realise that computers could not simply be added into a corporate mix; wider reorganisation was needed. Business is still coming to terms with that huge organisational task. Education is some way behind.

Then, there is the issue of potential. Business communities are not used to technologies whose power increases geometrically. The electric motor was a revolutionary technology. 'Electric motors powered machines separately, and therefore often required factories to be redesigned. Industrial architects knew nothing of electricity, and finding the proper layout and organization took much experimentation. Full adoption took 40 years.'[11] But electric motors – for all their disruptive effect on business – did not constitute a technology capable of geometric growth. Digital technologies do. Understandably, business people find it hard to see what such growth might mean in practice. They may know that computer chips went from incorporating about 275,000 transistors in 1987 to around 400,000,000 in 2005. But it is still hard to see the potential of machines which, in twenty years, may be a thousand times more powerful (and, possibly, in real terms, cheaper) than they are today. What might we do with such processing power? We can only guess.

It may seem hard to believe that highly paid, shrewd businessmen do not understand the revolution going on around them. But, for those who doubt it, we had a graphic demonstration of that fact in the financial carnival of the 1990s. Hardheaded business people invested hundreds of billions of dollars in pretty much anything with 'internet', 'digital' or 'telecoms' somewhere in the promotional literature. Notoriously, they threw money at companies which had never made a profit and never seemed likely to. Even allowing for inflation, billions were wasted on fragile dotcoms and obsolescent telcos. As Bunker Hunt once said, 'a billion here, a billion there, and pretty soon you're talking real money'. Showered with real money, conmen, CEOs, corporate shysters and crooked accountants made hay. Auditors were caught up in the irrational exuberance, and – in companies like Enron and WorldCom – participated in the profiteering. Finding they had to make a choice between their paymasters and their principles, many auditors chose the former. Investors, starry eyed, believed the fictional figures. They accepted the numbers; they followed where businessmen and venture capitalists led. Of course most invested funds, large and small, vanished; or vanished from where they were supposed to be. When the bubble burst it was small investors who, as always, suffered most. They had followed the lead of shrewd businessmen but, unlike them, were using their own savings. After the dotcom collapse, the world economy went into limited recession, multiplying investors' pain. There are several morals to all this – but one of them must be 'do not believe that businessmen always know what the next business will be'. Most of the financial community was, it seems, as dazed and confused as the rest of us by the nascent information age.

Nor were governments much better. The economist Joseph Stiglitz, writing of the US, notes that 'misguided deregulation and bad tax policies were at the core of the 1999 recession, and misguided deregulation, misguided tax policies and misguided accounting practices were at the core of the [post-2000] downturn'.[12] Corporations were aided by government funds, at the expense of infrastructure, education and basic research – the building blocks of post-industrial economies. The dotcom boom was related to new technologies only in demonstrating how poorly they were, and are, understood. In the long view, there is a central issue of adaptation – of digital technologies to us, and of us to them. This will not be quick. Like other innovations, digital technologies will take time to mature. 'The enabling technologies of the steel and electricity revolution... had arrived by the 1870s, but their full effects were not felt until well into the 1900s... Whether railroads or microchips, a revolution doesn't fully arrive until we structure our activities – our organizations and business methods – around its technologies, and until these technologies adapt themselves to us by becoming comfortable and easy to use... What's needed for the revolution to fully blossom are the 1,001 subtechnologies, arrangements, and architectures that adapt us to the new technologies and them to us. Their arrival takes time, and it defines the buildout period as one that creates the arrangements and subtechnologies that bring the new possibilities into full use.'[13]

We are still going through this adaptation process, and will be for years. Business people are still finding out what all this will mean for business and for education in the immediate future. Vision doesn't stretch much further, or deeper, than that. So it is hardly surprising that the business community has not paid close attention to schooling; and that the community does not know what kind of schools are needed for those who will work for business in the future – people whose working lives may span another four decades. But when business people do stop to think about it, they can be sure of one thing: our present pattern of schooling will not meet their needs. At some stage, the business community will collectively reach that conclusion. When it does, we shall see significant change in our schools.

---

[1] Pearn 1997
[2] BBC News Online 21.8.2005
[3] Christensen 2003
[4] Ibid
[5] Keep 2003
[6] Brynjolfsson 2004
[7] Porter and Ketels 2003
[8] Keep 2003
[9] Ibid
[10] Ibid
[11] Arthur 2002
[12] Stiglitz 2003
[13] Ibid

CHAPTER 19

POLITICIANS

If you don't get involved with politics, politics will get involved with you.
  Attributed to Lenin

Politicians who control school systems have several difficulties. The first is knowing just what they control. For most of us, direct experience of schools ends when we are in our teens and, since schools are not places of general interest, knowledge in depth ends there too. British politicians are further removed, for most have been part of our educational elite. They did not go to state schools, nor do they send their children to them. Some are nostalgic for the exclusive schools which gave them 'the best days of their lives' (a thought which most normal people find deeply depressing).

There is also an element of 'look where it got me'. Understandably, politicians regard themselves as successful people. If a certain sort of schooling helped them to reach their present eminence, then it must have been good. This goes some way to explain the political determination – which altered only briefly in the mid-sixties – to reinforce the traditional 80:20 model of British schooling. Among politicians, this backward view is still sometimes manifest as nostalgia for 'real school': that mythical schoolhouse where venerated teachers stand at the front of each class, dispensing information to clean, attentive, uniformed pupils, who sit silent, in orderly rows.

'Real school' may not be mentioned, but there have been a number of English measures apparently designed to return pupils to that lost scholastic garden. Among Britain's recent Prime Ministers, Mr Callaghan in 1976 made clear (if it had not been clear before) his support for retrogressive schooling and – which is not the same thing – for curricula which were more responsive to the putative needs of industry and commerce. These lines of thought opened a season of conservative attacks on state schools. Critics argued, among other things, that 'the freedom of schools to choose their own curriculum was a major cause of the low levels of attainment of the majority of pupils'.[1]

Mrs Thatcher (who followed Mr Callaghan to 10 Downing Street) shared the former tenant's view of schools. As Prime Minister, openly in favour of scholastic elitism, she strengthened it by encouraging the growth of private schooling, and by establishing a number of City Technology Colleges more generously funded and selective than the majority of state schools. CTCs were often successful in raising system-defined standards, but inevitably they increased inequality within the school system.

Mrs Thatcher's successor, John Major, proposed building grammar schools 'in every town' – his remembered towns 'of long shadows on cricket grounds, warm beer, invincible green suburbs'. In the event, Mr Major retired to the neighbourhood of a famous cricket ground before his envisioned schools could be built.

Since 1997, Mr Blair has followed his predecessors' example with a building programme for state-financed, but often privately controlled, city academies. He has also attempted to privatise at least the richer (or more religious) parts of the state school system. In this and other ways – and perhaps inadvertently – Labour's radical-right approach to schooling preserves, or covertly strengthens, existing social hierarchies and makes an already unbalanced school system more unequal.[2]

For other politicians, preserving hierarchies has been a more explicit aim. Though they may not say it aloud, some Ministers and their publicists have continued to believe that we are all in our allotted stations, and that to each there is appropriate education.[3] This seemed to be the conclusion at which the former education minister, Sir Keith Joseph, arrived. In a speech given in Birmingham he argued that 'the cycle of social deprivation... was attributed to a combination of the young and poor in a climate of sexual freedom perpetuating a deprived class with little effective hope of self-improvement'.[4] In this view, leaving your social station upsets a beneficent social order. It is a time-honoured outlook. As the educator Hannah More long ago explained, children in her care would learn 'on week-days, such coarse work as may fit them for servants'; to which she added that 'I allow no writing for the poor. My object is not to make fanatics, but to train up the lower classes in habits of industry and piety'.[5] And for politicians – both conservative and more ostensibly progressive – industry and piety remain scholastic aims. Mrs Thatcher, when Prime Minister, argued 'a strong practical case for ensuring that children at school are given adequate instruction in the part which the Judaic-Christian tradition has played in moulding our laws, manners, and institution... But I go further than this. The truths of the Judaic-Christian tradition are infinitely precious, not only, as I believe, because they are true, but also because they provide the moral impulse which alone can lead to that peace, in the true meaning of the word, for which we all long' – sentiments which would have been familiar to pupils of eighteenth-century ragged schools.[6] Since then, Mr Blair has supported the teaching of fundamental Christianity and creationism in state-financed schools, a stance some scientists have, kindly, attributed to the Prime Minister's 'lack of understanding'.[7] Mr Blair, 'said to be the most religious Prime Minister since Gladstone', has backed the millionaire car dealer Sir Peter Vardy in his attempt to take over seven comprehensive schools and turn them into Christian Academies promoting what purport to be Old Testament views of the world's creation. This may or may not (for the schools are reluctant to give details) include the claim that the world was made in six days, about 10,000 years ago.

There are, of course, many politicians who are not resistant to change in schools. Over the past decade there have been dozens of politically mandated top-down initiatives pressed upon the British school system. In terms of educational effect, many have been counterproductive. Those tend to last, since they fit the culture of the system. Others are well intentioned and promising: enterprise education, creative partnerships, personalised learning, continuous assessment, project-based examinations, 'leading edge initiatives', citizenship programmes, global development, digital curricula, among others. But, though there have been local successes, none of these has had a lasting systemic effect. When we look across the school system we see that the positive initiatives have fallen at the hurdles of large, ill-managed schools; inflexible and overcrowded curricula; political micro-management; academic hierarchies; didactic teaching; the one-to-many control ratio of our classrooms; our focus on teaching, rather than learning; our concentration on 'legitimate knowledge' and devaluation of personal knowledge; inadequate learning materials; the short timespan (and often inadequate funding) of centrally imposed innovations; inadequate teacher education (and consultation); insufficient time to prepare for the mandated initiative; or resistance – perhaps justified – from some of a targeted school's staff. In short, authoritarian innovations tend to stick; but, in an unfriendly culture, more positive initiatives are unlikely to last.

As a result, despite some political efforts to the bring schools into the twenty-first century, they remain fixed in the mould of a past era and a vanishing economy. As we have seen, the central and lasting innovations of recent years are (for those interested in learning) negative: school league tables, targeting and testing, micro-management, and the central imposition of 'basic curricula'.

Politicians – those who genuinely wish to modernise schools – face a more general difficulty: as we have seen, they find it hard to know what schools are for. Their child-minding function can be achieved through compulsory school attendance, sharper penalties for truanting (up to and including imprisoning the parents of truants), and by lengthening the school day, as is planned at the time of writing.

But 'preparing a future workforce' is a more difficult task. Like aging generals, politicians prepare (or prepare others) to fight the last war, and hope that the next will be much the same. The Prime Minister's office looks back to education for an industrial economy even as the Prime Minister speaks of information, globalisation and economic transformation.

Among Britain's government departments only the Treasury currently dissents, suggesting that schools might do things differently, without saying exactly how. And this absence of practical solutions is not surprising. In the last forty years we have had no serious systemic attempt at encouraging learning, individuation and equity. Despite the best efforts of researchers and thinktank philosophers, we still have no politically and educationally acceptable conception of comprehensive schooling to counter politicians' taken-for-granted elitism, and to replace the now commonly discredited comprehensive models of the mid-twentieth century.

For various reasons, then, politicians across the political spectrum are likely to be conservative (perhaps nostalgic, perhaps reactionary) when it comes to schools, and to present that conservatism as modernisation. Post-1997 Labour administrations have continued, and sometimes reinforced, the measures of previous governments. If we make the generous assumption that Mr Blair's governments are not essentially elitist, we must assume that Ministers believe these measures will improve the quality of schooling, and are appropriate for Britain's twenty-first-century post-industrial economy and society. If that assumption is true, we have a situation where Labour's rhetoric of the post-industrial age may be well intentioned but, in the last analysis, is almost as socially and economically damaging as their opponents' more open attachment to hierarchies of class.

Politicians, though, are not immune to pressure. When it comes to schools, they respond to articulate parents, to their favoured media, and to business lobbies. We have seen that all of these, in different ways, still underpin a conservative approach to the school system. That, though, will change. At some point universities will cease to base their entry procedures on school examinations, thus removing a main reason for parents to support anachronistic curricula and teaching methods. And, at some future date, business lobbies will push for education which prepares young people for a future economy, rather than for one now disappearing. When those changes happen, politicians will respond, and our school system will change. Whether the changes will benefit learners remains an open question.

---

[1] Young 1998

[2] The notion that Labour is making the school system more unequal 'inadvertently' is hard to defend after the government's reforms proposed in 2005 (see chapter 8).

[3] See chapter 4.

[4] Keith Joseph obituary, The Guardian 12.12.1994

[5] Roberts 1856

[6] Margaret Thatcher addressing the leaders of the Church of Scotland on May 21, 1988

[7] School attacked over evolution teaching, BBC News Online 22.3.2002

THE DISRUPTIVE TECHNOLOGY THAT DIDN'T

'Take this very important art and turn it into something as convenient as the pencil.'
George Eastman

'The network is the computer.'
Sun Microsystems

'In their capacity as a tool, computers will be but a ripple on the surface of our culture. In their capacity as intellectual challenge, they are without precedent in the cultural history of mankind.'
Esdger Dijkstra

Some technologies are sustaining: they encourage you to do today (hopefully better) what you did yesterday. Some technologies – the disruptive ones – do not. They undermine, and eventually transform, an earlier way of working.

Almost everywhere, computers and networks are disruptive technologies: they change the way organisations, and people, work. They are changing the way we live. Except in schools. In schools, computing has become a sustaining technology. Schools have tamed digital networks: drawn their teeth. As Papert has said of school computing 'what had started as a subversive instrument of change was neutralised by the system and converted into an instrument of consolidation'.[1] To take just one example, electronic whiteboards – a widely acclaimed twenty-first century innovation in British schools – are so clearly digital cousins of the traditional chalkboard that they have hardly ruffled the surface of the didactic paradigm.

There are several reasons for this negation of computing's potential. One, noted earlier, is the confusion and inefficiency of the political process in the commissioning of information technology. Over past decades large amounts of money have been spent on IT – much of it not spent well. 'The [British] government already spends £14bn a year on computer systems and services, the highest figure in Europe, and double the sum spent in 1999. The public sector accounts for 55 per cent of the whole UK market for IT.'[2] Does the country get value for this significant sum of money? 'The government's confidence in IT to drive new policies is remarkable, given the reputation for failure of public sector computer projects.'[3] There are good reasons for these failures. One is 'inexperience among civil servants and the frequent lack of a senior figure capable of getting a grip on a project that is going awry'.[4] As of 2005 'seventy risky Whitehall computer projects have received secret "red warnings" that they will fail to deliver unless immediate action is taken to rectify problems'.[5] Some of these projects may

185

have been educational (despite being publicly funded, they were not named 'for reasons of commercial confidentiality') but it is unlikely, for it is hard find evidence when educational IT projects are going wrong; or, indeed, when they are going right.

That is due to the self-referential nature of school systems. Since there are no shareholders, and few reality checks, school systems can, and do, get away with getting things wrong. Information technology is one of the more expensive mistakes. If a business misconceives its computer systems, if they are misused, or if they terminally malfunction, the firm either goes broke (and, globally, this is a main cause of business bankruptcy) or it rapidly puts things right. In the case of schools, that rarely happens. Instead, teachers and pupils adapt to mistakes. They have no choice. In closed systems, mistakes are not evident, except to those who must live with them.

The trouble started last century when politicians first saw computers as a transformative technology – a way of modernising schools systems. But that missed the point. It was not computers which were transformative: it was networks, and the ways in which both were used. On the part of those who specified technology for schools, concentrating on machines – and the wrong sort of machines – was not a small miscalculation, like buying one brand rather than another; something to be rectified at the next upgrade. It was a category error, which is proving hard to undo.

In the 1980s, administrators started, and have continued, to buy desktop machines: a policy which has had significant educational consequences. It is hard to uncover either technological or educational reasons for this decision. Certainly it was not in response to teacher demand. Unsurprisingly, most teachers had a poor understanding of computers when they started coming into schools and (at least in the early days) found that computers made working life more difficult. The desktop purchasing policy, however, was supported by politicians, most of whom had, and have, a limited understanding of computing.[6] Useful guidance could have been found in the work of educational computing's pioneers – Papert, Kay, Minsky – but those sources were unknown or ignored. As a result, quantities of large computers have been bought and installed in schools. Many of those machines were put into 'computer suites' or 'computer labs': both convenient terms for rooms with a number of computers. Over the last decade it has become common also to find one or more desktop machines in classrooms and school libraries. A growing number of teachers now have laptops, either their own, or belonging to the school. Very few pupils are so equipped. This spread of computing kit has led to much uninformed and self-congratulatory discussion of 'pupil-computer ratios' – yet the fundamental difficulties of on-demand networked access for teachers and learners remain unchanged.

In the nineties most British schools were 'networked', but these networks are, as a rule, hard-wired, and were used mainly for connecting one machine to another. More recently, government sources have publicised the (quite high) percentage of schools 'connected to the internet'. This, however, does not tell us much about learners' usage, any more than 'the number of houses with electric power' would tell us about householders' use of electrical devices. Anecdotal evidence suggests that very few pupils – and not too many teachers – have on-demand access to the net. Schneiderman rightly notes that 'as long as school administrators only count how many classrooms are connected to the internet, or how many computers have been purchased, there will be little educational progress'.[7]

In most schools now, when you want to use a machine, you go to where it is, and hope that it is not already in use. It is a long time since Negroponte remarked that we should 'move bits, not atoms'; computing power and digital content should come to us, not we to it. It has taken even longer to get the message through to schools, for fixed desktop machines imply several things. One is rationing: since there are fewer machines than students, anyone's time with the computer will be limited. It will be very limited if the computers are in a suite, for then the room has to be booked in advance, and pupils must move there at the appointed moment.

Installed in schools in the 1990s, computers became, in a sense, sacralised: they were objects to be approached respectfully. The short history of educational computing brings to mind an earlier technology worship, at the start of the twentieth century. Then Henry Adams saw electricity and its great generators as sacred artefacts. Adams felt about electricity generation, he said, 'much as early Christians felt about the cross'.[8] Writing of one well-crafted generator – at which he spent whole days in contemplation – Adams confesses that, 'before the end, one began to pray before it; inherited instinct taught the natural expression of man before silent and infinite force'.[9]

Today's silent and infinite force, both electric and digital, is embodied in schools' computers. These are in line of descent from teaching machines, those unhappy attempts to bring electronic technologies into late-twentieth-century schools. Teaching machines are, as the name implies, a part of schools' didactic paradigm. Since the original computing configuration made machines – not the network – primary, schools looked for things which stand-alone machines could do: repetitive instruction (given the oxymoronic label 'programmed learning'); word processing; spreadsheets; database construction, and so on. In the UK there are even 'computer curricula' which, as someone said, is rather like having a curriculum for pencils.

Since they have no efficient means of rectifying systemic mistakes, school systems become expert in rationalising them. Thus with static computing: there are firms which specialise in supplying more and more inappropriate machines; we have advisors telling teachers how to use them; we have shelves loaded with documentation on computer-assisted teaching; and we have IT experts maintaining these anachronistic networks. An early British advisory quango – the National Advisory Council for Educational Technology (NCET) – succumbed to a form of technological necrophilia: it pressed upon schools a series of technologies clearly in their death throes. Its renamed successor, the British Educational Communications and Technology Agency (Becta), has a better track record. But, as part of education's closed system, Becta is still inclined to uncritical applause of whatever its state paymasters may decide.

At one remove from schools there are academic centres which specialise in 'educational technology'. Some of these are part of the rationalisation industry: they find new – and not always useful – ways of using the unsuitable kit now in schools. Other groups are more adventurous: they invent or develop cool digital gadgets, most of which are, in classroom terms, solutions looking for problems. Few, within schools or without, admit that it is schools' computers themselves, their networks, and the pedagogies they support, which are at the heart of the educational problem.

THE MOBILE AND THE PHONE BOX

Co-opted into the teaching machine tradition, computers have been robbed of their transformative potential to enhance learning. In the early years of this century, the problem for schools is to restore that possibility: to turn computers and networks into tools for research, into aids to learning, and a window on the world outside the classroom. The question now is: how do we do that? To which the answer is twofold: first, we need to change the technology; and, second, we need different ways of using it.

By analogy, the technology change will be a shift from phone box to mobile. Mobile phones go where you go. Phone boxes are of course fixed. You go to them. At base, they are both phones – but their uses, their affordances, are very different. For school computing, the mobile phone model assumes that learners will have their own lightweight computer, or wireless-networked device, which goes where they go, rather than having learners go to where the computer is.

When people on the move had to rely on phone boxes, usage was relatively low. Often it was (and still is) hard even to find a phone box. When you did find one there was no guarantee it would be working. Phone boxes did just three things. They got you out of the rain and, if they worked, and if you had the right change, they took your cash and let you make a voice call. Those calls were likely to be made with some urgency, and to be relatively brief.

Mobiles are different. They are personalised; they go with you. They are easy to use. They can do, if you want, fifty different things. Billions of voice calls, text messages, picture messages, diary entries, business cards, calculations, spreadsheets, photos, songs, websites, ringtones, payments, articles, radio programmes, television programmes, games and videos are sent to and from mobile phones every week.

Similarly, the different models of school computing have different patterns of use. As we have seen, pupils can use fixed computers only sporadically – when teacher says; when the person ahead has finished; or, with a computer suite, when the room has been booked. We would think it odd if a classroom had only two ballpoints, which pupils shared; but, with computers, that is an accepted pattern. Limited access has several consequences. One is that 'computing' can become a limited end in itself, with its own curriculum, aims and targets. Pupils have to learn applications which do more efficiently what could be done with pencil and paper.

Another consequence is that computers are used to deliver 'independent learning systems' and other training programs for drill and practice in low-level skills.

There are things, too, which fixed computers, shared among many, cannot do. Generally they cannot be used to support active learning, or pupils' research, or continuous assessment. Phone box computing is commonly confined to sporadically supporting the lower levels of school work.

The mobile computing model is radically different, both in hardware and software, and what can be done with both. In the mobile model all learners have a computer terminal which goes where they want it. We cannot say just what this personalised educational device might be like – since we don't yet have an ideal example – but we can describe its characteristics. It will have a screen and either a keyboard of usable size or very good handwriting recognition; or both. It will be wireless-networked, light, cheap, and reasonably rugged. It will have long battery life. It might be a thin client; it might be in tablet format. Until someone comes up with a better name, call it a workpad. At the time of writing, the closest approximations are India's Simputer and the 'hundred dollar laptop' (HDL) prototypes from MIT's Media Lab.

How practicable is this vision of personalised mobile educational computing? If we thought of a standard laptop for each learner, it would fall at the first hurdle for, though laptop costs are dropping, the national cost, even for richer countries, would be formidable. But if we work on the analogy of a mobile phone for each person, it becomes practicable. After all, in richer countries, most of us now carry phones. So we need to start from scratch and consider a machine made specifically for education and training – like the HDL – and for mass purchase. It would be a device simplified to do only what it absolutely needs to do; probably more than the Simputer, but less than a standard laptop. Construction cost and profit would need to be cut to the bone, so that we could afford, from a year's information technology budget, to give a workpad to every pupil and trainee in Britain.

Would a machine priced between $US100 and $US150 be an attractive proposition for a manufacturer? It might, if we consider the international market which, conservatively, might be in the order of several hundred million workpads. Even with, say, $20 profit per machine, that would be a significant sum; leaving aside the publicity value of making a real contribution to global education and training. At the time of writing, MIT is confident that its HDL will be manufactured at, or near, the advertised price point.

What would follow, if all students had a workpad, or an HDL, with them whenever they were learning? There are many possibilities. One is that the computer would be taken for granted, as ballpoints are taken for granted. We don't have classes in ballpoints, or curricula for them. They become simply a tool for doing something more interesting. Another possibility for workpads is personalising the machines, so that your screen shows only your own programs and your own work. Though it would not be easy to arrange, personalisation could lead to individuation (or quasi-individuation), so that a number of learners together could be working with different curricula, or different assignments, or different learning styles (text-based or graphic, for example).

We can imagine two learners sitting side by side, one researching, say, the effects of altitude on athletic performance, the other setting out the arguments for and against the testing of drugs on animals. If the two girls had different learning styles, their curricula would allow for that. The difficulties, and cost, of such individual programming have to be weighed against the social and educational advantages. (It would certainly be a better investment than Britain's expensive exercises in 'digitising the curriculum'.)

Individuation would solve one of the persistent problems with comprehensive schooling. Comprehensives are socially desirable but, in learning as elsewhere, one size does not fit all. We all learn in different ways, at different speeds. We want to learn different things. However we configure traditional classrooms, one teacher cannot simultaneously offer different curricula – or even different styles of teaching and learning – to twenty or thirty pupils. But mobile computers could do that, freeing the teacher to help those who need help, when they need it, on a tutorial basis.

Today most approaches to individuation openly or covertly undermine the comprehensive principle by separating, streaming, setting or selecting pupils, often on the basis of arbitrary 'academic' criteria (see chapter 8). Clearly this practice is socially regressive and perpetuates the English disease of educational discrimination. Separating academic sheep from non-academic goats – as schools commonly do – also works against the innovative principle of the knowledge-based economies in which young people may spend their working lives. A knowledge economy depends on a high level of productive and sustainable innovation. But any study of innovation shows that sheep do not, in this arena, perform particularly well.

Workpads will offer universal wireless connectivity to the web, giving learners access to the visual arts, to new technologies, to the history, the present and the future of the natural sciences, to news, to indices of climate change, to video… a window on the endlessly rich and various world outside the classroom.

Such ambient information has wide implications for current school-system practice. Though educators are sometimes reluctant to say so, memorising facts has always been central to schooling. But if millions of facts and figures are within instant reach, does it make sense to memorise them? In the twenty-first century, why should we continue with present patterns of memorisation for its own sake? It may have been sensible to remember the succession of kings, or the number of genes in a nematode, when such information was hard to find. It makes little sense when information is immanently available on the web, on extranets and on intranets.

Of course this does not mean there is nothing we need to remember. We cannot find information we want unless we know where to look for it. Nor will it be useful, once found, unless we know how to assess it, and have the intellectual structures which will set it in context. In other words, information makes sense only when we have a mental context in which we can first find it and (a related task) set it in a conceptual framework. Only then can we judge it. For this century, creating those mental and epistemological contexts will be a central task of school systems.

Individual workpads open other possibilities. It is generally agreed that we learn best when we are finding out about something that interests us. In dignified terms, this is self-selected research. It is hard to organise learners' individual research in traditional classrooms, partly because of their information poverty. A pupil is unlikely to find answers to her questions among a classroom's books, unless the teacher has already prepared answers for those questions; and that means the learner is researching a question of the teacher's choice, not her own. Universal access to the web changes that. Thereafter, the problem may not be information poverty, but information overload. The learner's skill – a valuable one these days – will be knowing how to winnow the information, to assess its provenance, its worth, and its truth value.

To date, the real lesson of two decades of school computing is that (to paraphrase a commercial slogan) it is the networks, not the computers, which are at the heart of the matter. Schools are, to a large degree, closed environments, intellectually and physically separated from the community around them. Data networks lessen that separation. They put learners in closer touch with the world outside school. We already see pupils in email (or, more rarely, audio or video) contact with other students, in this country or abroad. Other pupils get in touch with experts for answers to problems they cannot solve at school. Mobile computing would enlarge those possibilities. We can now envisage international networks of schools and learners which would have been impossible a decade ago.

Finally, individual workpads would transform assessment. Most assessment now happens too late to be of much use (see chapter 7). Unless she gets a hundred per cent in a test, the learner finds that she could have done better. But there is no chance to do better, because the assessment refers to a closed case: to work that has been done, and cannot be undone or redone. A sophisticated school network could offer something different – continuous assessment which not only monitors pupils' progress, but suggests new directions at points of intellectual impasse. Like individualised curricula, continuous assessment programs would be difficult and expensive to build. But the rewards, in terms of learning and creativity, would make the effort worthwhile.

Of course if school pupils had wireless-networked workpads, teachers too would need to have – and use – wireless networked machines. The only way to be easy with networks is to make use of them constantly. Contrary to official belief, 'short courses in computing for teachers' are no substitute for that familiarity which comes from digital experimentation and the regular use we make of networks when we find that they do make at least some things in life a little easier and more interesting.

In summary, it is technically and financially possible to change the model of school computing – and associated models of learning – from phone box to mobile. Something similar has been accomplished in the world outside schools. Mobile computing in schools is educationally and socially desirable. It can be done now. Sooner or later, it will be. The question is, how soon? Or how late?

There is a wider issue, beyond putting right past mistakes. It is a commonplace, but true, that there are rapid – and sometimes radical – changes in the networked world. Significant decisions in the education system are at the opposite pole: they are, as a rule, made and implemented very slowly. It follows that we should, now, occupy ourselves in assessing where electronic networks will be in five years time. We should be preparing schools, and educating teachers, for that future. To date, education's generals have been resolutely fighting the last digital war. In a fast-moving field, they might now turn their attention the next.

---

[1] Papert 1992
[2] Cross, M, *Prospect* October 2005
[3] Ibid
[4] Ibid
[5] Hencke, D, *The Guardian* 5.7.05
[6] By 2002 the Parliamentary Select Committee on Information reported that still 'few Members have effective systems for dealing with the host of e-mails which come into their offices each day', noting too that email is one of the simplest computer-assisted applications.
http://www.publications.parliament.uk/pa/cm200102/cmselect/cminform/1065/106505.htm#a9
[7] Schneiderman 2002
[8] Adams 1995
[9] Ibid

VI SCHOOLS FOR THE FUTURE

CHAPTER 21

SCHOOLS FOR THE TWENTY-FIRST CENTURY

'What kind of education will best prepare students for life in a knowledge society? Typical answers to this question list characteristics that such education should foster: flexibility, creativity, problem-solving ability, technological literacy, information-finding skills, and above all a lifelong readiness to learn... But there is another way of approaching the question. It is to consider what kind of experience offers the best preparation for life in a knowledge society. The obvious answer is experience in a learning organization. The implications of this disarming answer are quite radical, however. For if schools are to constitute the learning organizations in which students gain experience, the role of students must change from that of clients to that of members, workers. This means changing the function of the school from that of service provider to that of a productive enterprise to which the students are contributors. But what is that productive enterprise? What are the students contributors to?'
　　Marlene Scardamalia and Carl Bereiter

'As perceptions change regarding the economic necessity to improve basic skill levels and provide access to learning for all on a lifetime basis, technologically assisted methods of teaching and other "learning technologies" must move centre stage.'
　　Alan Burton-Jones

'The economic product of the United States has become predominantly conceptual.'
　　Alan Greenspan

Assume that politicians will (at some point) decide that the nation needs in its workforce more people who are innovative, inventive, curious and critical – and that will imply, among other things, a reshaping of our school system. Given contemporary economic trends, the early twenty-first century might be a good time to undertake that reshaping.

There are not many fortunate junctures in the history of schooling, but this may be one of them. Perhaps for the first time in history, the needs of national economies are converging with the needs of learners. We are moving toward a new type of economic structure (see chapter 14) which will make new demands of our school system, and open new doors for pupils. According to Britain's Chancellor of the Exchequer, speaking in 2005, 'if China and India are turning out 4 million graduates a year, then we cannot afford to waste the talent of any child, write off the potential of any young person, discard the abilities of any adult. It is because the skills of workers are the new commanding heights of the economy, it is because the skills of working people are now the most critical means of production, it is because increasingly it is the skills of working people that gives companies value and gives nations comparative advantage, that new principles must guide education and training in ensuring good well paying jobs for the future.'[1]

All that, of course, depends on the quality of education and training. If the coming economy needs people who are generally smarter, readier to adapt to change, and will continue learning through life, these are surely qualities that any school should foster. But most do not. They cannot, for they were designed to serve economies that preferred obedience to intelligence in their workers. A school system which caters efficiently for a vanishing social and industrial order cannot also prepare for one that is new.

So how might schools take advantage of the opportunities that new economies offer? How can they begin to do what educators have desired since the time of Socrates – give precedence to learning, adaptability and creativity? How can schools turn themselves into learning organisations?

A first step is to isolate the training component in schooling. We may still need a centrally imposed linimal qualification without which no one should leave school: we all need to be literate, to count, and to be competent with the technologies of a networked society. But that is as far as a national prescription for training should go. It may be that more specialised pursuits (biogenetic analysis, sculpting, engineering, film making, and so on) will need their own regimes of basic training, but clearly these are not subjects for central prescription.

In all of these cases it's reasonable to say that, since training has defined outcomes, we can find optimal instructional methods – though, as many people have pointed out, we may not have found them yet. After all, we have been teaching reading for centuries. The evidence suggests that we have not become much better at it.

Training should be an important, but quite limited, part of schooling. If it becomes dominant – as it often is now – we ought to ask why. Is it because schools are doing it badly, and training routines take more time and effort than they should? Or is it because those who run schools confuse training with education? Is it because training exercises are easier to devise and to mark? Whatever the answer, we are getting it wrong. We should be doing things otherwise. And, if we are to have a national curriculum (with associated and centrally planned micro-management), it should be limited to the training sector of the school system. We cannot micro-manage real education.

With training defined and delimited, schools could concentrate on the more important task: fostering pupils' ability, and wish, to learn. This of course is anathema to those who believe that a teacher's task is to transmit information through instruction. And in a sense, the traditionalists are right. Information transmission and genuine learning are incompatible. Being lectured has never been a good way to learn. It certainly does not foster interest in continuing to learn. What traditionalists find hard to accept is that, as between learning and instruction, learning is, by some distance, the more important. The British government's 2005 proposals for reforming schools show that politicians, too, find the distinction difficult (see chapter 8).

Moving schools' focus to learning is a paradigm shift: one that depends on a change both in political attitudes and in teachers' philosophy and practice. That is an easy thing to recommend and – for reasons outlined above – hard to do. It implies a change in control, in hierarchies and in mindset. Central control of school knowledge, deskilling of teachers and micro-management of teaching are designed to underpin instructional regimes (though the jury is out on whether they successfully do that). But even the most optimistic administrator would not argue that these structures encourage individual learning, creativity or independent initiative.

The histories of autocracy and democracy show how hard it is to replace centrally ordered hierarchies with more flexible and more democratic ways of working. Yet that is what we shall have to do, if we want schools well adapted to a century in which looser, nimbler and more adaptive organisations are likely to be the norm.

Which brings us back to a structural problem common to all school systems. As noted, we have a traditional classroom pattern of one teacher to many pupils – which lends itself to instruction, and is not conducive to individual learning. We all want to learn different things at different times, and we learn in different ways. But most of the time, in most classes, the teacher is instructing the whole class. It is hard to treat students as individuals: classroom structure prevents any real move toward individuation of learning. As Scardamalia puts it, 'Why won't teachers turn higher levels of cognitive responsibility over to students? Answers may be sought in the need to maintain a position of authority and in disbelief in the capacity of students to shoulder such responsibility. But prior to these is a concrete fact of life: the ratio of one teacher to 30 or so students. This condition not only favours a centralized management structure; it also severely constrains the kind of discourse that can go on. As analysts of classroom discourse have observed, classroom exchanges are usually both initiated and terminated by the teacher... a typical exchange will start with the teacher asking a question, followed by a response from a student, and terminated by a remark by the teacher, often followed immediately by the initiation of a new exchange; e.g., "Right. And what did the British do then?" With such a discourse structure, it should not be surprising that all the higher-level control of the discourse is exercised by the teacher. The students are cast into a perpetually reactive and receptive role.'[2] But, given that this is the way schools are – one teacher to many pupils – how do we achieve a learning environment: how do we achieve what Scardamalia calls 'a sharing of cognitive responsibility'?

A large part of the answer lies in another radical shift: a move from schools' traditional didactic mode (chapter 5) to one better adapted to learning and to individuation. In the twenty-first century, that implies new uses of digital technologies and networks (or uses which are at least new to school systems). At some point schools will make a radical shift from didactic and print-based technologies to their successors. That shift, when it happens, will not be about doing better today what we did yesterday: technological transformation is worthwhile only if it is linked with radical improvements in teaching and learning; a rethinking of what is to be learned, and how it might be learned.

The socioeconomic opening to new scholastic structures has come at an historic moment when new technologies make its implementation more possible. Inevitably we will at some stage move to the provision of a personal networked device for each learner (chapter 20). Well used, these will open new avenues for individual learning.

As schools change, teaching practice must change. Learning in school is a concomitant – but not a necessary consequence – of good teaching. In a reorganised school system, teachers will be more important, and more autonomous, than they are today; but they will work in a digital and networked, rather than print-based, system. Teachers will no longer be students' principal source of information. That will be the internet, or some other searchable data network. Teaching will move toward a tutorial model; and, within appropriate intellectual structures, learning will be more a matter of students' active research rather than passive absorption of information.

Some of the likely changes have been noted earlier, and are here only briefly recalled:

Rethinking memorisation. We have seen that memorisation of facts still takes up much of the time pupils spend at school but, when most of the facts we might need can be drawn instantly from ambient data networks, why would we continue to memorise them? David and Foray note that 'new technologies, which first emerged in the 1950s and then really took off with the advent of the internet, have breathtaking potential. They enable remote access to information and the means of acquiring knowledge. In addition to transmitting written texts and other digitizable items (music, pictures), they also allow users to access and work upon knowledge systems from a distance (e.g. remote experimentation), to take distance-learning courses within the framework of interactive teacher-student relations (tele-education) and to have unbelievable quantities of information – a sort of universal library – available on their desktops.'[1]

Knowledge context. The ambient availability of information does not mean there is nothing we need to remember. We cannot find what information we want – nor can we convert it into knowledge – unless we know where and how to look for it. Nor will information be useful, once found, until we know how to assess it, and have the intellectual structures that will set it in context. Learners need teachers' help in knowing not only what information to find, but also how to assess its provenance, validity and its truth value. Cultivating such critical awareness is (or should be) schooling's province.

Simulation. Information technologies have another powerful, and so far under-exploited, use in schools. With exponential growth in computing power we can simulate, for learners, increasingly complex environments and processes. These may be processes or settings which are too dangerous for students (like chemical plants); places where students are unlikely to be allowed (like corporate planning meetings for new projects); or areas where access for outsiders is unlikely (like high-technology laboratories or defence installations). There are of course many other possibilities for well-programmed simulation: configurable science labs, for instance. Once built, these simulations would allow students to take part virtually in processes, and virtually to visit places, that would otherwise be closed to them.

Digital gaming. Most teachers shun digital games – either because they fail to understand them, or because they are labelled violent and destructive. As indeed many are. But computer gaming, whether single-player or massively multiplayer, opens immense possibilities for education. Inspired by games like Sims, MIT's Games-to-Teach Project 'hopes to offer students a chance to explore the worlds of math, science, and engineering through new and exciting game models. A major challenge will be how to create a next-generation games that allow students to engage in critical problem solving, creative expression, and rich social relationships – [games] that appeal to a broad audience.'[4]

Individuation. A networked terminal for each student (see chapter 20) will allow schools to move toward individualised curricula. This will solve one of the perceived problems of comprehensive education: it is socially desirable for all young people in a neighbourhood to attend local inclusive schools – but of course students learn in different ways, at different speeds, and want to learn different things.

Taking this further, we can imagine schools which could, virtually, cater for students who want to take subjects – philosophy, say, or microbiology – for which it would be impracticable to hire specialist teachers. Such virtual teaching and learning would need to revisit the work of earlier curriculum reform movements, rather than that of current British providers, led by the BBC's *soi disant* 'bite-size curricula'. When it comes to learning, one size does not fit all.

Curriculum and learning materials. These are also known as textbooks (and, more accurately, as teaching materials) though many now come in digital form. But the medium is not the message: media have little bearing on often questionable quality. Quality is governed by many things, among them the history of textbook production. Historically, educational publishers had an ideal business model. Teachers, who hoped for money, or an escape from the classroom, would labour unpaid on schoolbook manuscripts. Publishers, who had invested almost nothing in developing the work, would choose among writers' offerings, would publish the best (or most marketable), and would in due course pay the author a small percentage of any net profit on the book.

Life is now more difficult: publishers may have to invest significant sums in the development of teaching and learning materials. What has changed less is the quality of the published offerings. Forty years ago the physicist Richard Feynman was asked to review the textbooks about to be imposed on Californian schools. He was dismayed: 'the reason was that the books were so lousy. They were false. They were hurried. They would try to be rigorous, but they would use examples (like automobiles in the street for "sets") which were almost OK, but in which there were always some subtleties. The definitions weren't accurate. Everything was a little bit ambiguous – they weren't smart enough to understand what was meant by "rigor." They were faking it. They were teaching something they didn't understand, and which was, in fact, useless, at that time, for the child. ... Finally I come to a book that says, "Mathematics is used in science in many ways. We will give you an example from astronomy, which is the science of stars." I turn the page, and it says, "Red stars have a temperature of four thousand degrees, yellow stars have a temperature of five thousand degrees ..." – so far, so good. It continues: "Green stars have a temperature of seven thousand degrees, blue stars have a temperature of ten thousand degrees, and violet stars have a temperature of ... (some big number)." There are no green or violet stars, but the figures for the others are roughly correct. It's vaguely right –but already, trouble! That's the way everything was: everything was written by somebody who didn't know what the hell he was talking about, so it was a little bit wrong, always! And how we are going to teach well by using books written by people who don't quite understand what they're talking about, I cannot understand. I don't know why, but the books are lousy; universally lousy!' Publishers will of course say: well, that was a long time ago; things are better now. They may be. But educational publishers follow the school system principle of self-reference; teaching materials are produced and reviewed by those within the education system. If we had contemporary textbook reviews by scientists of Feynman's calibre, it would be interesting to hear their opinions.

More seriously, it is rare to find leading scientists involved in the development of teaching or learning materials. It is worth looking back to a time (a fairly brief time) when that did happen, in what was known as the American Curriculum Reform Movement (USCM). The Curriculum Reform Movement was in part a response to the 1959 launch of a Soviet earth satellite. Many Americans reached the by-no-means-obvious conclusion that a country which could launch Sputnik must have a broad-based, advanced and successful education system. That proved not to be the case but, for a while, it concentrated US attention, and funding, on the public education system. There was an unprecedented (though relatively brief) American effort to make areas of science and technology accessible to learners outside – and sometimes within – higher education. USCM had many interesting features, but what made it particularly noteworthy was the participation of distinguished research scholars, and the fact that each project was guided by a steering committee of scientists and engineers. More generally, most of those in the movement subscribed to the idealistic belief that 'any subject can be taught effectively in some intellectually honest form to any child at any stage of development'.[5] This proposition may not finally have been proven, but *trying* to prove it made USCM one of the most ambitious and exciting educational enterprises of the twentieth century. It took forward discussions on intellectual structure and on learning which are significant, if unresolved, today.

A similar knowledge-building enterprise in Britain would now be digital and interactive, in more genuine ways than is usual for that often-abused term. It would not be cheap, and would need to be a collaboration between funding bodies and commercial publishers, who might have a better project management record than either or American or British academics.[6] Though expensive, such advanced curriculum projects would be a worthwhile investment if we are serious about offering students the best of contemporary thinking – and if we take seriously the Chancellor's contention that 'we face the most dramatic restructuring of global economic activity since the industrial revolution... with Asia moving from the fringes to the centre of the new world economic order' and that the 'speed and scale of technological change'[7] has never been so fast.

Professional networking. New technologies will have other roles, among them mitigating the professional isolation of teachers and the hermetic nature of schools. When schools are fully networked, teachers can be, at will, in contact with professional colleagues within or without the school. From being an isolated, and isolating, task, networked teaching becomes collaborative; even collegial. While still keeping pupils safe – as parents understandably demand – schools will be more open to the surrounding community, and to exterior life. We may in future see our school system as a single networked entity rather than as separate – and often unequal – units.

Assessment. One way of making schools more genuinely educational, more closely involved with the world outside their walls, is to unravel the argument – constructed over the past thirty years – that how schools teach, and what they teach, should be controlled and evaluated by central government. As we have noted, this is an argument, in football terms, for having a referee who makes the rules, judges the play, takes part in it and, on occasion, moves the goal posts. For schools, we need to replace this judge-and-jury arrangement with one that escapes the hermetic sphere of an enclosed and politicised system. We need to monitor pupils' performance through a system of constructive assessment that helps the learner through her work in ways that allow teachers' intervention when it is most needed. In the wider world, we need to measure schools' performance, not against school-and-government-generated tests, but against school-leavers' performance in the world outside the education system. And of course we need to separate school assessments from university entrance.

We cannot say whether twenty-first century schools will in fact resemble the sketch above. But we can predict, with reasonable certainty, that there will come a point when it is clear that traditional schooling is not supporting a new and knowledge-based economy. At that point our school system will change, or be changed. As educators our task is to see that this change benefits learners, as well as the economy. We need to remind politicians of their own words: for example, Mr Brown's statement that 'we know education is a precondition of progress personal and national – the very best anti-poverty strategy, the best economic development program'[8]; or Mr Blair's assertion that 'the knowledge economy is our best route for success and prosperity. But we must be careful not to make a fundamental mistake. We mustn't think that because the knowledge economy is the future, it will happen only in the future. The new knowledge economy is here, and it is now ...our job is to help people with that change. Not to resist it, and so suffocate opportunity.'[9] We might, too, remind Mr Blair of his advice that, in helping people with the coming change, 'learning is the key to individuals succeeding in the new economy... at school, in further education, throughout people's working lives. The key capability for people to survive and thrive in the new economy is their capacity to learn, and then to apply that learning.'[10] The Prime Minister's education policies, across the school system, now seem designed to discourage learning; but this does not change the validity of his diagnosis, or the urgency of the prescription.

That urgency is underlined if we take seriously – or even half-seriously – the more pessimistic predictions around climate change ('in as little as 10 years, or even less... the point of no return with global warming may have been reached'[11]) and advanced oil depletion (our oil-starved civilisation will revert to a Hobbesian state of nature[12]). The forecasts may be overblown (we must hope they are) but many of the global changes now happening are not benevolent. And these problems foretold are not minor inconveniences which can be solved by politicians, scientists, writers, teachers, technologists – or any other single group. It is banal but true: these things involve us all, and affect all our lives. Which makes it vital that schools shift their backward gaze toward what is happening in the world today, and what may happen tomorrow.

---

[1] Gordon Brown, quoted in *The Guardian* 14 September 2005
[2] Scardamalia 2002
[3] David and Foray 2003
[4] Games-to-Teach http://www.educationarcade.org/gtt/vision5.html . In England, Nesta Futurelab is doing interesting work in the same field.
[5] Bruner 1963
[6] Britain's Teaching and Learning Technology Programme (to take just one example) was a classic case of well-intentioned mismanagement.
[7] Gordon Brown, quoted in *The Guardian* 14 September 2005
[8] Statement from the Rt Hon Gordon Brown MP to the IMFC on Sunday 29 April 2001
[9] Mr Blair, speaking at the 'Knowledge 2000' conference: London: DTI 2000
[10] Ibid
[11] *The Independent* 24.1.2005
[12] Kunstler 2005

BIBLIOGRAPHY

Adams, H. (1995). *The education of Henry Adams* (ed Jean Gooder), Penguin.

Adnett, N. and Davies, P. (2002). *Markets for schooling*, Routledge .

Aghion, P. and Howitt. P., Appropriate growth policy: A unifying framework: The 2005 Joseph Schumpeter Lecture, delivered to the 20th Annual Congress of the European Economic Association, Amsterdam, August 25, 2005. http://post.economics.harvard.edu/faculty/aghion/papers/Appropriate_Growth.pdf

Aldrich, R. (1982). *An introduction to the history of education*, Hodder and Stoughton.

Aldrich, R. (1995). School and society in Victorian Britain, The College of receptors.

Aldrich, R. (ed 2002). *A century of education*, Routledge Falmer.

Aldrich, R., Crook, D., Watson, D. (2000). *Education and employment*, Institute of Education, University of London.

Amrein, A.L. & Berliner, D.C. (2002). High stakes testing, uncertainty, and student learning.

Apple, M.W. (1979). *Ideology and curriculum*, Routledge.

Apple, M.W. (1988). *Teachers and texts: A political economy of class and gender relations in education*. New York: Routledge.

Apple, M.W. (1996). *Cultural politics and education*. Buckingham: Open University Press.

Apple. M.W. (1982). *Education and power*. New York: Routledge and Kegan Paul.

Bailey, J. (2002) *After thought: The computer challenge to human intelligence*, Basic Books.

Ball, S. (1993). Education markets, choice and social class: The market as a class strategy in the UK and USA, *British Journal of Sociology of Education, 14* (1).

Ball, S. (1994) *Education reform: A critical and post-structural approach*. Buckingham: Open University Press.

Barlowe, A. & Mack, H. (2004). *Looking for an argument?: An inquiry course at Urban Academy Laboratory High School*. New York: Teacher to Teacher Press.

Barnett, C. (1986). *Audit of war*. Macmillan.

Barrow, J.D. (1999). *Impossibility: The limits of science and the science of limits*, Vintage.

Beare, H. (2001). *Creating the future school*, Routledge.

Becta: Computer games in Education Project Report, *Becta/TEEM* 2003.

Bennett, R. (2005, April). Keynote Speech at "First international conference on urban education and intercultural relations," D'Youville College, Buffalo, NY.

Bentley, T (1998). *Learning beyond the classroom*. Routledge Demos.

Berliner, D. & Biddle, B. (1995). *The manufactured crisis: Myths, fraud and the attack on America's public schools*. Reading, MA: Addison-Wesley.

Bobbitt, P (2000). *The shield of Achilles*, Allen Lane.

Booth, J (1858). *On the self-improvement of the working classes*. Leeds; no publisher credited.

Bourdieu, P. (1998). *Acts of resistance: Against the tyranny of the market*. New York: The New Press.

Bowles, S. & Gintis, H. (1986). *Democracy and capitalism: Property, community and the contradictions of modern thought*. New York: Basic Books.

Bracey, G. (June 2005). No child left behind: Where does the money go? Education Policy Studies Laboratory. Tempe, AZ: Arizona State University. Available at: http://edpolicylab.org.

Brodkin, K. (1994). How Jews became white. In S. Gregory and R. Sanjek (Eds.) *Race* (pp. 78-102). New Bruswick, NJ: Rutgers University Press.

Bruner, J. S. (1963). *The process of education*, Vintage.

Bruner, J. S. (1996). *Toward a theory of instruction*, Harvard University Press.

Brynjolfsson, E. (2004). Productivity's technology iceberg, http://www.technologyreview.com/articles/wo_brynjolfsson_031004.asp?trk=nl

Brynjolfsson, E. & Kahin, B. (eds.2002). *Understanding the digital economy*, MIT.

Buckingham, D (1999). Young people, politics and news media, *Oxford Review of Education, 25* (1-2).

Buckingham, D. (2000). *The making of citizens*, Routledge

Burke, J. & Ornstein, R. (1995). *The axemaker's gift: A double-edged history of human culture*, Grosset/Putnam .

BIBLIOGRAPHY

Burn, A. (2003). English teaching, *Practice and Critique, 2*(2).
Burton-Jones, A. (1999). *Knowledge capitalism: Business, work and learning in the new economy.*Oxford: OUP.
Butler, R. A. (1971). *The art of the possible*, Hamish Hamilton.
Cairncross, F (1997). *The death of distance*, Orion Business Books.
Cala, W. (2002, September 24). [Letter to the editor], *Education Week.*
Capellaro, C. (2004). Blowing the whistle on the Texas miracle: An interview with Robert Kimball.
Capital Strategies (2000). *The business of education: An analysis of business developments in the education and training marketplace.* London: Capital Strategies Ltd.
Carnoy, M., Castells, M., Cohen S. & Cardoso, F.H. (1996). *The new global economy in the information age*, Penn State Press.
Carpentier, V. (2003). Public expenditure on education and economic growth in the UK, 1833-2000, *History of Education, 32*(1).
Castells, M. (2000). *The rise of the network society*, Blackwell.
Castells, M. (2003). *TheInternet galaxy*, Blackwell.
Castells, M. (1989). *The informational city.* London: Blackwell.
Castells, M. (1998). *End of the millennium.* London: Blackwell.
Chancellor, V. E. (1970). *History for their masters*, Adams and Dart.
Christensen, C.M. (2000). Meeting the challenge of disruptive change, in Harvard Business Review on innovation, *Harvard Business Review* 2001.
Christensen, C.M. (2003). *The innovator's dilemma*, Harper Business Essentials.
Counts, G. (1932). *Dare the school build a new social order?* New York: John Day.
Covey, S. R. et al (1994). *First things first*, Simon and Schuster.
Crosland, S. (1982). *Tony Crosland*, Coronet.
Cullingford, C. (1992). *Children and society: Children's attitudes to politics and power*, Cassell.
Dale, R. (1989). *The state and education policy.* Milton Keynes: Open University Press.
David, P. A. and Foray, D. (2003). Economic fundamentals of the knowledge society, *Policy Futures in Education, 1.*
Davies, H. (2002). *The Howard Davies review of enterprise and the economy in education.* London: HMSO.
Davies, N. (2000). *The school report*, Vintage.
Davies, W. (2005). *Modernising with a purpose: A manifesto for digital Britain*, IPPR.
Davis, E. (1998). *TechGnosis: Myth, magic and mysticism in the age of information.* Three Rivers Press.
Davis, S. (2001). *Lessons from the future*, Capstone.
De Geus, A (2002). *The living company: Habits for survival in a turbulent business environment*, Harvard Business School Press.
Deakin, N. and Parry, R. (2000). *The treasury and social policy*, Macmillan Press.
Dean, M. (2002). Liberal government and authoritarianism, *Economy and Society, 31*(1), 37-61.
Denning, P. J. (ed, 2002). *The invisible future.* McGraw-Hill.
Department for Trade and Industry and Department for Education and Employment (2001). *Opportunity for all in a world of change.* London: DTI and DfEE.
Dertouzos, M. (1997) *What will be*, Platkus.
Dewey, J. (1915, May 5). *The New Republic 3* (28) 42-3.
Dewey, J. (1916). *Democracy and education.* New York: Macmillan.
Drucker, P. F. (1996). *The concept of the corporation*, Transaction Publishers.
Drucker, P. F. (1998). *Post-capitalist society*, Butterworth Heinemann.
Drucker, P. F. (2000). *Management challenges for the 21st century*, Butterworth Heinemann.
Eaglesham, E. (1956). *From school board to local authority.* London: Routledge and Kegan Paul.
Eaglesham, E. (1967). *The foundations of twentieth century education in England.* Routledge and Kegan Paul.
Ebeling, R. (2000). It's time to put public education behind us: The future of freedom foundation commentaries. Available at: www.fff.org/comment/ed0200f.asp.edu/soc/faculty/kollock/papers/design.htm.
Education Policy Analysis Archives, 10(18). Available at: http://epaa.asu.edu/epaa/v10n18/.
Edwards, T. & Tomlinson, S. (2002). Selection isn't working: Catalyst environments. Paper presented at the European Association for Research on Learning and Instruction, Nijmegen, The Netherlands.
Evans, P. and Wurster, T. S. (2000). *Blown to bits*, Harvard Business School Press.

Fenwick, K. and McBride, P. (1981). *The government of education*, Methuen.
Feynman, R. P. (1985). *Surely you're joking, Mr Feynman!*, WW Norton & Company.
Feynman, R. P. (1999). *Six not-so-easy pieces*, Penguin.
Florida, R. (2002). *The rise of the creative class*, Basic Books.
Fones-Wolf, E. (1994). *Selling free enterprise: The business assault on labour and liberalism 1945-1960*. Urbana: University of Illinois.
Frame, J. (1982). *To the is-land*, Women's Press.
Freeman, C. and Louca, F. (2001). *As time goes by*, Oxford University Press.
Freire, P. (2000). *Pedagogy of the oppressed*, Continuum.
Friedman, M. (1953). *Essays in positive economics*, Chicago University Press.
Friedman, M. (1962). Capitalism and Freedom, University of Chicago Press.
Friedman, M. (1995, June 23). Public schools: Make them private, Cato Institute Briefing Paper No. 23,. Available at: www.cato.org/pubs/briefs/bp-023.html.
Friedman, T. (1999). Semiotics of sim city, *First Monday*, Issue 4.
Fukuyama, F. (2003). Profile Books.
Future Surveyed: 150 Economist Years. The Economist (September 11, 1993) F70(3).
Fyvel, T. R. (1961). *The insecure offenders*, London.
Gardner, H. (1997). *Extraordinary minds*, Weidenfeld and Nicolson.
Gewirtz, S. (2002). *The managerial school: Post-welfarism and social justice in education*. New York: Routledge.
Gilder, G. (2000). *Telecosm*, Touchstone.
Gilpin, R. (2000). *The challenge of global capitalism*, Princeton University Press.
Gilpin, R. (2001). *Global political economy*, Princeton University Press.
Goodson, I. (1988). *The making of curriculum*, The Falmer Press.
Goody, J. & Watt, I. (1962). The consequences of literacy, *Comparative Studies in History and Society*, 3.
Goody, J. (1986). *The logic of writing and the organisation of society*, Cambridge University Press.
Gosden, P.H.J.H. (1969). *How they were taught*, Blackwell.
Greenfield, S. (2003). *Tomorrow's people*, Penguin.
Guile, D. (1998). *Information and communication technology and education*. London: Institute of Education.
Guile, D. (2003). From 'credentialism' to the 'practice of learning: Reconceptualising learning for the knowledge economy, *Policy Futures in Education*, 1.
Hakkarainen, K. (1995). Collaborative inquiry in computer-supported intentional learning environments. Paper presented at the European Association for Research on Learning and Instruction. Nijmegen, Netherlands
Handy, C. (2001). *The elephant and the fly*, Hutchinson.
Haney, W. (2000). The myth of the Texas miracle in education, *Education Policy Analysis Archives*, 8(41). Available at: http://epaa.asu.edu/epaa/v8n41/
Haney, W. (2003). Attrition of students from New York schools, invited testimony at public hearing 'Regents Learning Standards and High School Graduation Requirements' before the New York Senate Standing Committee on Education, Senate Hearing Room, New York, 23 September. Available at: http://www.timeoutfromtesting.org/testimonies/923_Testimony_Haney.pdf.
Hakkarainen, K. (1995). Collaborative inquiry in the computer-supported intentional learning environments. Paper presented at the European Association for Research on Learning and Instruction, Nijmegen, The Netherlands.
Hanushek, E. A., Some simple analytics of school quality' (undated).
Hargreaves, D. (2001). *Mosaic of learning*, Demos.
Hatcher, R. (2003, December 12). Business agenda and school education in England. Retrieved from: http://socialist-teacher.org/dossiers.as?pd=y&id=75 .
Hayden, C. (2001, May 7). Letter to the Hon. Richard Brodsky and the Hon. Richard Green, New York State Assembly.
Hertz, N. (2002). *The silent takeover*, Arrow.
Hertz, N. (2004). *IOU: The debt threat and why we must defuse it*, Fourth Estate.
Hickox, M. and Moore, R (1991). Post-fordism and education, in Brown, P and Lauder, H (eds), *Education and economic survival*, Routledge.
Hirschman, O. (1970). *Exit, voice and loyalty*, Harvard University Press.

BIBLIOGRAPHY

Howard, A. (1987). *RAB: The life of R. A. Butler*, Cape.
Hursh, D. & Apple, M.W. (1983). The fiscal crisis, politics and education: A critical analysis of the report of the National Commission of Excellence in Education, unpublished manuscript.
Hursh, D. (2004). Undermining democratic education in the USA: The consequences of global capitalism and neoliberal policies for education policies at the local, state, and federal levels. *Policy Futures in Education, 2*(3-4), 601-614.
Hursh, D. (2005a). Neo-liberalism, markets and accountability: Transforming education and undermining   democracy in the United States and England. *Policy Futures in Education. 3*(1), 3-15.
Hursh, D. (2005b). The growth of high-stakes testing in the USA: Accountability, markets and the decline of educational equality. *British Educational Research Journal. 31*(5), 605-622.
Hyndman, M. (1978). *Schools and schooling in England and Wales*, Harper and Row.
Illich. I. (1970). *Deschooling society*, Marion Boyars.
Johnson, D. C. & Salle, L. M. (2004). *Responding to the attack on public education and teacher unions*. Menlo Park: CA: Commonwealth Institute. Available at: www.commonwealinstitute.org.
Jones, K. (1989). *Right turn*, Hutchinson Radius.
Kaku, M. (1998). *Visions: How science will revolutionise the twenty-first century*, OUP.
Katz, R. (1998). *Japan: The system that soured*, M.E.Sharpe.
Katznelson, I. (2005). *When affirmative action was White: An untold history of racial inequality in twentieth-century America*. New York: W. W. Norton.
Keep, E. (2000). Learning organisations, lifelong learning and the mystery of the vanishing employers. SKOPE Research Paper No.8.
Keep, E. (2003). No problem. *The Guardian* 16.12.03.
Kennedy, P. (1989). *The rise and fall of the great powers: Economic change and military conflict from 1500-2000*, Fontana.
Kleinfield, N. (2002). *The elderly man and the sea? Test sanitizes literacy texts*, New York Times, June 2, p. A-1.
Kliebard, H. (1983). *The struggle for the American curriculum: 1893-1958*. New York: Routledge Press.
Kollock, P. (2001). Design principles for online communities, http://www.sscnet.ucla.
Kozol, J. (2005). *The shame of the nation: The restoration of apartheid schooling in America*. New York.
Krugman, P. (1999). *The return of depression economics*. Allen Lane: The Penguin Press.
Kuhn, T. S. (1970). *The structure of scientific revolutions*, Chicago UP.
Kunstler, J. H. (2005). *The long emergency*, Atlantic Books.
Kurzweil, R. (1999). *The age of spiritual machines*, Phoenix.
Landes, D. S. (1988). *The wealth and poverty of nations*. Little Brown.
Lave, J. and Wenger, E. (2002). *Situated learning: Legitimate peripheral participation*, Cambridge University Press.
Lawson, J. and Silver, H. (1973). *A social history of education in England*. London: Methuen.
Levinson, R. and Turner, S. (2001). *Valuable lessons: Engaging with the social context of science in schools*, The Wellcome Trust.
Levitas, R. (1998). *The inclusive society?: Social exclusion and new labour*. London: Macmillan.
Lipman, P. (2004). *High stakes education: Inequality, globalization, and urban school reform*. New York: Routledge Falmer.
Lipman, P. (2005). We're not blind. Just follow the dollar sign: Chicago's "Renaissance" could mean dark ages for public schools. *Rethinking Schools, 19*(4), 54-58.
Littky, D. (2004). *The big picture: Education is everyone's business*, ASCD.
Little, J. W. & McLaughlin, M.W. (1993). *Teachers' work: Individuals, colleagues, and contexts*. New York: Teachers College Press.
Macdonald, G. (2004). School computing: The mobile and the phone box. *Educational Computing and Technology, 9.*
Machin, S. & Vignoles, A. (eds, 2004). *What's the good of education? The economics of education in the UK*, Princeton University Press.
Machin, S., Vignoles, A. & Galindo-Rueda, F. (2003). Sectoral and area analysis of the economic effects of qualifications and basic skills. DfES.
Maclure, J. S. (1986). *Educational documents: England and Wales 1816 to the present day*. London, Methuen.

Margolis, M. & Resnick, D. (2000). *Politics as usual*, Sage.

Martina, C., Hursh, D., Markowitz, D., Hart, K. & Debes, P. (2003). Contradictions in educational policy: Developing integrated problem-based curriculum in a high stakes environment, paper presented at the annual meeting of the American Educational Association, Mexico City, October 30-November 2.

May, T. (2002). *The Victorian schoolroom*, Shire Publications.

Mayer, M. (1990). *The greatest-ever bank robbery: The collapse of the savings and loan industry*, Charles Scribner's Sons.

McLuhan, M. (1964). *Understanding media*, Routledge.

McNeil, L. & Valenzuela, A. (2001). *The harmful impact of the TAAS system of testing*. Texas: Beneath.

McNeil, L. (2000). *Contradictions of school reform: Educational costs of standardized testing*. New York: Routledge.

Meier, D. (1995). *The power of their ideas: Lessons for America from a small school in Harlem*. Boston: Beacon Press.

Meier, D. (2005). 'No Child Left Behind' and democracy. In D. Meier, A. Kohn, L. Darling-Hammond, T.R. Sizer & G. Wood (Eds.) *Many children left behind: How the No Child Left Behind Act is damaging our children*. Boston: Beacon Press, 66-78.

Messer-Davidow, E., Shumway, D. R., Sylvan, D.J. (eds,1993). *Knowledges: Historical and critical studies in disciplinarity*, University of Virginia Press.

Miner, B. (1999/2000). *Testing: full speed ahead*. A Report on the National Education Summit, Rethinking

Miner, B. (2004). Seed money for conservatives. *Rethinking Schools*, *18*(4), 9-11.

Mokyr, J. (1990). *The lever of riches*. Oxford University Press.

Monbiot, G. (2000). *Captive state*, Macmillan.

Monk, D., Sipple, J. & Killeen, K. (2001). Adoption and adaptation: New York State school districts' responses to state imposed high school graduation requirements: An eight-year retrospective, a condition study prepared for the New York State Education Finance Research Consortium, 10 September. Available at: http://www.albany.edu/edfin/CR01_MSK_Report.pdf.

Moss, P. & Tilly, C. (1996). "Soft" skills and race: An investigation of Black men's employment problems. *Work and Occupations*, *23*(3), 52-276.

Mulgan, G. (2005). 'Charles Tilly', *Prospect*, September 2005.

National Commission on Excellence in Education (1983). *A Nation at risk: A report to the nation and the Secretary of Education*. Washington, DC: US Department of Education.

National Defense Act (1958). Public Law 85-864, 85th Congress, September 2, 1958.

Naughton, J. (1999). *A brief history of the future*, Weidenfeld and Nicolson.

Negroponte, N. (1995). *Being digital*, Coronet.

New York State School Boards Association (16 September 2002) Title I Accountability Status, updated for 10 March 2003.

No Child Left Behind Act (2001). 20 USC, para. 6301.

Noam, E. (1995). Electronics and the dim future of the university. *Science Magazine*.

Noble, D. (1997). *The religion of technology*, Knopf.

Nonaka, I. & Nishigucki, T. (eds, 2001). *Knowledge emergence*, Oxford University Press.

North, D. C. (1990). Institutions, institutional change and economic performance, Cambridge University Press.

Olssen, M., Codd, J.& O'Neill, A.M. (2004). *Education policy: Globalization, citizenship and democracy*. Thousand Oaks, CA: Sage.

Ong, W. (1982). *Orality and literacy: The technologizing of the word*, Methuen.

Orfield, G. & Eaton, S. (1996). *Dismantling desegregation*. New York: New Press.

Orfield, G., Losen, D., Wald, J. & Swanson, C. (2004). *Losing our future: How minority youth are being left behind by the graduation rate crisis*. Contributors: Advocates for Children of New York, The Civil Society Institute. Cambridge, MA: The Civil Rights Project at Harvard University.

Ostrom, E. (1990). *Governing the commons: The evolution of institutions for collective action*, Cambridge University Press.

Paige, R. & Jackson, A. (2004, November 8). Education: The civil rights issue of the twenty-first century. Hispanic Vista. Available at: http://www.hispanicvista.com/HVC/Opinion/Guest_Columns/110804.

Papert, S. (1992). *The children's machine*, Basic Books.

Parenti, C. (1999). Atlas finally shrugged: Us against them in the me decade. *The Baffler, 13*, 108-120.

Pearn, M. (1997). A question of survival', in Royal Society of Arts: *For life – A vision of learning for the 21st century*. London: RSA, 11-13.

Pesce, M. (2000). *The playful world*, Ballantine.

Peters, M. A.(2003). Education policy in the age of knowledge capitalism. *Policy Futures in Education, 1*.

Peters, M. (1994). Individualism and community: Education and the politics of difference. *Discourse, 14*(2), 65-78.

Phillips, K. (2002). *Wealth and democracy*, Broadway Books.

Phillips, R. & Furlong, J. (2001). *Education reform and the state: Twenty-five years of politics, policy, and practice*. New York: Routledge Falmer.

Pinzur, M. (2003, August 8). State schools fail to meet New Federal Test Standards: Federal, state results differ, *Miami Herald*.

Porter, M. E. & Ketels, C. H. M. (2003).UK competitiveness: Moving to the next stage. DTI Economics paper No. 3 5.2003.

Postman, N. (1971). *Teaching as a subversive activity*, Delta.

Postman, N. (1990). Informing ourselves to death. A speech given at a meeting of the German Informatics Society (Gesellschaft fuer Informatik) on October 11, 1990 in Stuttgart.

Postman, N. (1996). *The end of education*, Vintage Books.

Postman, N. (1998). Five things we need to know about technological change. Speech given in Denver, Colorado, March 27, 1998.

Prahalad, C. K. (2005). The fortune at the bottom of the pyramid, Wharton School Publishing.

Preston, C. (2004). *Learning to use ICT in classrooms*, Mirandanet.

Pullman, P. (2003). Lost the plot, *The Guardian* 30.9.03.

Putnam, R. D. (2000). *Bowling alone*, Simon and Schuster.

Randall, L. (2005). Smashing open the universe. *Prospect*, September 2005.

Reich, R. B. (1992). *The work of nations*, Vintage Books.

Reich, R. B. (2002). *The future of success*, Vintage Books.

Rethinking Schools, 19(1). Available at: http://www.rethinkingschools.org/archive/1901/tex191.shtml.

Rifkin, J. (2004). Return of a conundrum. *The Guardian* 2.3.04.

Rifkin, R. (1995). *The end of work*, Tarcher Putnam.

Rifkin, R. (2000). *The age of access*, Penguin.

Rivera, M. (2003, June 19) Personal communication.

Road_Paige-Alphonso_Jackson.htm.

Roberts, W. (1856). *Memoirs of the life of Mrs Hannah More*. London: n.p.

Robertson, S. (2000). *A class act: Changing teachers' work, the state, and globalization*. New York: Falmer Press.

Romer, P. M. (1993). Ideas and things: The concept of production is being retooled (The future surveyed: 150 Economist years). *The Economist* (September 11, 1993).

Romer, P. M.(1999). Economic growth, in *The Fortune encyclopedia of economics* (ed David R Henderson), Warner Books.

Romer, P. M. (1996). *Changing tastes: How evolution and experience shape economic behaviour* (Oscar Morgenstern Memorial Lectures) Cambridge University Press.

Rose, M. (1995). Possible lives: *The promise of public education in America*. Boston: Houghton Mifflin.

Rose, N. (1999). *Powers of freedom: Reframing political thought*. Cambridge: Cambridge University Press.

Rosen, P. (2002). *Framing production*. MIT Press.

Ruddick, J. (1991). *Innovation and change*. Milton Keynes: Open University Press.

Rugg, H. (1923). *The social studies in the elementary and secondary school, twenty-second yearbook of the National Society for the Study of Education*, Part II, Bloomington, Ill: Public School Publishing Co.

Rugg, H. (1929-1932). *Man and his changing society: The Rugg social science series of the elementary school course* (Vols. 1-6) (pp. 1-27). Boston: Ginn.

Salen, K. and Zimmerman, E (2003). *Rules of play*, MIT Press.

Sassen, S. (1994). *Cities in a world economy*. Thousand Oaks: Pine Forge Press.

Sayer (1995). *Radical political economy: A critique*. Oxford: Blackwell

Scardamalia, M. (2002). Collective cognitive responsibility for the advancement of knowledge. In B. Smith (ed.), *Liberal education in a knowledge society* (pp. 67-98). Chicago: Open Court.

Scardamalia, M. and Bereiter, C. (1999). Schools as knowledge-building organisations, in Keating, D and Hertzmann, C. (eds) *Today's children: tomorrow's society*, Guilford.

Scardamalia, M., & Bereiter, C. (2003). Knowledge building in *Encyclopedia of education* (2nd ed., pp. 1370-1373). New York: Macmillan Reference.

Schneiderman, B. (2002). *Leonardo's laptop*, MIT Press.

Schumpeter, J. A. (1950). *Capitalism, socialism and democracy*, Harper Perennial.

Schwartz, P. (2003). *Inevitable surprises*, Free Press.

Seely Brown, J. and Duguid, P. (2000). *The social life of information*. Harvard Business School Press.

Selwyn, N. (2004). Literature review in citizenship, technology & learning, NestaFuturelab Report, 3.

Shaw, L. (2004, October 21). US education secretary quizzed, *Seattle Times*.

Simon, B. (1974). *The two nations and the educational structure 1780-1870*, Lawrence & Wishart.

Simon, B. (1974a). *The politics of educational reform 1920-1940*, Lawrence & Wishart.

Simon, B. (1988). *Bending the rules: The Baker 'Reform' of Education*, Lawrence & Wishart.

Skidmore, P. (2003). *Beyond measure*, Demos.

Smith, B. (ed.) *Liberal education in a knowledge society* (pp. 67-98), Open Court.

Sneyd-Kynnersley, E. M., (1913). *Some passages in the life of one of HM inspectors of schools*, Macmillan and Company.

Spar, D. (2001). *Pirates, prophets and pioneers*, Random House.

Spring, J. (1998). *Education and the rise of the global economy*, Lawrence Erlbaum Associates.

Steer, W. B. (undated). *Our public elementary schools and how they are staffed*, London n.p.

Stevens, P. and Weale, M. (2003). *Education and economic growth*. London: NIESR.

Stiglitz, J. (2002). *Globalisation and its discontents*, Penguin.

Stiglitz, J. (2003). *Roaring nineties*. Allen Lane.

Stiglitz, J. The fruits of irrationality. *The Guardian* 24.9.03.

Tabb, W. (2002). *Unequal partners: A primer on globalization*. New York: The New Press.

Tawney, R. H. (1952). *Equality*, Allen and Unwin.

Taylor, F.W. (1911). *The Principle of scientific management*. New York: Harper and Brothers.

The accountability rhetoric', in G. Orfield & M.L. Kornhaber (eds) *Raising standards or raising barriers? Inequality and high stakes testing in public education* (pp. 127-150). New York: Century Foundation Press.

Thrupp, M. & Willmott, R. (2003). *Education management in managerialist times: Beyond the textual apologists*. Maidenhead: Open University Press.

Timmins, N. (1996). *The five giants*, Fontana.

Todd, E. (2003). *After the empire: The breakdown of the American order*, Constable.

TTA (1999). *Initial teacher training national curriculum for the use of information and communications technology in subject teaching*. London: HMSO.

Turing, A. M. (1936). On computable numbers, with an application to the Entscheinungs Problem. *Proc. London Math. Soc*, 42.

Turing, A.M. (1950). Computing machinery and intelligence. *Mind, 59*, 433-460.

Turkle, S. (2004). How computers change the way we think. *The Chronicle of Higher Education, 50*(21) 1.

US Department of Education (April 2002). *What to know and where to go: A parents' guide to No Child Left Behind'*. Washington, DC: US Department of Education, Office of the Secretary.

US Department of Education (September 2002). *No Child Left Behind: A desk reference*. Washington, DC: US Department of Education, Office of Elementary and Secondary Education.

Utterback, J. M. (1996). *Mastering the dynamics of innovation*, Harvard Business School Press.

Vilas, C. (1996). Neoliberal social policy: Managing poverty (somehow). *NACLA report on the Americas, 29*(2), 16-21.

Von Krogh, G., Ichijo, K., Nonaka, I. (2000). *Enabling knowledge creation*, Oxford.

Walford, G. (1994). Choice and equity in education, Cassell.

Whitty, G., Power, S. & Halpin, D. (1998). *Devolution and choice in education: The school, the state and the market*. Philadelphia: Open University Press.

209

BIBLIOGRAPHY

Wiener, M. J. (1992). *English culture and the decline of the industrial spirit 1850-1980*, Penguin.
Wiggins, G. & McTighe, J. (1999). *Understanding by design*, Alexandria, VA: Association for Supervision and Curriculum Development.
Williams, R (1961). *The long revolution*, Penguin.
Winerip, M. (2003, August 13). The 'zero dropout' miracle: alas! alack! A Texas tall tale. *New York Times*, B7.
Winerip, M. (2003, March 12). Passing grade defies laws of physics. *New York Times*, A22 & B7.
Winter, G. (2004). Worst rates of graduation are in New York', *New York Times*, 26 February, B3.
Wolf, A. (2002). *Does Education Matter?*, Penguin.
Wolmar, C. (2005). *On the wrong line*, Aurum Press.
Young, I. M. (2000). *Democracy and inclusion*, Oxford: Oxford University Press.
Young, M. F. D. (1998). *The curriculum of the future*, Falmer.
Young, M. F. D. (1999). *Knowledge, learning and the curriculum of the future*, London: Institute of Education.

Printed in the United Kingdom
by Lightning Source UK Ltd.
113329UKS00001B/37